Volume 1: The Green, the Bleh and the Fuzzy

THE GREEN, THE BLEH AND THE FUZZY

First Edition

Copyright © 2012 Rebecca Hicks
dba Lunasea Studios

No part of this book may be used or reproduced (except for review purposes) by any electronic or mechanical means without express written permission from Lunasea Studios or an agent of Lunasea Studios.

Requests for permission to reproduce any parts of this work should be addressed to: Lunasea Studios, 9450 Mira Mesa Blvd. Ste. C-107, San Diego, CA 92126

Contact Rebecca Hicks at rhicks@lunasea-studios.com

ISBN 978-0-9799290-4-5

For James, who loves me more than coffee.

That's a lotta love.

Introduction

The classic western *The Good, the Bad and the Ugly* is a story of greed, betrayal, and epic ponchos.

The story of the Little Vampires is nothing like that at all. Their story doesn't begin with a shoot-out, but with a random observation made by my husband, James, a diabetic. He showed me the marks on his fingertips that were made by the needle of his blood glucose meter.

"Look at my fingers. They look like they're being nibbled by little vampires."

The image of mischievous little vampires nomming on James's fingertips popped into my mind. And like adorable but unwelcome house guests, the little biters just wouldn't leave. I was trying to focus on other creative projects at the time, specifically the comic book that I was writing. But I kept drawing little vampires, and I couldn't stop thinking about their personalities and their world. It wasn't long before I had a fully formed story about little vampires and their attempts to be big and fierce.

We had bought a small press table at the 2007 San Diego Comic-Con for the purpose of promoting the comic book. In June, a month before the convention, James asked if I could possibly maybe write and draw that Little Vampires story into something that he could then possibly maybe turn into a book after he did some research into learning how to do book binding.

It's amazing what impossible things he and I will commit to when we don't realize they're impossible.

We had 50 impossibly hand-bound *Little Vampires* books on our table at the beginning of Comic-Con. We left with only 10 copies remaining, with fans wanting more Little Vampires stories, and with an invitation to do a book signing in October. James and I excitedly realized that these characters had great appeal, and that I should continue writing and drawing their misadventures. Then we less-than-excitedly realized that we needed to have more books made by October.

One of the first Little Vampire sketches, drawn on a sticky note.

For the sake of James's fingertips, we decided to skip the book-binding and have the book printed. We drove to Sacramento for the signing, hosted by the lovely woman that I still consider my patron goddess, Margaret Mannatt.

I was still an elementary school teacher at the time, but we brought the Little Vampires to comic-book and pop-culture conventions whenever and wherever we could. I began to realize, more and more, that this was what I was meant to do. Making one of the hardest decisions of my life, I left teaching and dedicated myself to the arts full time.

In the summer of 2009 I wrote and illustrated *Little Vampires and Friends*, which introduced the introverted Frank and energetic Wolfie. James performed another feat of impossible book-binding, and we premiered this hand-bound sequel at Comic-Con 2009. I still had more stories that I wanted to tell, but printing and publishing books based on all of those ideas would be far too expensive.

So I began the Little Vampires webcomic in October of 2009. I had been a webcomics fan for years, and had made many friends in the industry that encouraged me to run and away and join their artistic circus.

Which brings us here, to this book, the first collection of Little Vampire webcomics. My hope is that you find it all good, and not the least bit bad, ugly, or epic poncho-wearing.

-Rebecca Hicks
March 2012

Thank You

Thank you. Yes, you. Thank you for supporting the independent arts.

Thanks to James, my husband, who could simply walk into Mordor. He's just that awesome.

Thanks to Margaret and Phil, the loveliest of patrons, and thank you Jerlene, the loveliest of mentors.

Thank you to Daniel and Dawna and Goblin Boy, to Alina and Layne, to Neal and Kristen, and to Dane and Ashlie for the emotional and creative support.

Thanks to all my family and friends for not always understanding why I have so little free time, but for supporting me anyway. And thank you Peter and Kim for all the editing help.

Special thanks to my Ma, for getting me that typewriter in high school.

Thank you to all my teachers, to all my friends still in the teaching profession, and to all my students.

Cast Of Characters

Little Vampires

The Little Vampires try to be as fierce and deadly as human-sized vampires, but they fail spectacularly at it. This doesn't prevent them from trying.

Despite their continued efforts, the Little Vampires are perceived as more friendly than fierce, and more endearing than deadly.

Frank

Frank is more introverted and intellectual than his friends. He doesn't often show emotion, but he has a romantic soul. Though he can come across as a little on the boring side, he has a lot of fascinating interests and skills that he is very passionate about.

Wolfie

Wolfie is the most athletic and energetic of his peers, and loves a good competition. He's also mischievous and fun-loving, and fiercely loyal to his friends and family.

Elsa

Elsa is the pop-culture geek of the group. She loves comics, movies, and video games. She also loves playing a wide variety of sports.

Little Vampire Girls

The Little Vampire Girls are not as obsessed with being fierce as the Little Vampires are. They'd rather spend their time reading.

Mumsy

Mumsy is often grumpy. But you'd be grumpy too if your friends kept trying to turn your clothes into gift wrapping.

Little Zombies

Brainsbrainsbrains.

The Cat

The Little Vampires practice being fierce by trying to scare The Cat. The Cat tolerates them because they sometimes bring him tuna.

Blood Oranges

The Little Vampires think blood oranges actually have blood in them. The truth would devastate them.

October 28, 2009 • Little Vampire vs. Piano: Round One

BEHIND THE SCENES

The weeks leading up to the premiere of the Little Vampire webcomic were hectic. James and I were both busy with our usual convention planning and with the design of the comic website. We turned down several invitations for social engagements, including one to our friend Dave's piano recital.

I decided that the best way to apologize to Dave was to honor his craft in the first comic.

We did get to attend a later recital. I was delighted to find that Dave is a master jazz pianist, and that his piano did not honk at all.

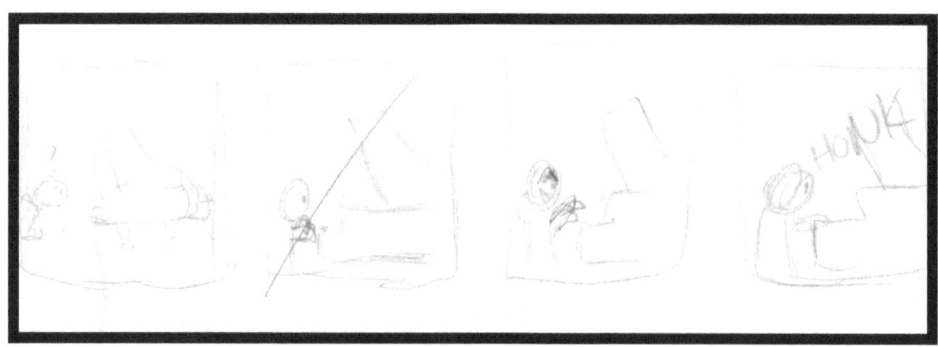

Thumbnail sketch of the first comic strip. I left out the second panel in the final comic because it slowed down the comedic pacing. The next comic would utilize a beat panel.

November 4, 2009 • Little Vampire vs. Piano: Round Two

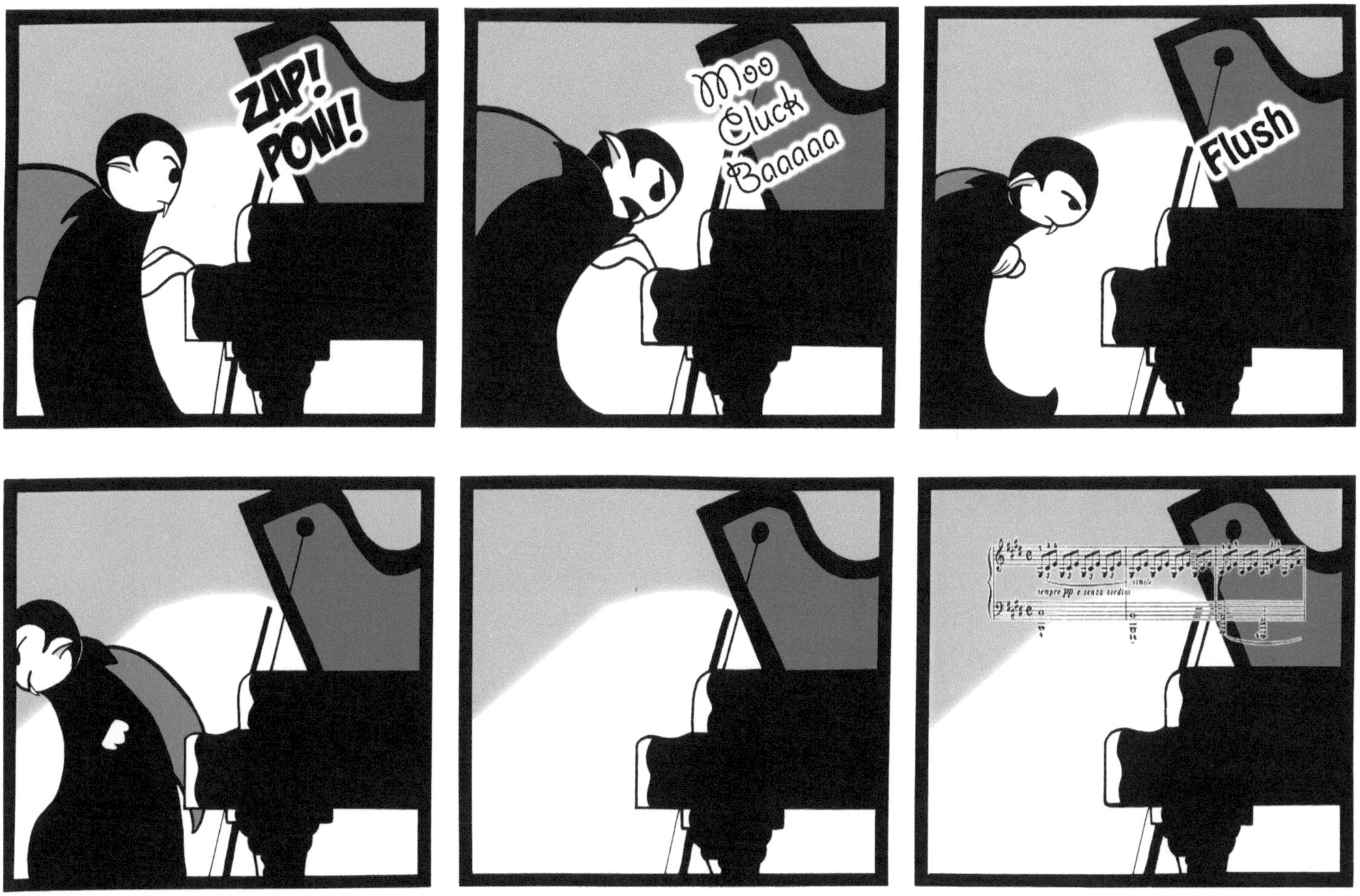

ZAP!
POW!
Moo
Cluck
Baaaaa
Flush
simile

BEHIND THE SCENES: SFX

Creating sound effects for a medium that has no sound is just one of the many fun, yet maddening parts of my job. Some sound effects that I considered using in this comic included *booga booga, eeeyooop, phhhhbbbt, cluckbuhguck, toot,* and *choo choo*.

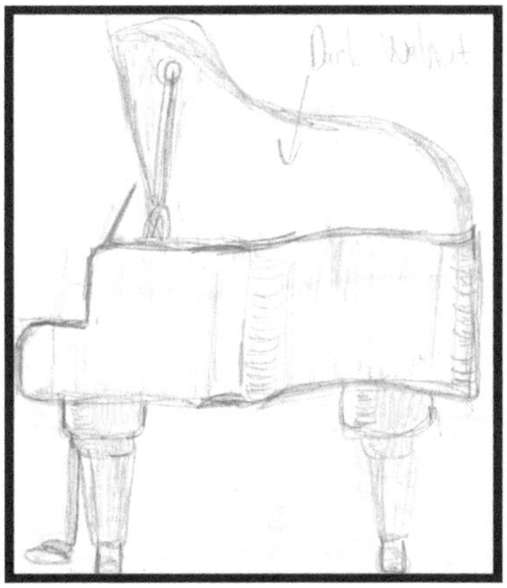

The musical score is from the beginning of Beethoven's *Moonlight Sonata*, one of the Little Vampires' favorite pieces of classical music.

November 11, 2009 • Rise and Shine with Frank

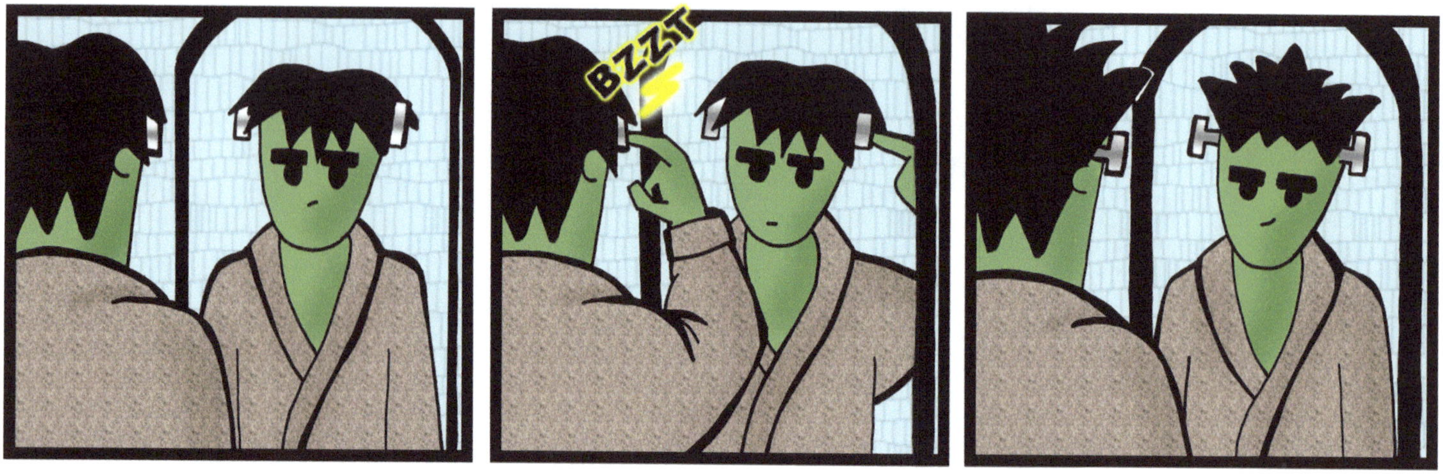
BZZT

MEET THE CAST

I decided early on that Frank was a fellow that cared quite a bit about his personal grooming. This would lead me to have him develop a love of costuming and cosplay (costume play).

November 18, 2009 • Sparkle

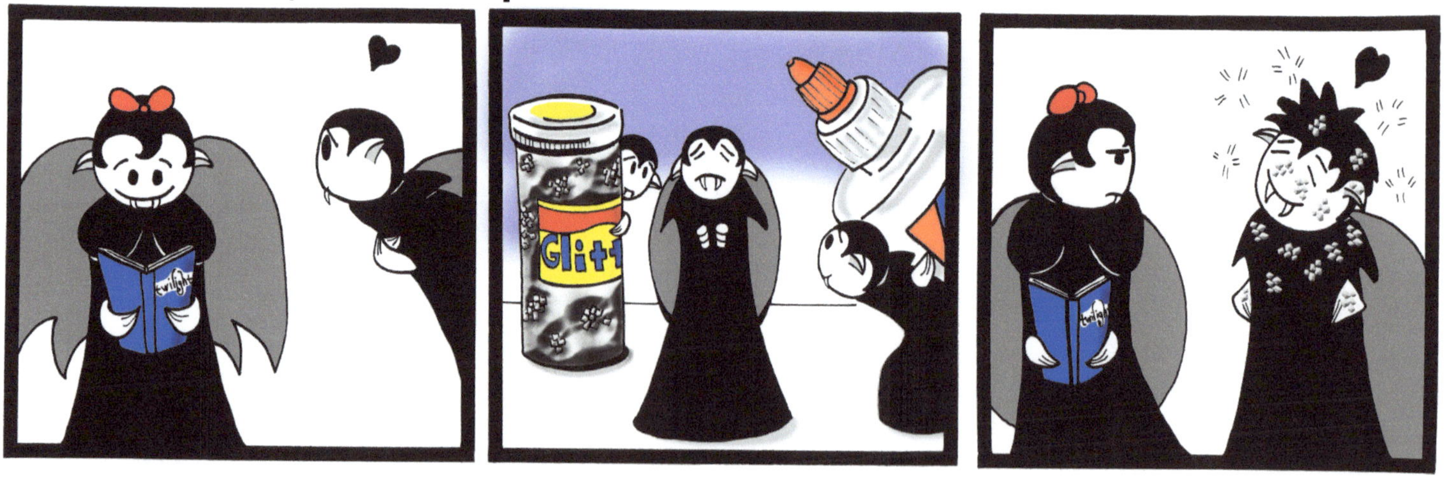
Glitt

BEHIND THE SCENES

The Little Vampires don't sparkle. But they will do what it takes to impress the ladies. This fun little poke at the *Twilight* phenomenon wound up becoming one of my best-selling art prints.

November 25, 2009 • Happy Thanksgiving!

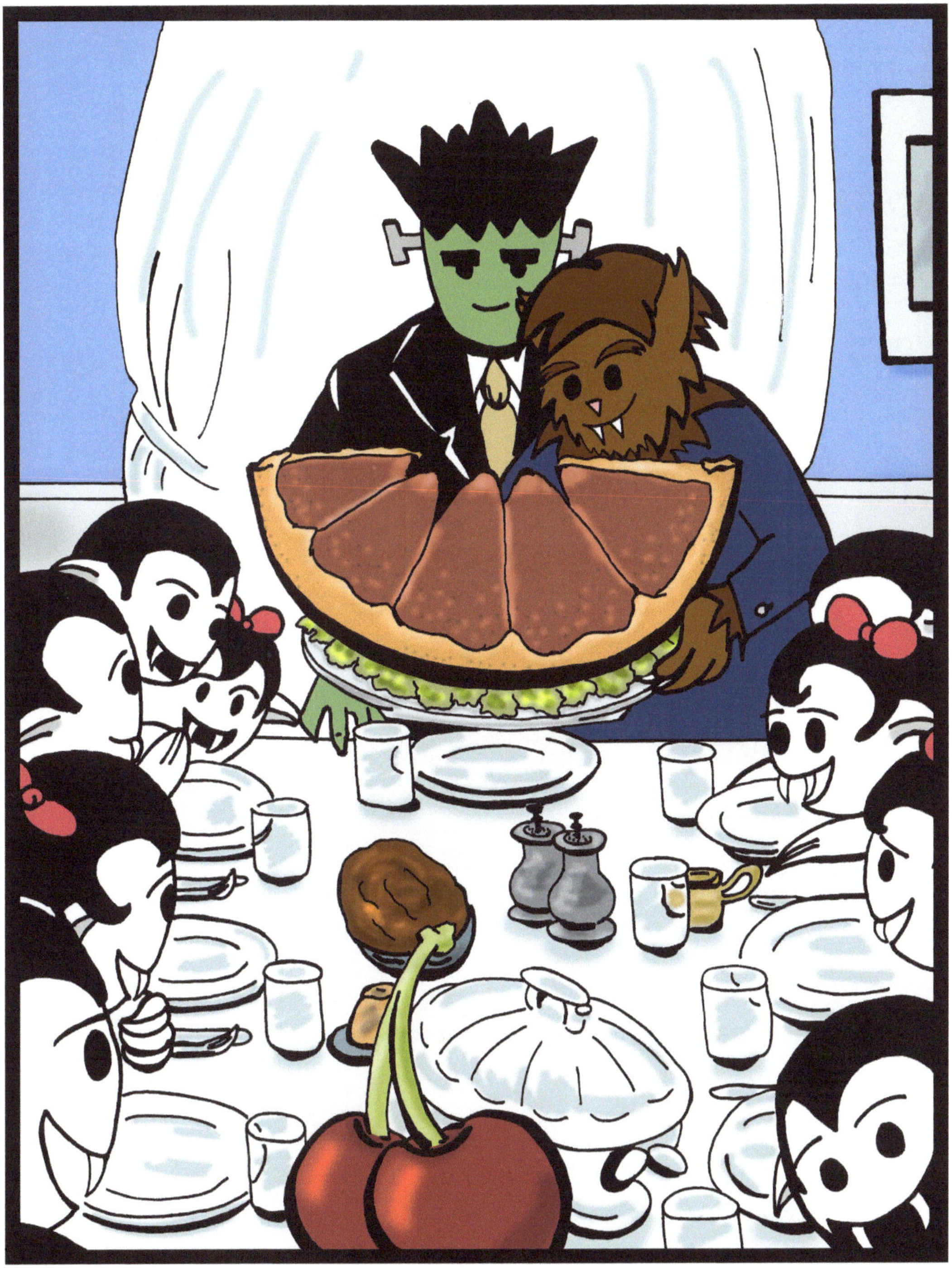

ART DIRECTION

The "turkey" is a slice of a blood orange in this homage to Norman Rockwell's famous painting *Freedom From Want*. This is not the last time I would visit my love of art history in the comic.

December 2, 2009 • The Cat

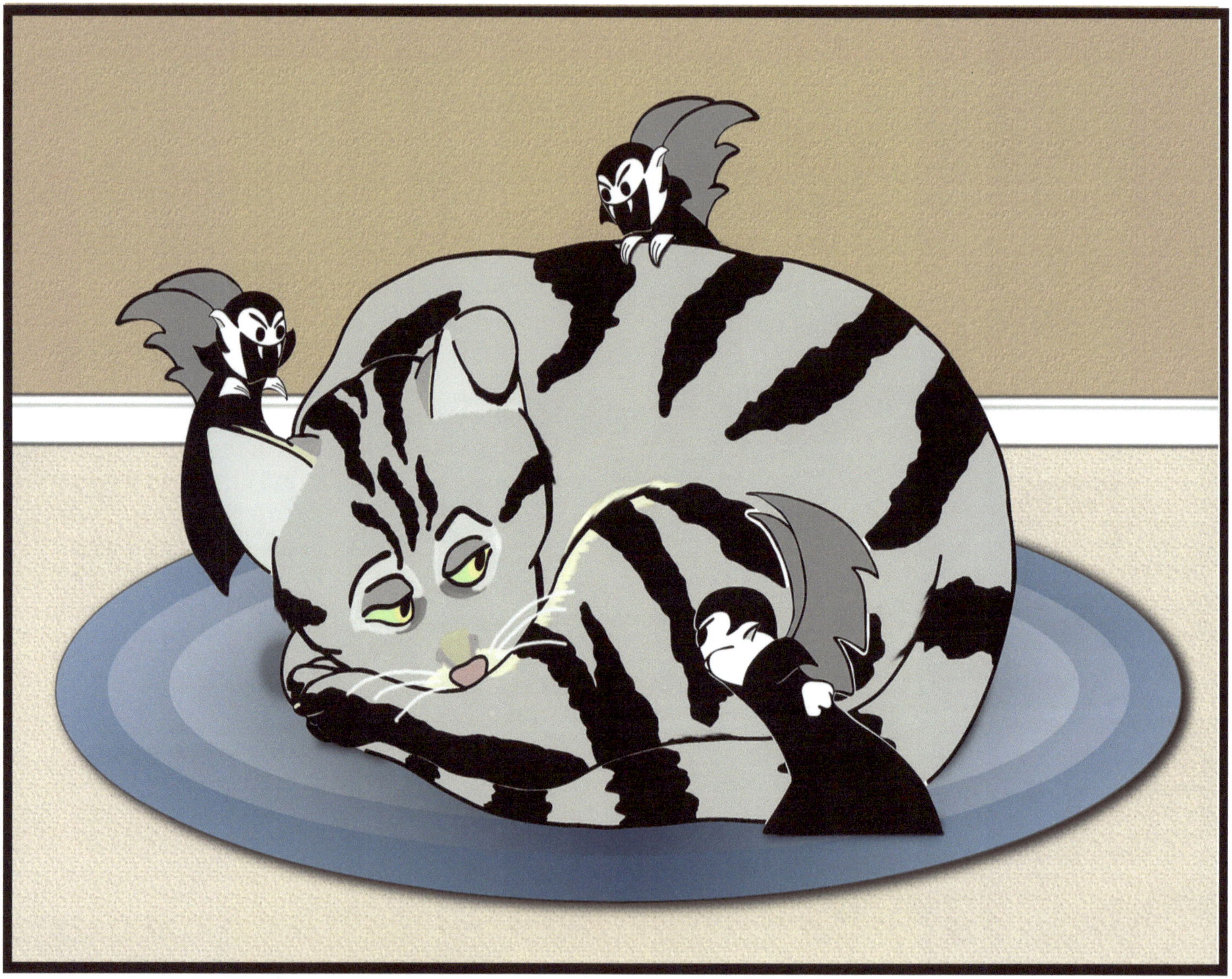

BEHIND THE SCENES

The Cat in the Little Vampires universe is based on our cat, Matt. Matt the Cat was diagnosed with cancer in late November of 2009, and I honored his fight with this comic. Matt died in January of 2011. It gives me great comfort knowing that he lives on in the Little Vampires books and comics.

December 9, 2009 • Bzzt

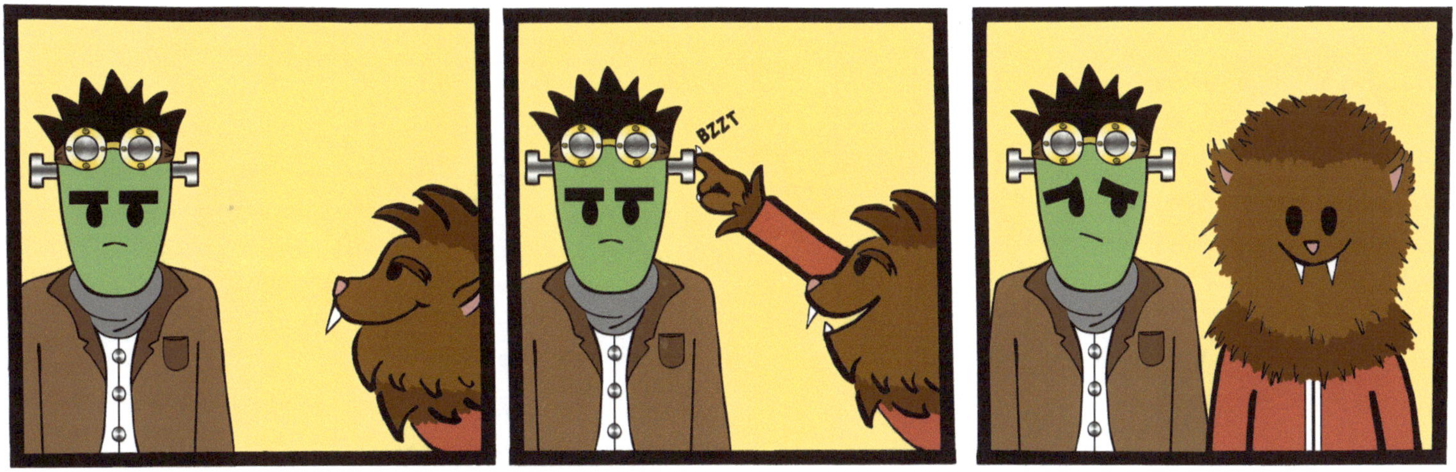
BZZT

December 16, 2009 • Wheeee!

BEHIND THE SCENES

This was the art for my annual Christmas card. I love the sense of freedom and joy I was able to convey with this comic.

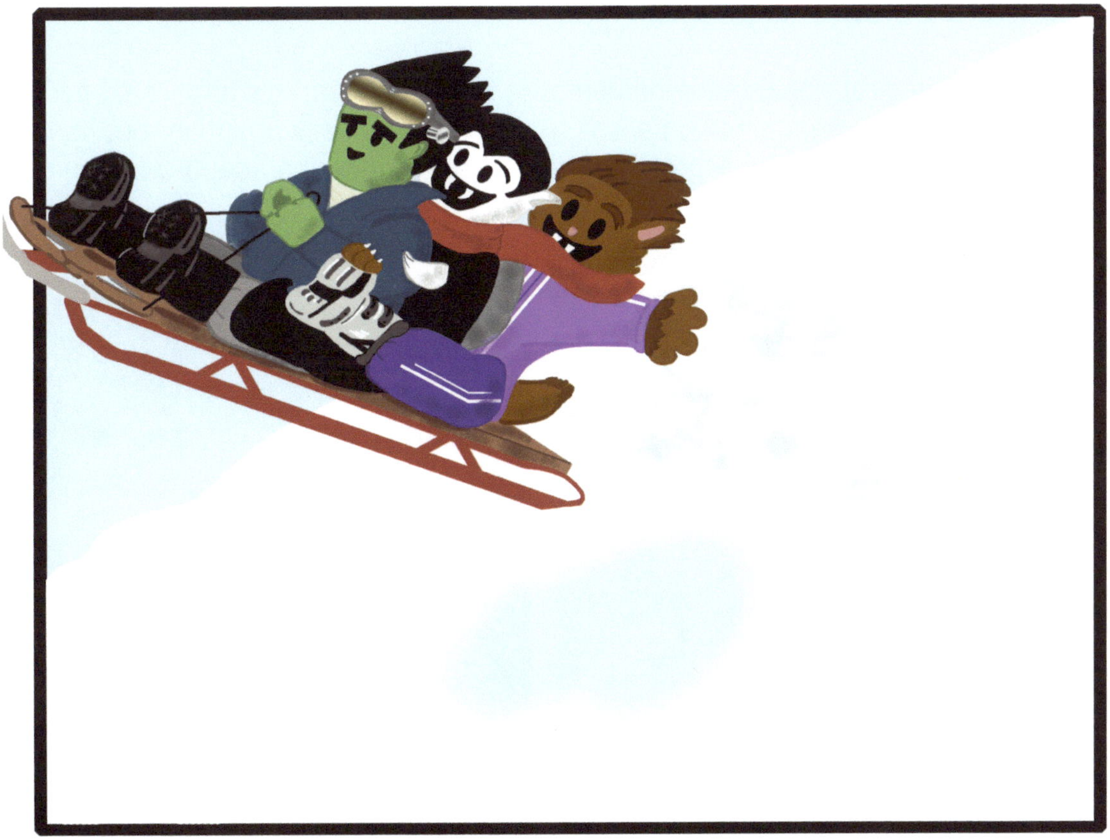

December 23, 2009 • Happy Holidays to All Except Mumsy

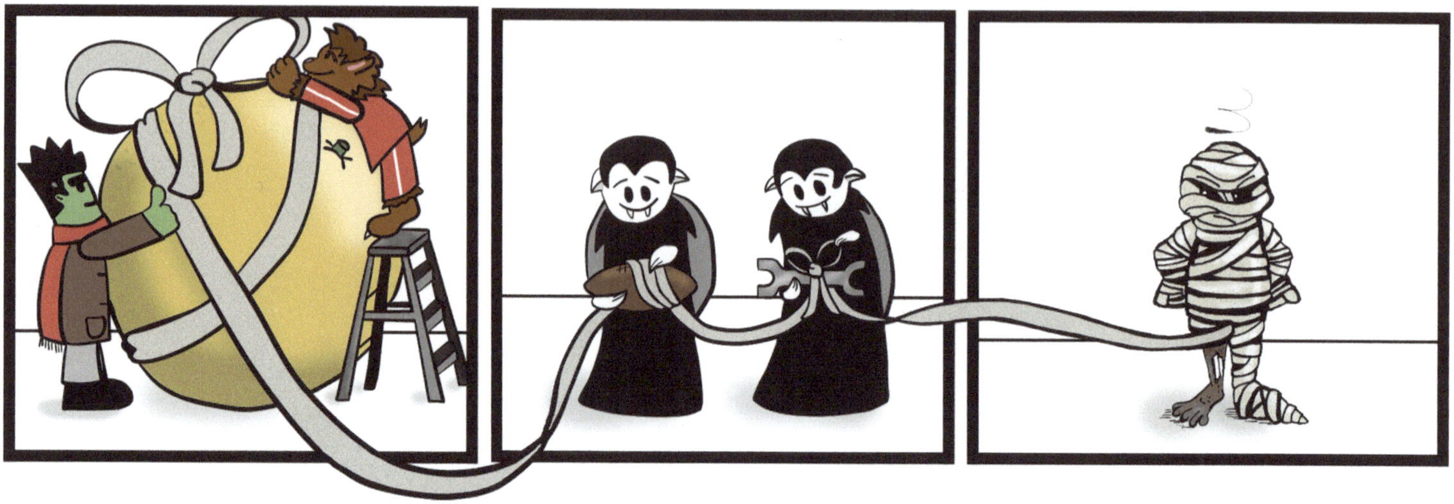

MEET THE CAST

This marks the first appearance of Mumsy in the Little Vampires universe. I named him Mumsy because it sounded British. I imagined that he was, of course, originally Egyptian, but had spent so many centuries as a resident of the Egyptian wing of The British Museum that he adopted British mannerisms.

December 30, 2009 • Happy New Year!

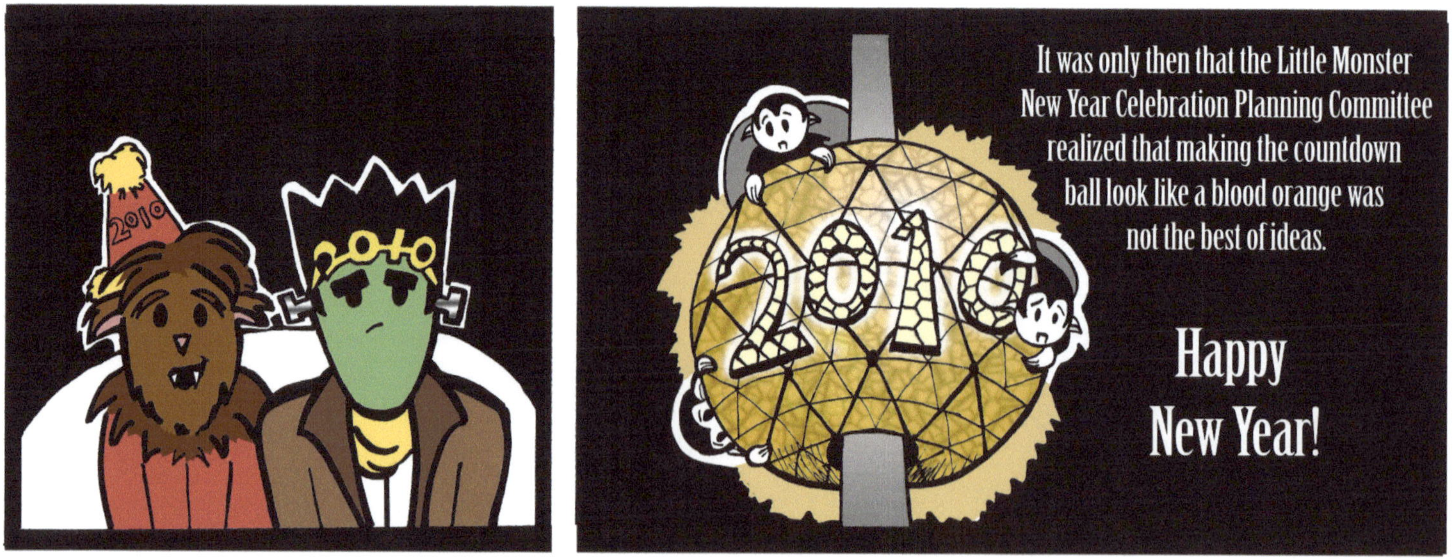
2010
2010
2010
It was only then that the Little Monster New Year Celebration Planning Committee realized that making the countdown ball look like a blood orange was not the best of ideas.
Happy New Year!

January 6, 2010 • The Blood Orange of the Baskervilles

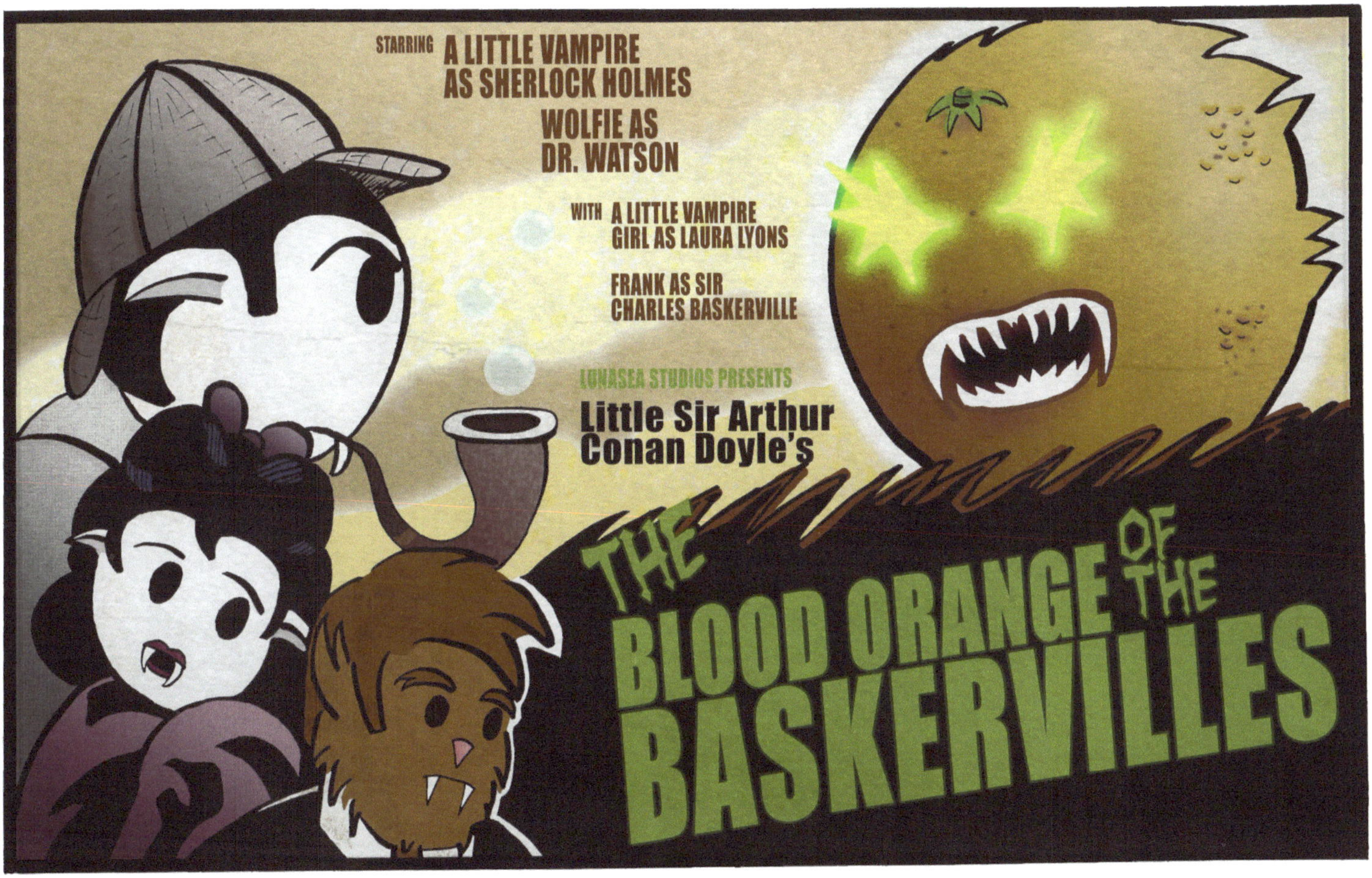
STARRING A LITTLE VAMPIRE AS SHERLOCK HOLMES
WOLFIE AS DR. WATSON
WITH A LITTLE VAMPIRE GIRL AS LAURA LYONS
FRANK AS SIR CHARLES BASKERVILLE
LUNASEA STUDIOS PRESENTS
Little Sir Arthur Conan Doyle's
THE BLOOD ORANGE OF THE BASKERVILLES

BEHIND THE SCENES

Sherlock Holmes has been a passion of mine since I was a little girl. I devoured all of the original Doyle stories, and have enjoyed just about every depiction of Holmes and Watson in other media. This includes the 2009 *Sherlock Holmes* movie starring Robert Downey Jr. and Jude Law. Seeing that movie with my family inspired this comic, which I based on the posters for the 1939 *The Hound of the Baskervilles*, starring Basil Rathbone and Nigel Bruce.

I am a huge fan of the BBC's 2010 modernization of Sherlock Holmes, *Sherlock*. The Little Vampires are big fans of the flowing black coat that Benedict Cumberbatch wears in that series.

January 13, 2010 • Zombie Hockey

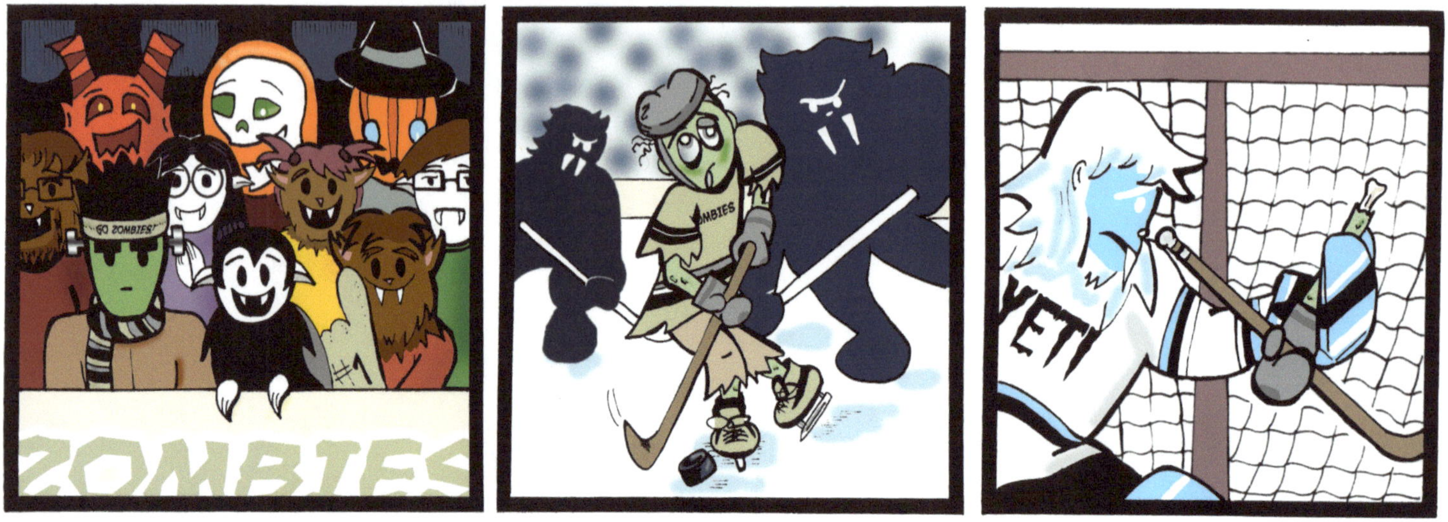
GO ZOMBIES!
ZOMBIES
ZOMBIES
YETI

January 20, 2010 • Zombie Hockey Victory

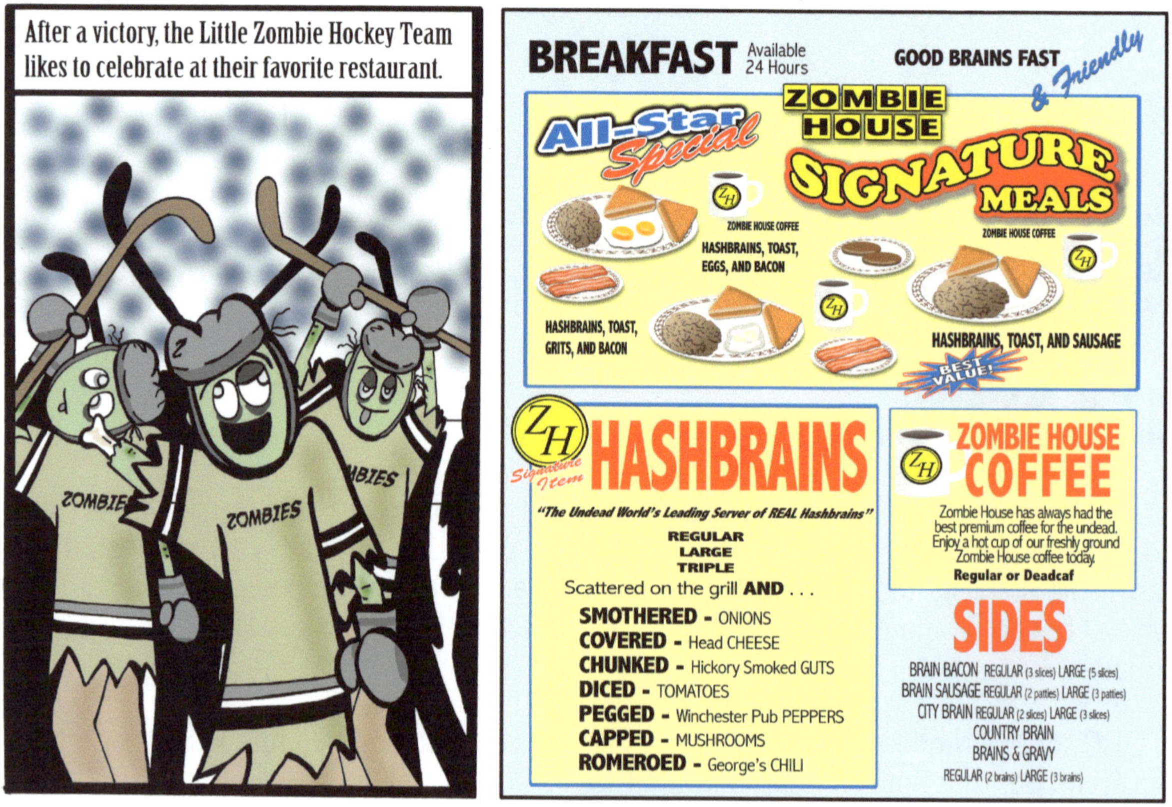
After a victory, the Little Zombie Hockey Team likes to celebrate at their favorite restaurant.
ZOMBIES
ZOMBIES
ZOMBIES
BREAKFAST Available 24 Hours
GOOD BRAINS FAST & Friendly
All-Star Special
ZOMBIE HOUSE
SIGNATURE MEALS
ZOMBIE HOUSE COFFEE
HASHBRAINS, TOAST, EGGS, AND BACON
ZOMBIE HOUSE COFFEE
HASHBRAINS, TOAST, GRITS, AND BACON
HASHBRAINS, TOAST, AND SAUSAGE
BEST VALUE!
ZH Signature Item
HASHBRAINS
"The Undead World's Leading Server of REAL Hashbrains"
REGULAR
LARGE
TRIPLE
Scattered on the grill AND . . .
SMOTHERED - ONIONS
COVERED - Head CHEESE
CHUNKED - Hickory Smoked GUTS
DICED - TOMATOES
PEGGED - Winchester Pub PEPPERS
CAPPED - MUSHROOMS
ROMEROED - George's CHILI
ZOMBIE HOUSE COFFEE
Zombie House has always had the best premium coffee for the undead. Enjoy a hot cup of our freshly ground Zombie House coffee today.
Regular or Deadcaf
SIDES
BRAIN BACON REGULAR (3 slices) LARGE (5 slices)
BRAIN SAUSAGE REGULAR (2 patties) LARGE (3 patties)
CITY BRAIN REGULAR (2 slices) LARGE (3 slices)
COUNTRY BRAIN
BRAINS & GRAVY
REGULAR (2 brains) LARGE (3 brains)

BEHIND THE SCENES

The crowd in the Zombie Hockey comic includes "Little Vampire-ized" characters from the *Monster Commute* and *Weregeek* web-comics.

Zombie House is an homage to the Waffle House chain of restaurants.

January 27, 2010 • How 'Bout the Power of Flight

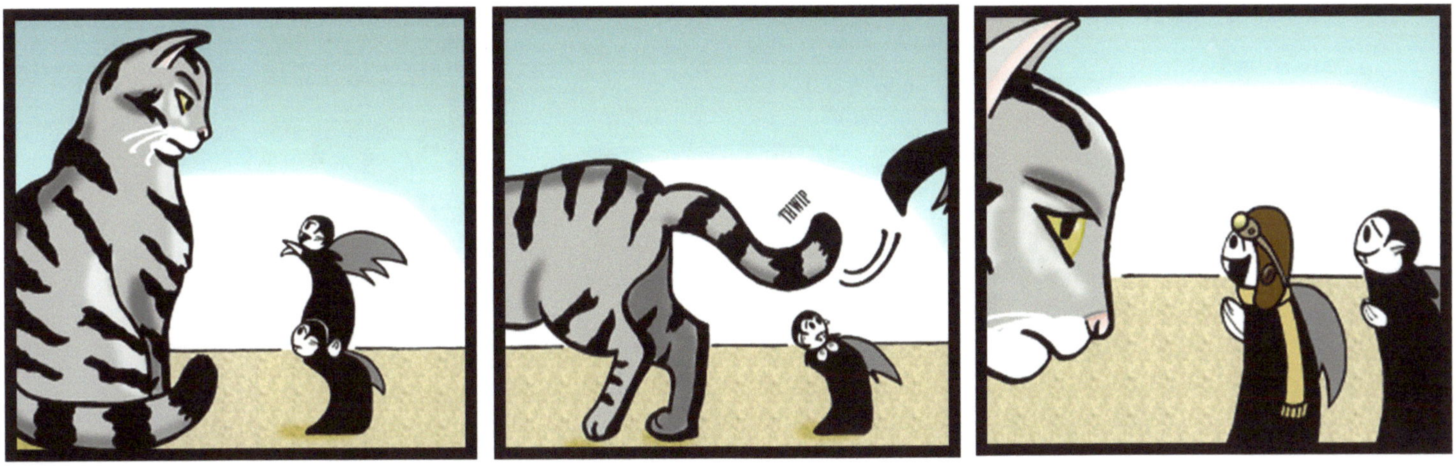
THWIP

MEET THE CAST

The Little Vampires try to be like big vampires as much as possible. Since several vampire tales grant them the power of flight, I decided that the Little Vampires would try to fly as well. Their wings are more useful for expressing their emotions than they are for sustained flight.

February 3, 2010 • Corgisailing

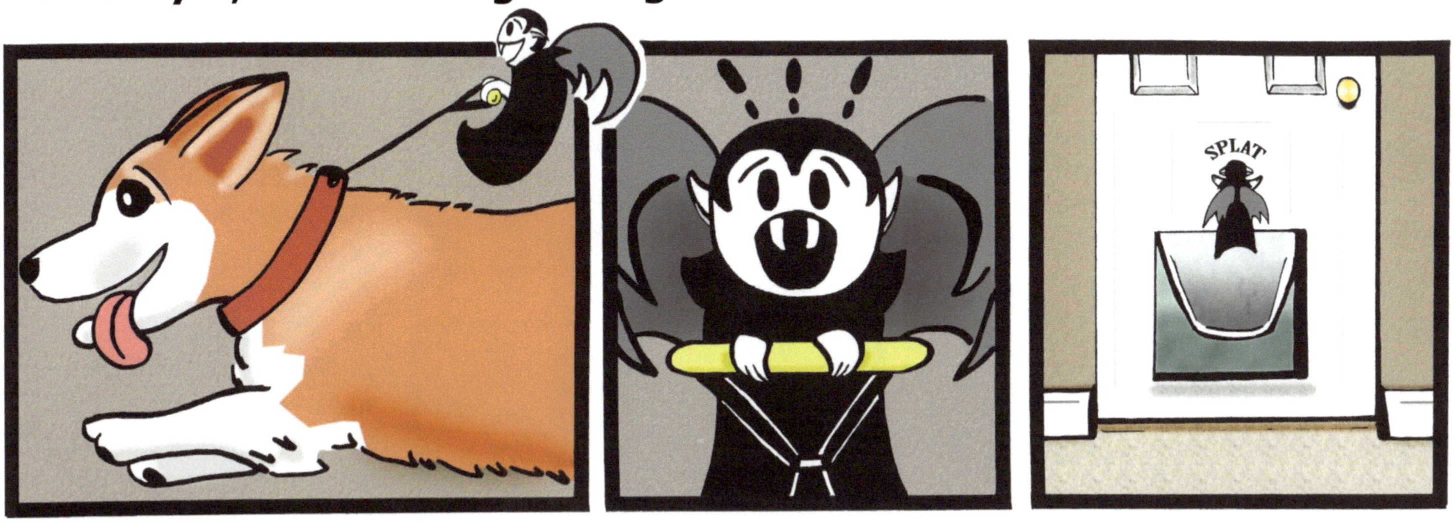
SPLAT

BEHIND THE SCENES

I asked readers to vote for a dog breed to be used in one of the comics. Corgi won by a landslide.

February 10, 2010 • Valentines

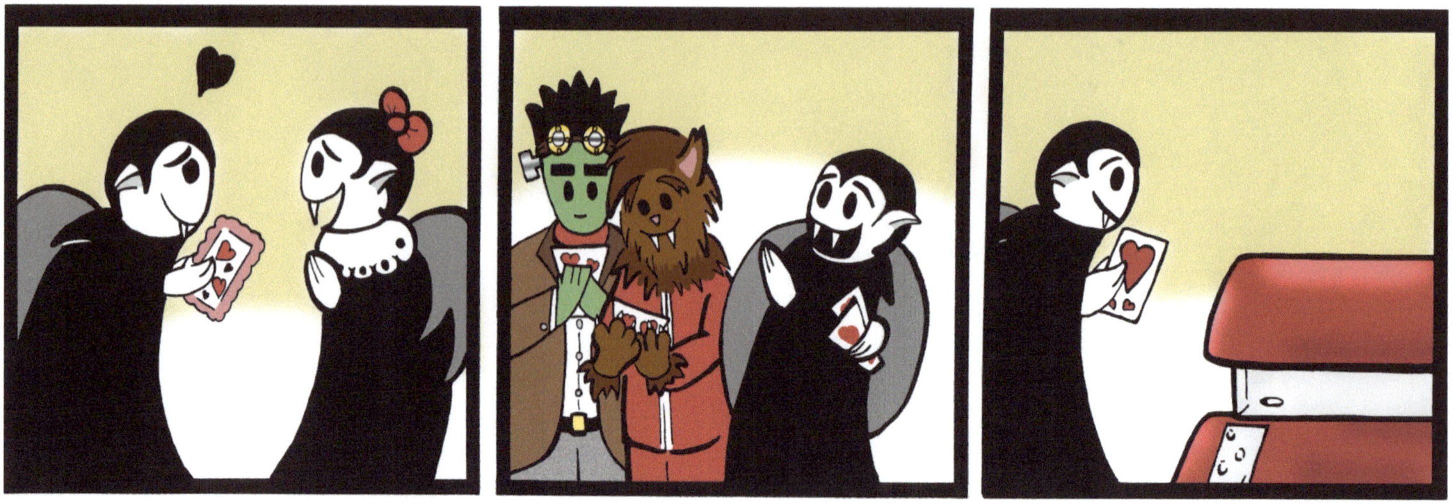

February 17, 2010 • Little Monster Winter Olympics

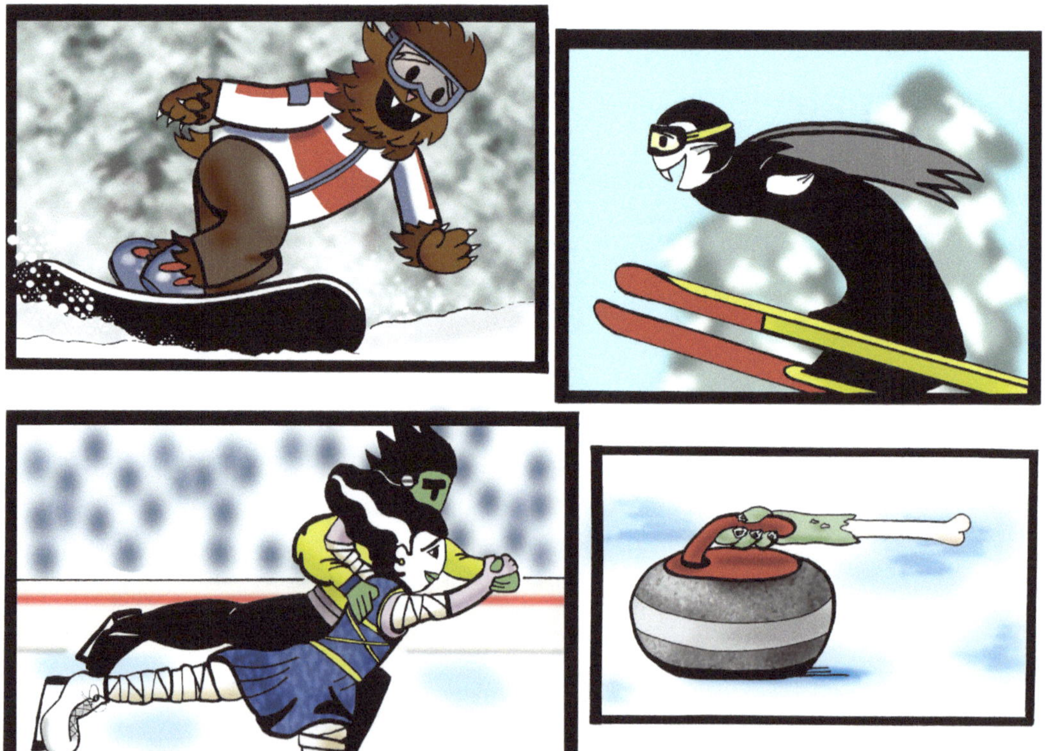

BEHIND THE SCENES

While watching the 2010 Olympic Winter Games, I realized that curling, that much-maligned cold weather sport, was actually awesome.

The Games were held in Vancouver, British Columbia, so maybe it was the Canadian love of curling that infected me through the television. But for whatever reason, I became a lifelong curling fan because of the 2010 Olympics.

February 24, 2010 • Zam"boney"

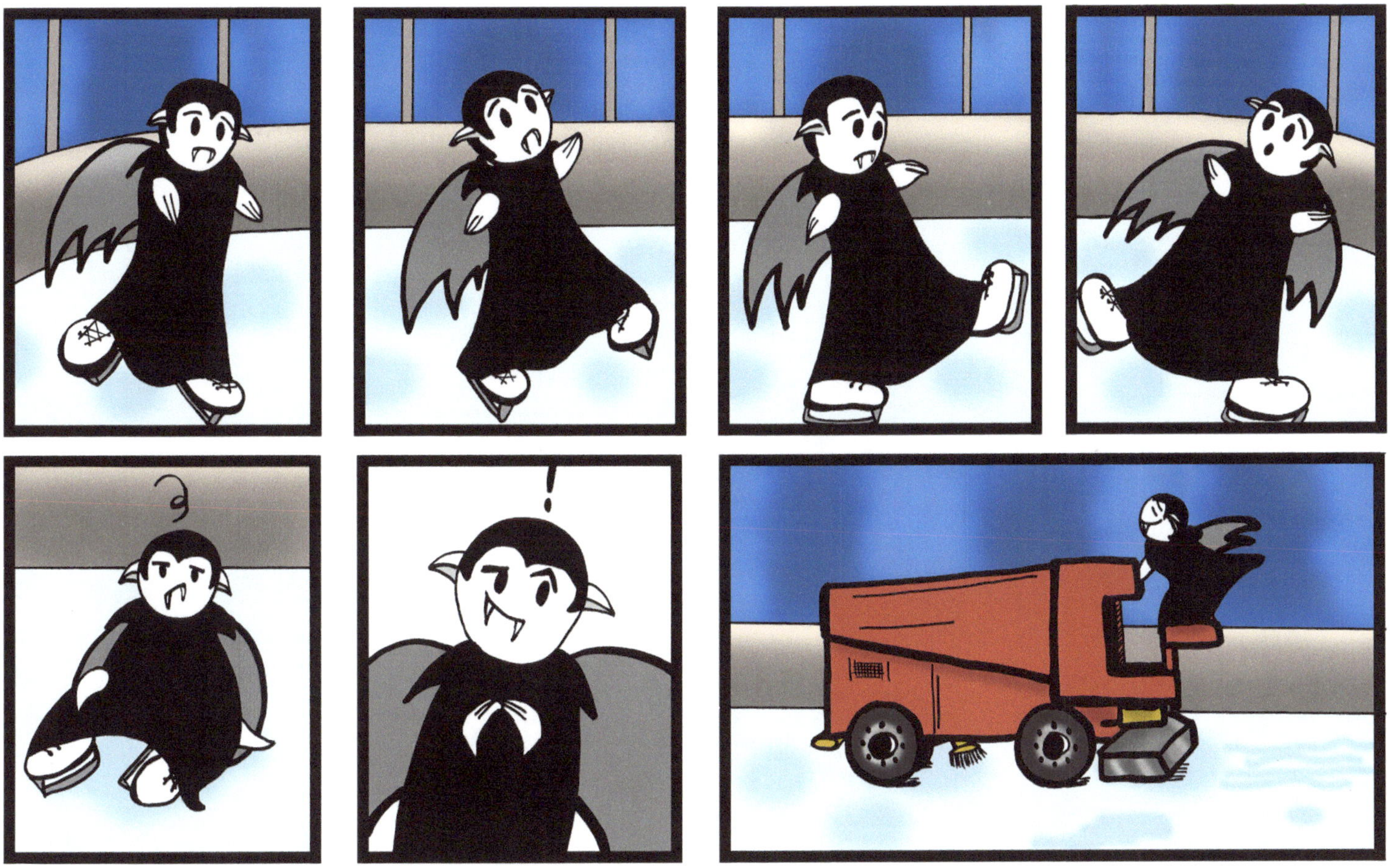

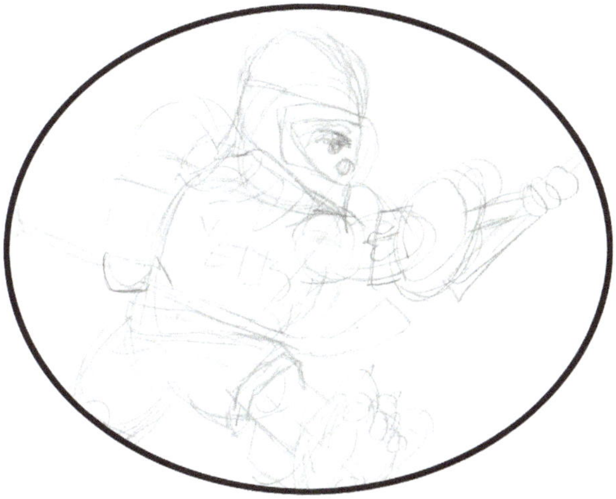

Studies for the zombie hockey comic strip.

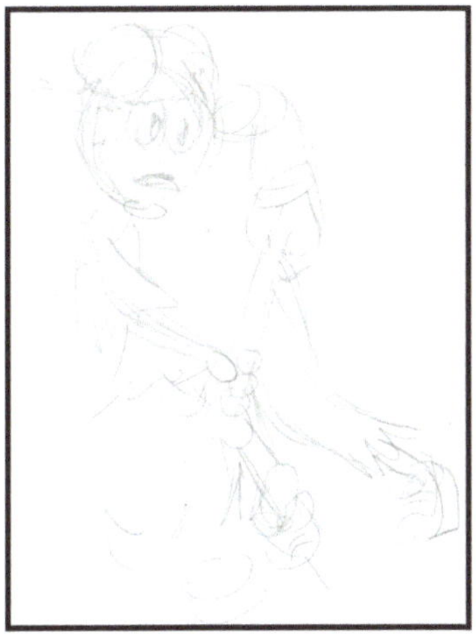

March 3, 2010 • Staple Wranglin'

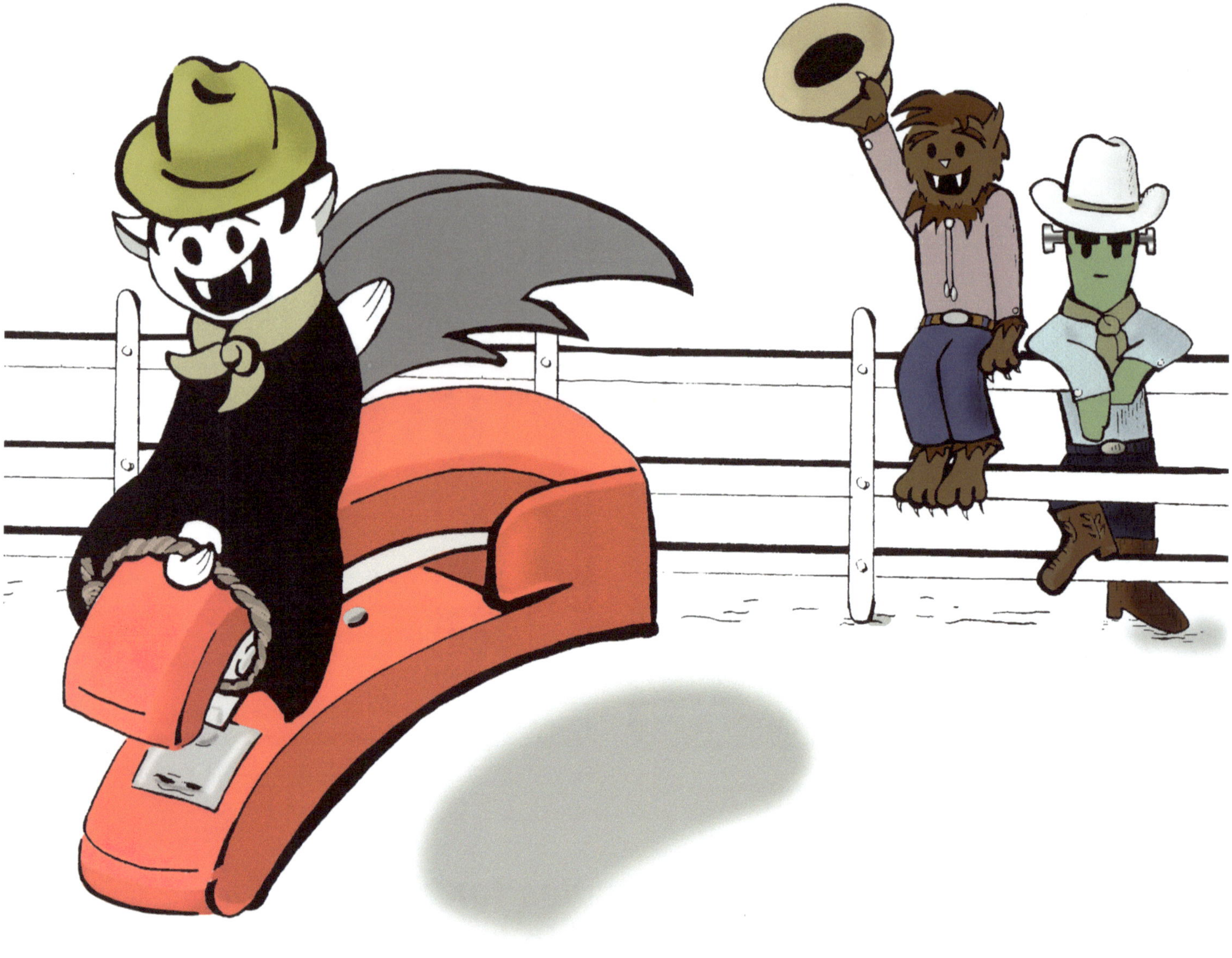

ON LOCATION

We attend a variety of conventions, big and small, in a variety of places, big and small. In March of 2010 we exhibited at Staple! The Independent Media Expo in Austin, Texas. Austin is a fun, quirky city, and Staple! is a fun, quirky show. This comic was inspired by the show's symbol, a red stapler.

March 10, 2010 • The Little Fremont Troll

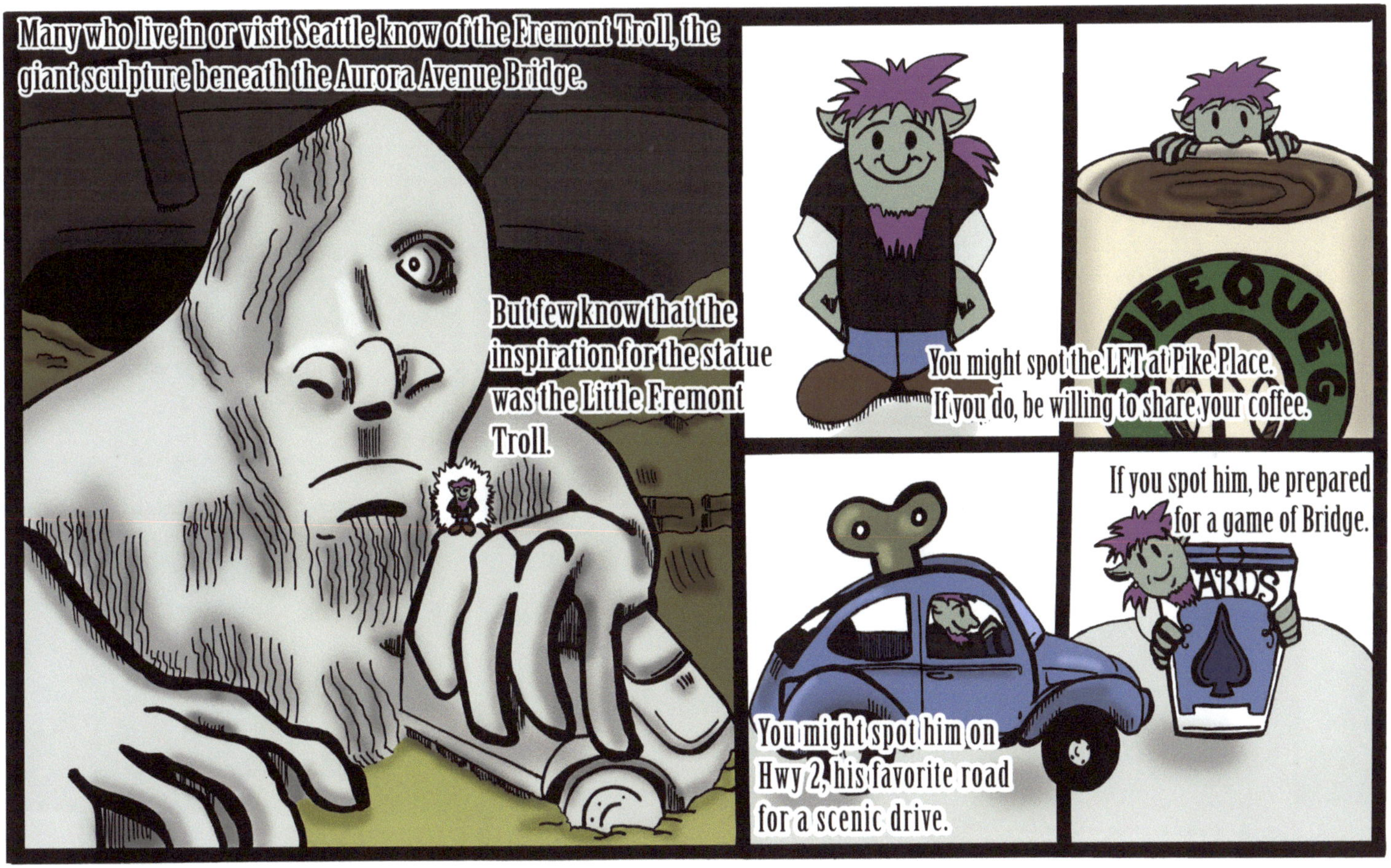
Many who live in or visit Seattle know of the Fremont Troll, the giant sculpture beneath the Aurora Avenue Bridge.
But few know that the inspiration for the statue was the Little Fremont Troll.
You might spot the LFT at Pike Place. If you do, be willing to share your coffee.
You might spot him on Hwy 2, his favorite road for a scenic drive.
If you spot him, be prepared for a game of Bridge.

ON LOCATION

The weekend after Staple! in Texas we were in Seattle, Washington for Emerald City Comicon. Staple! celebrates independent writers and artists, and is one of the smaller shows we exhibit at. Emerald City Comicon celebrates all pop culture, and is one of the larger shows we exhibit at. Both are great shows in great cities.

Seattle is fun and quirky like Austin, and is also one of the geekiest cities in the United States. It has the Science Fiction Museum and Science Fiction Hall of Fame, hosts the Penny Arcade Expo for gamers, and has a giant statue of a troll beneath the Aurora Bridge. The Fremont Troll is one of my favorite pieces of American public art, and I just couldn't resist using it in a comic.

March 17, 2010 • Banshee of the Dance

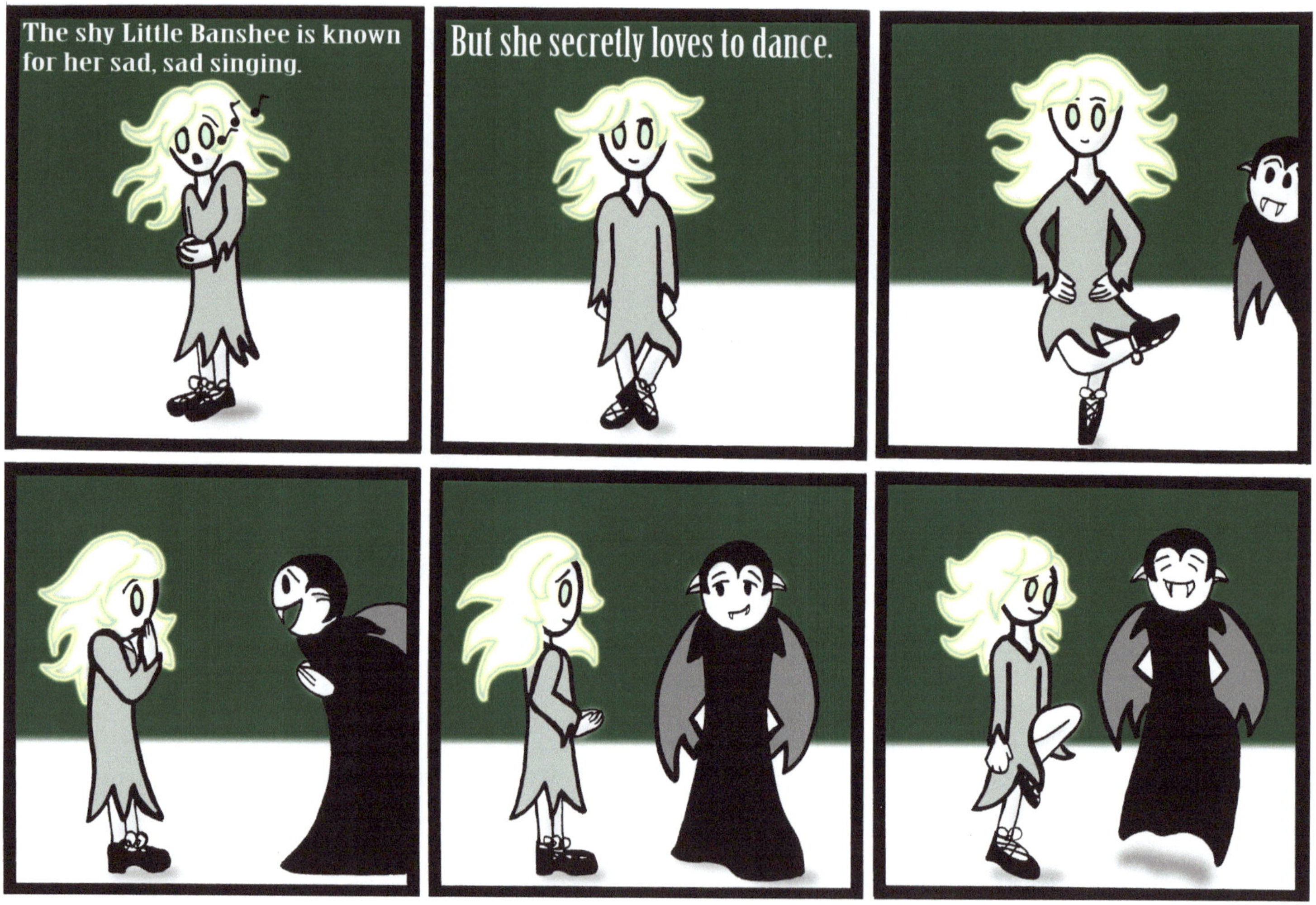
The shy Little Banshee is known for her sad, sad singing.
But she secretly loves to dance.

BEHIND THE SCENES

This comic is a little shout-out to my Irish heritage. I love mythology and folklore from around the world, and this includes the stories of my ancestors. I've always been extra fascinated by the tales of the banshees, fairy spirits that sing a wailing song when someone is about to die. I wondered what they did in their spare time, when they weren't foretelling death with high-pitched laments. Since I am a fan of Irish dancing, I decided to make this banshee a fan as well.

March 24, 2010 • Go Big Blue

ON LOCATION

Two weekends after Emerald City Comicon in Seattle, I headed to Kentucky for the Powell County Reading Celebration. I'm a graduate of Powell County High School, and am forever grateful to many of the teachers there for encouraging my passion for arts and literature.

There are so many things I love about Kentucky. I love all the family and friends I have there. I love the beautiful natural landscape. And I love the University of Kentucky Wildcats basketball program. So when Wolfie dreams of playing college basketball, he dreams he plays for the Wildcats. I know, I know, it's funny for a little werewolf to play for a team with a cat mascot, but I created Wolfie, so there.

It's not like I'd have him play for UK's rivals, the Duke Blue Devils. That would just be wrong.

Concept sketches for Wolfie. He started out more dog-like than man-like. As his personality developed and I realized that he was the athlete of the group, I decided that I wanted to be able to draw him playing a variety of sports. So I gave him a more humanoid shape.

March 31, 2010 • San Francisco WHEEEEEE!

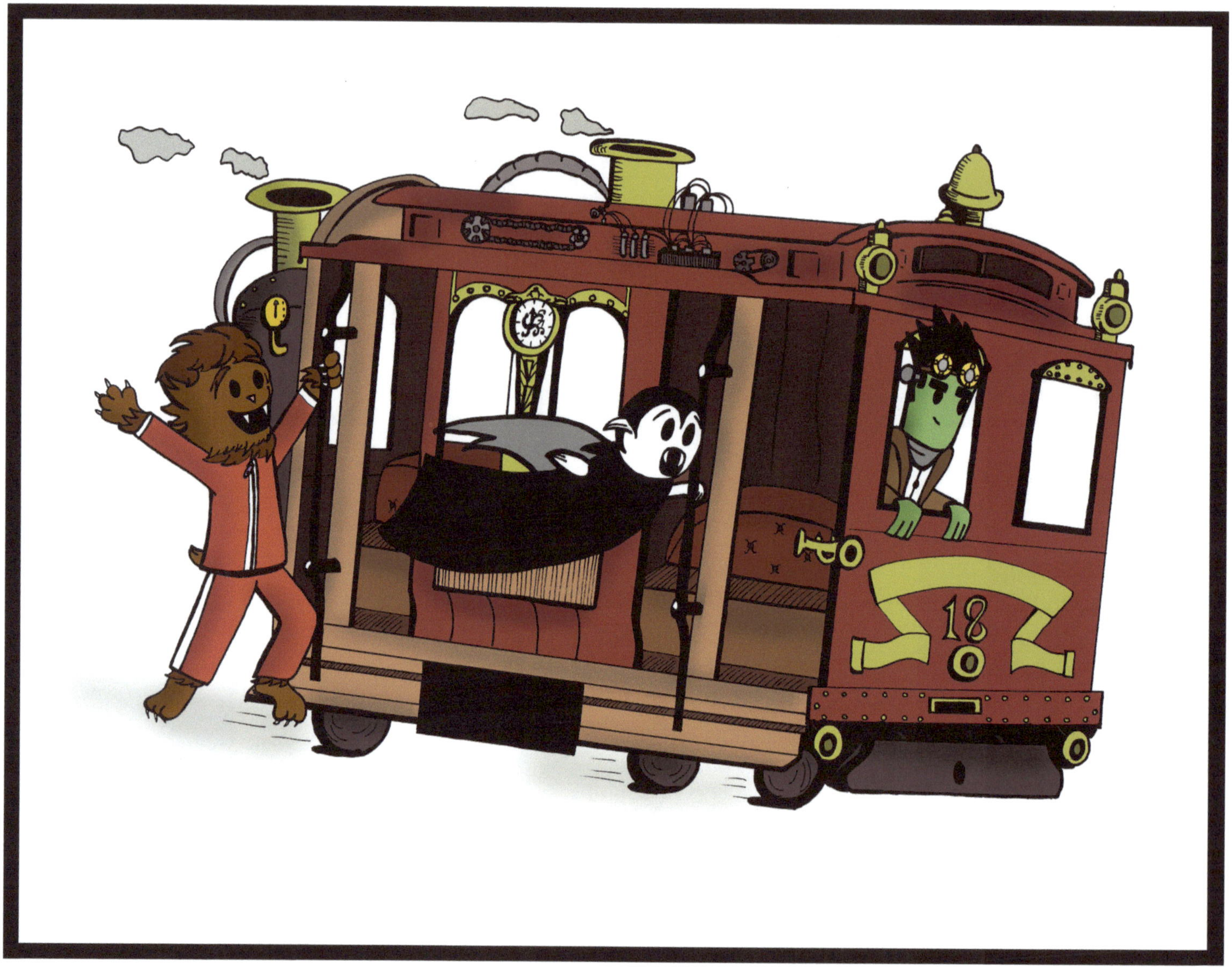
18

ON LOCATION

March Madness applies to more than college basketball. It applies to conventions as well. The weekend after returning from Kentucky, James and I were in San Francisco, California for WonderCon. Luckily for us, it was easy to find coffee near the Moscone Convention Center. We sure did need it.

April 7, 2010 • Reverence

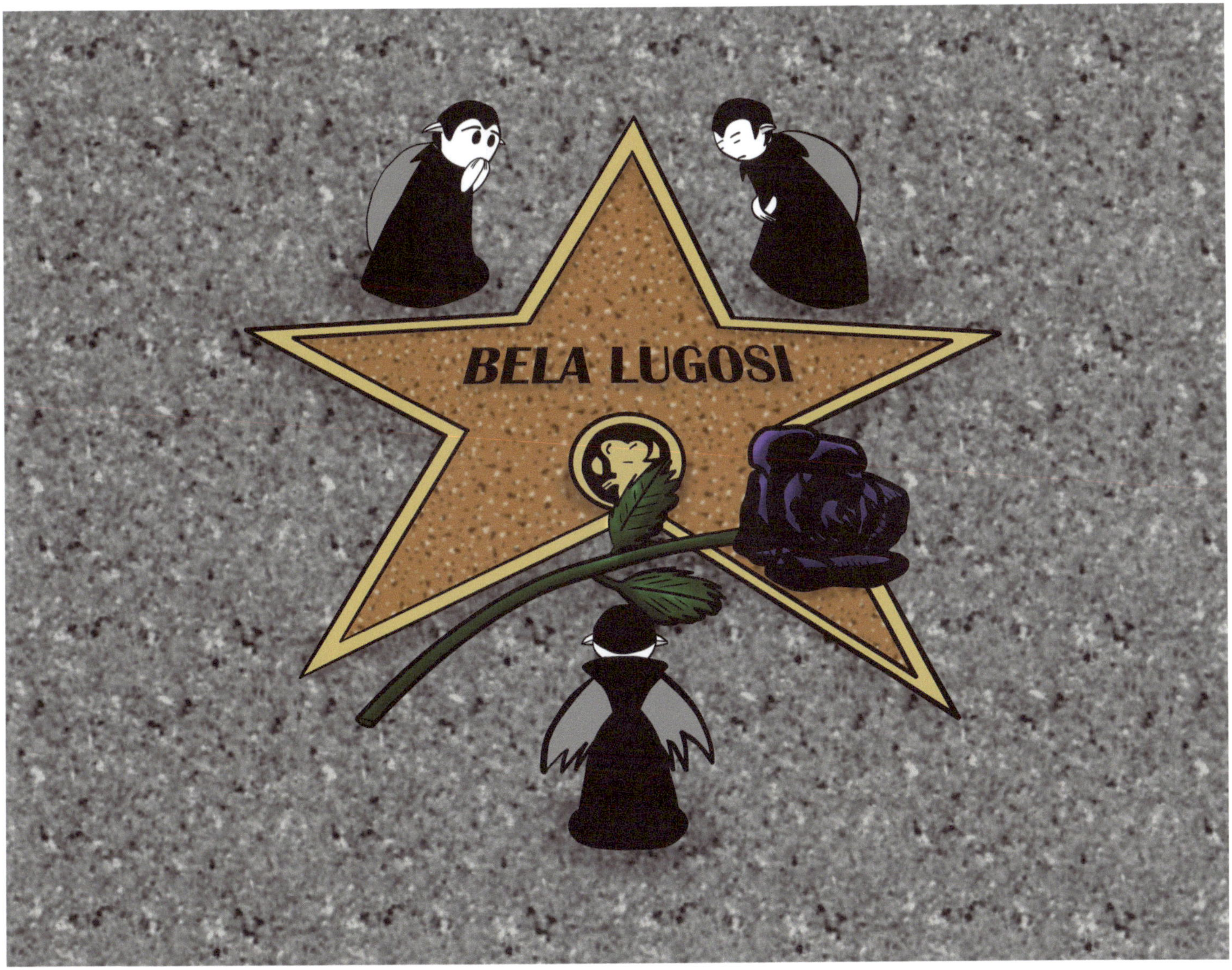
BELA LUGOSI

ON LOCATION

The weekend after WonderCon was Monsterpalooza in Burbank, California. It's a great horror convention that is, thankfully, closer to home. Amazingly, I got to meet Bela Lugosi Jr., son of the original movie Dracula, at Monsterpalooza. More amazingly, he bought a copy of the first *Little Vampires* book. Wow.

April 14, 2010 • The Vampire-est Place on Earth

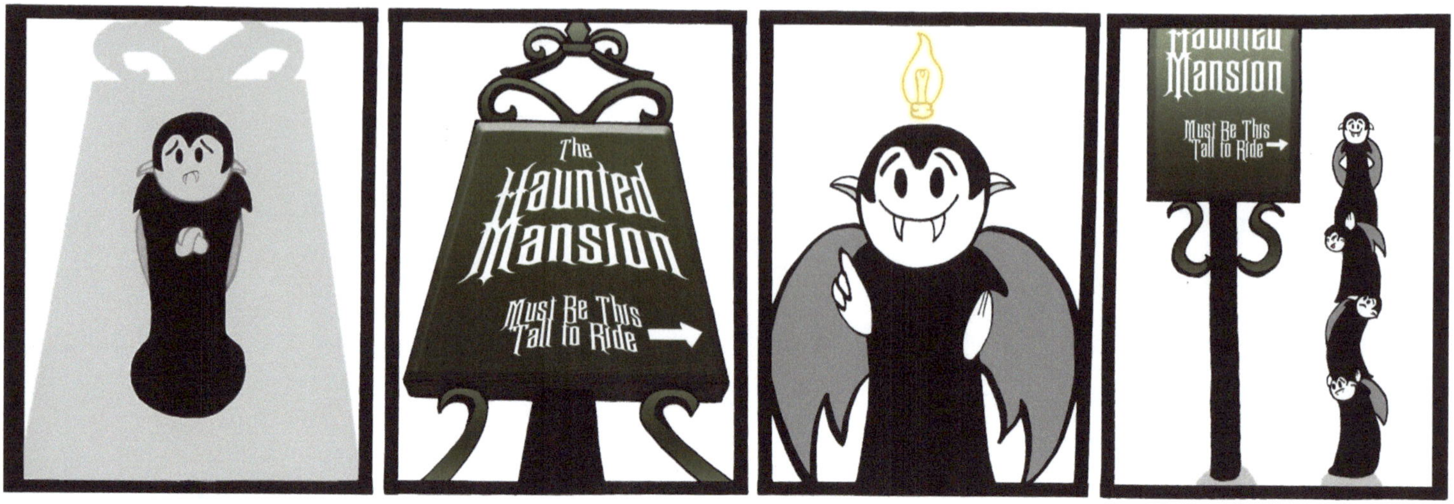
The Haunted Mansion
Must Be This Tall to Ride
Mansion
Must Be This Tall to Ride

ON LOCATION

After Monsterpalooza, we exhibited at the Wizard World Anaheim Comic Con. The Anaheim Convention Center is right by Disneyland, so I had the Little Vampires pay a visit to the happiest place on Earth.

April 21, 2010 • Earth Day with Frank

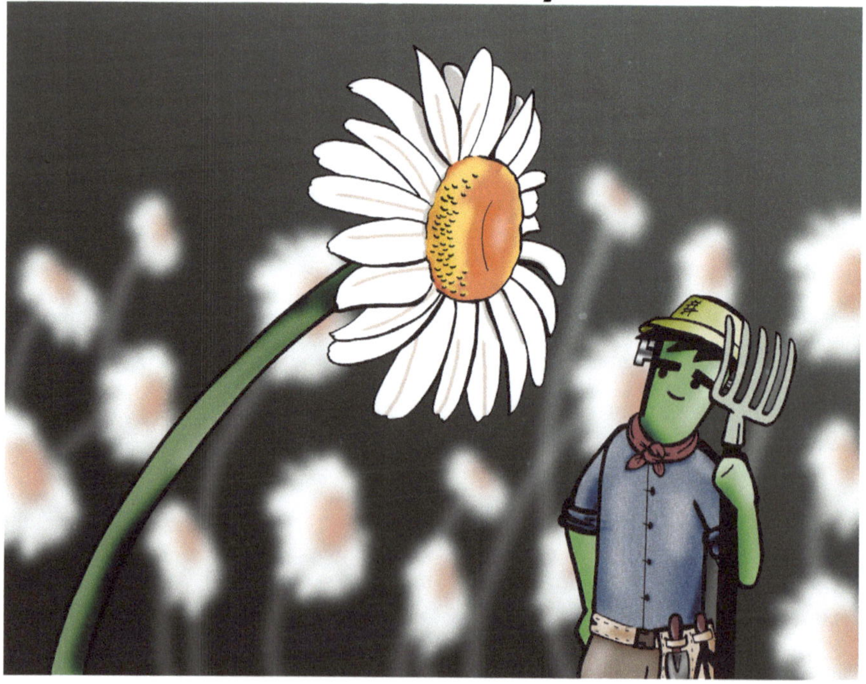

BEHIND THE SCENES

After more than a month of back-to-back conventions, it was wonderful to be able to take some time to stop and smell the flowers.

In the classic *Frankenstein* starring Boris Karloff, the Monster befriends a little girl who enjoys throwing flowers into a lake. The Monster wants to throw flowers into the lake too, but gets carried away and throws little Maria into the lake. Oops.

I decided that Frank would love flowers in a less lethal manner.

April 28, 2010 • Bzzt Revisited

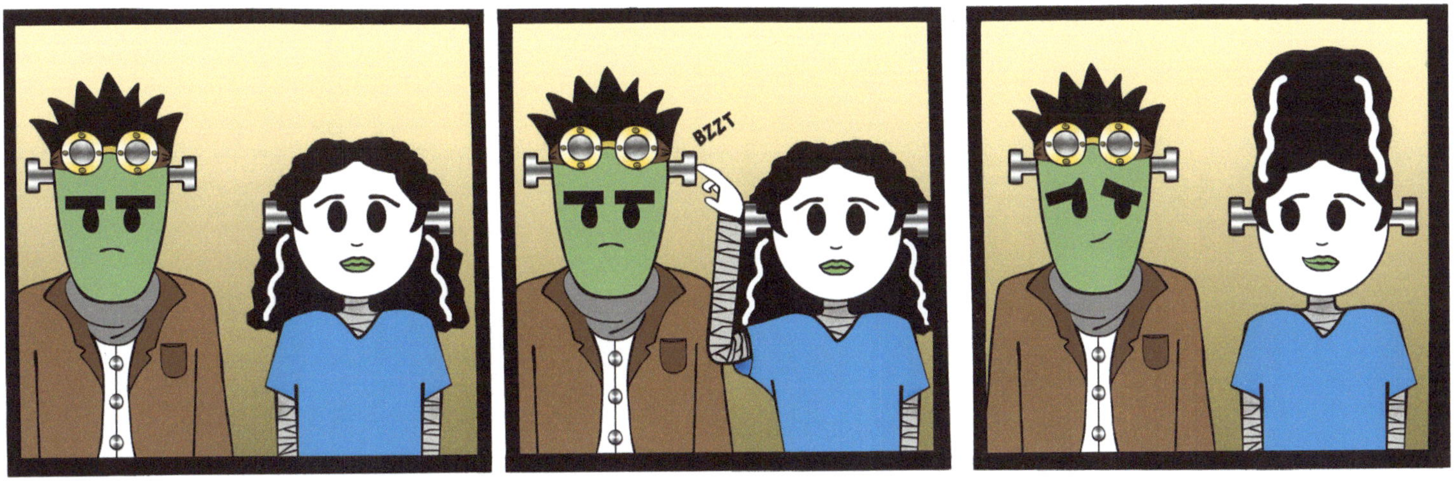
BZZT

MEET THE CAST

Elsa is named after Elsa Lanchester, the wonderful actress who played the Bride in *Bride of Frankenstein*. I didn't want to name her the Bride because she and Frank are just good friends.

May 5, 2010 • Does Whatever an Iron Can

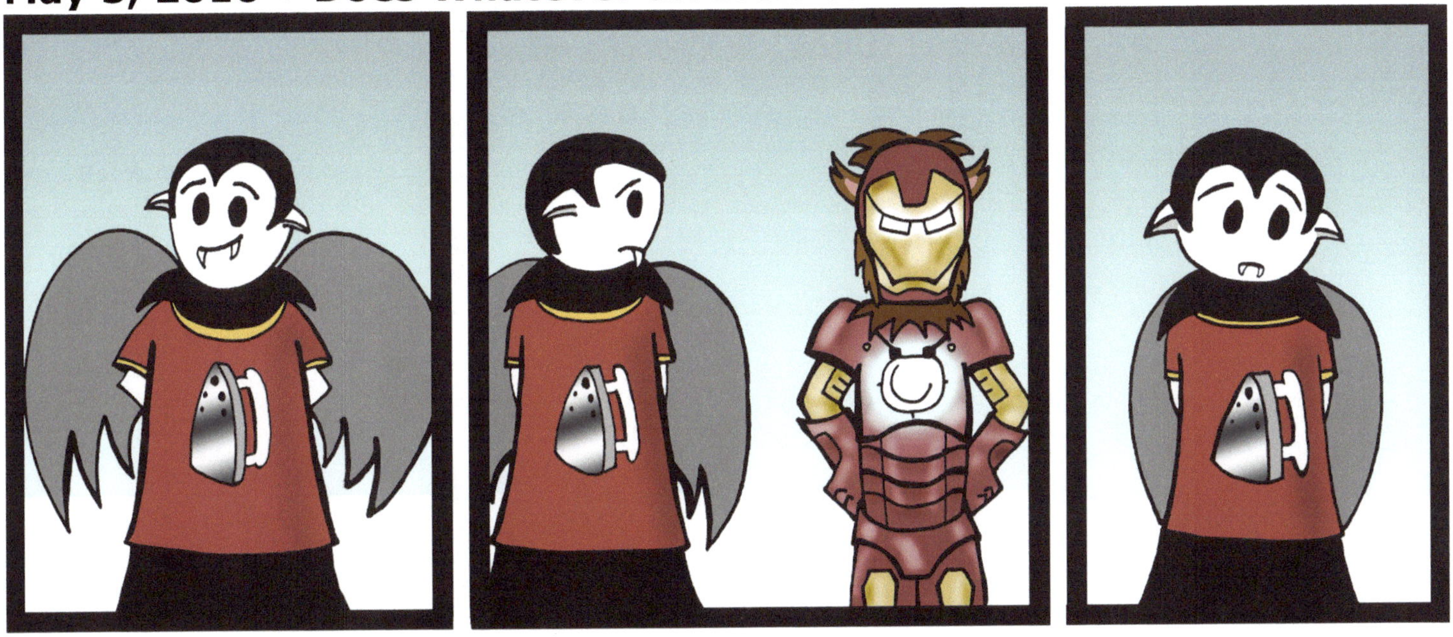

May 12, 2010 • Blood Orange Parcel Service

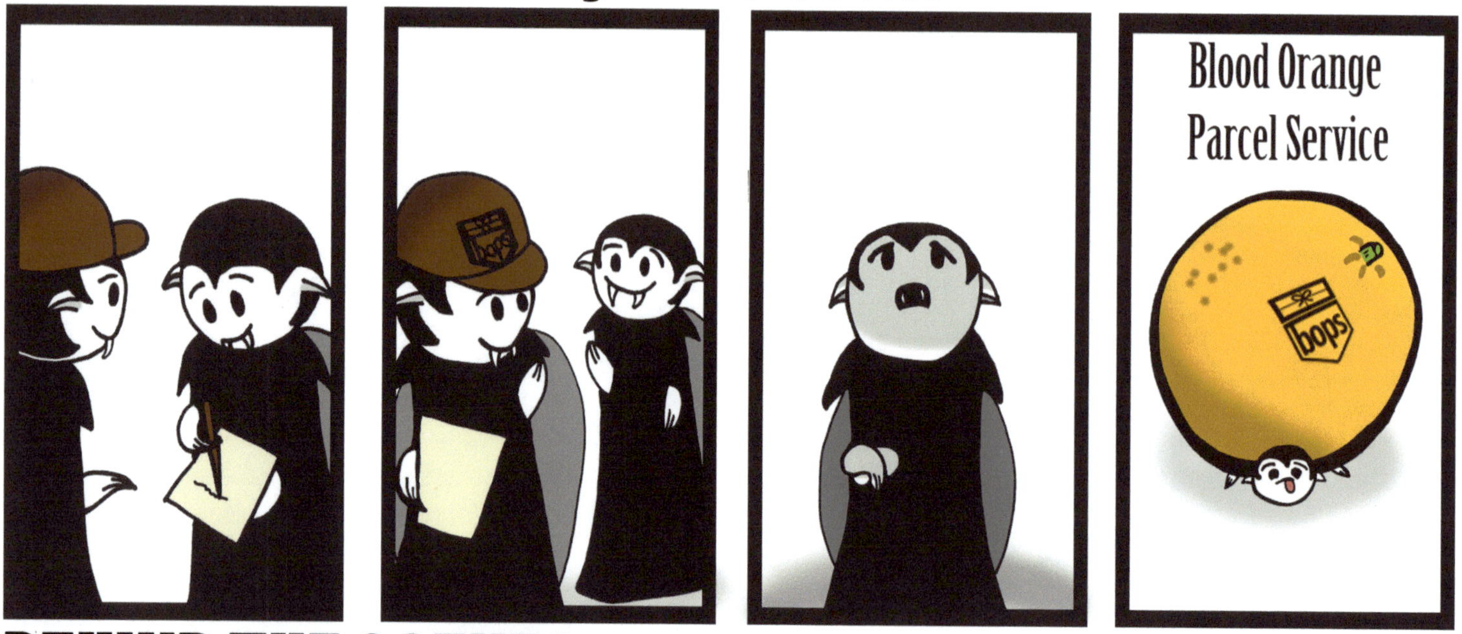
Blood Orange
Parcel Service
bops

BEHIND THE SCENES

My father was a UPS delivery truck driver when I was growing up in New York. I don't think he delivered any blood oranges to vampires, but he might have.

May 19, 2010 • The Adventures of Wolfie Hood

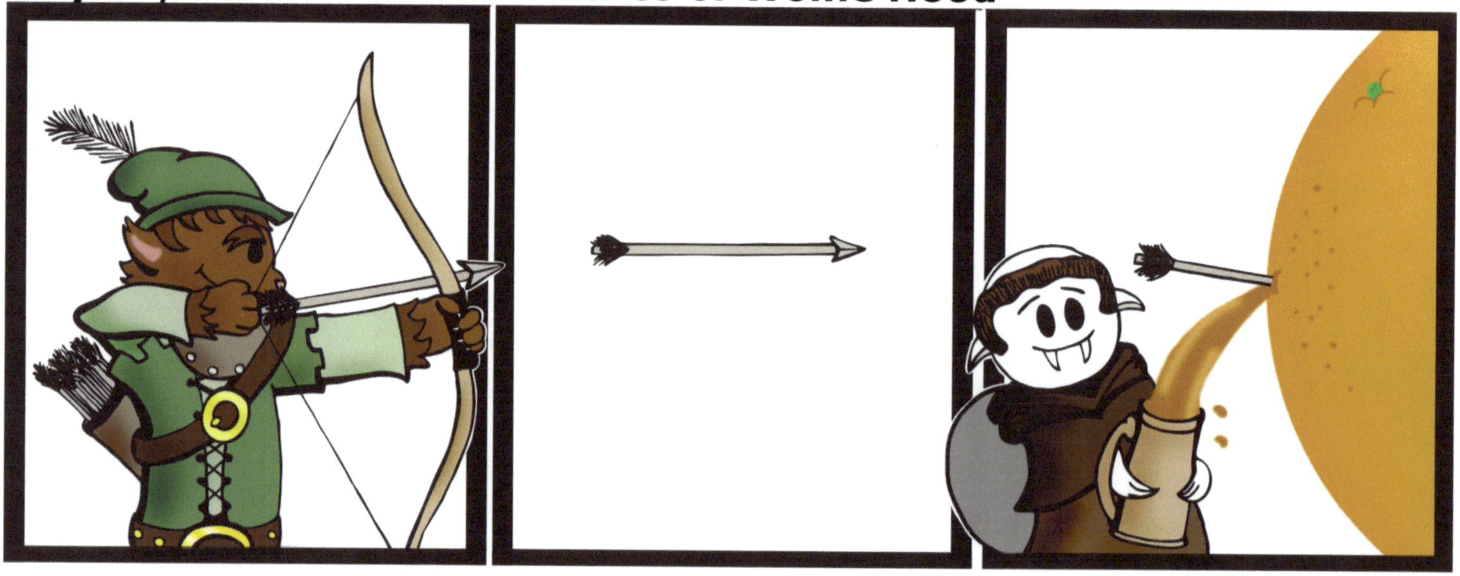

May 26, 2010 • Little Vampire vs. Cactus

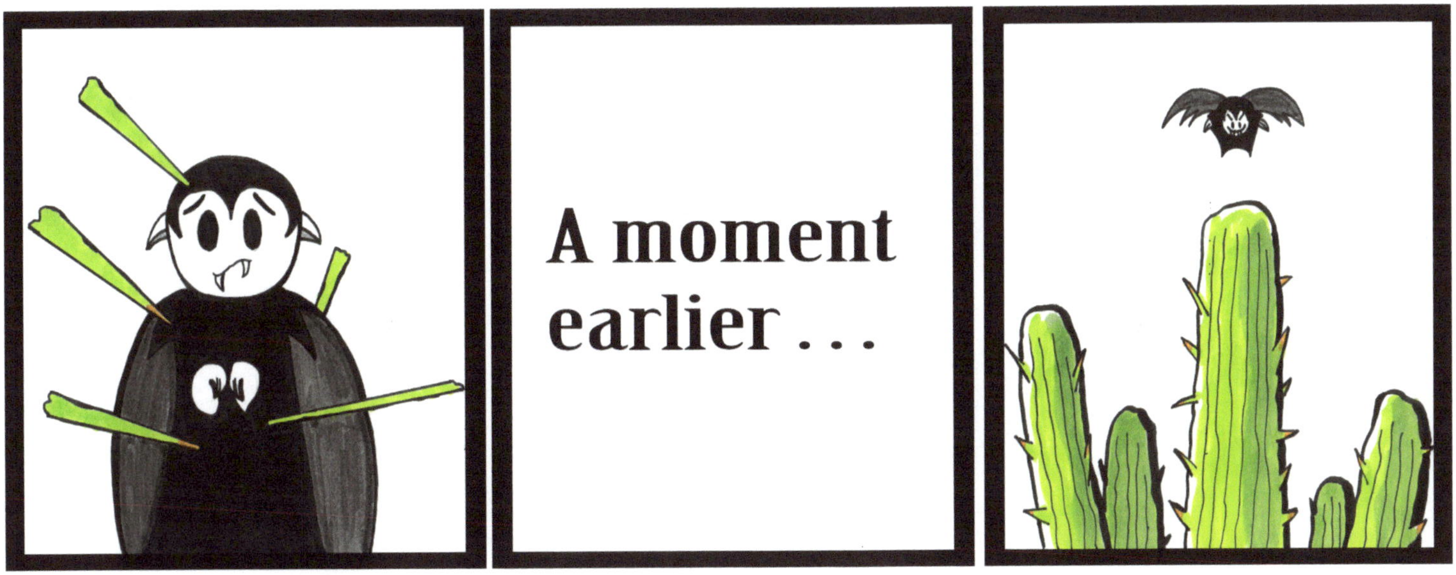
A moment earlier . . .

ON LOCATION

We drove to the Phoenix, Arizona area twice in May of 2010, once to exhibit at LepreCon, a science-fiction convention, and again for Phoenix Comicon. I normally color the comic using Photoshop, but used Copic markers for this strip honoring Arizona. No Little Vampires were harmed in the making of this comic.

June 2, 2010 • Cosplay Fail

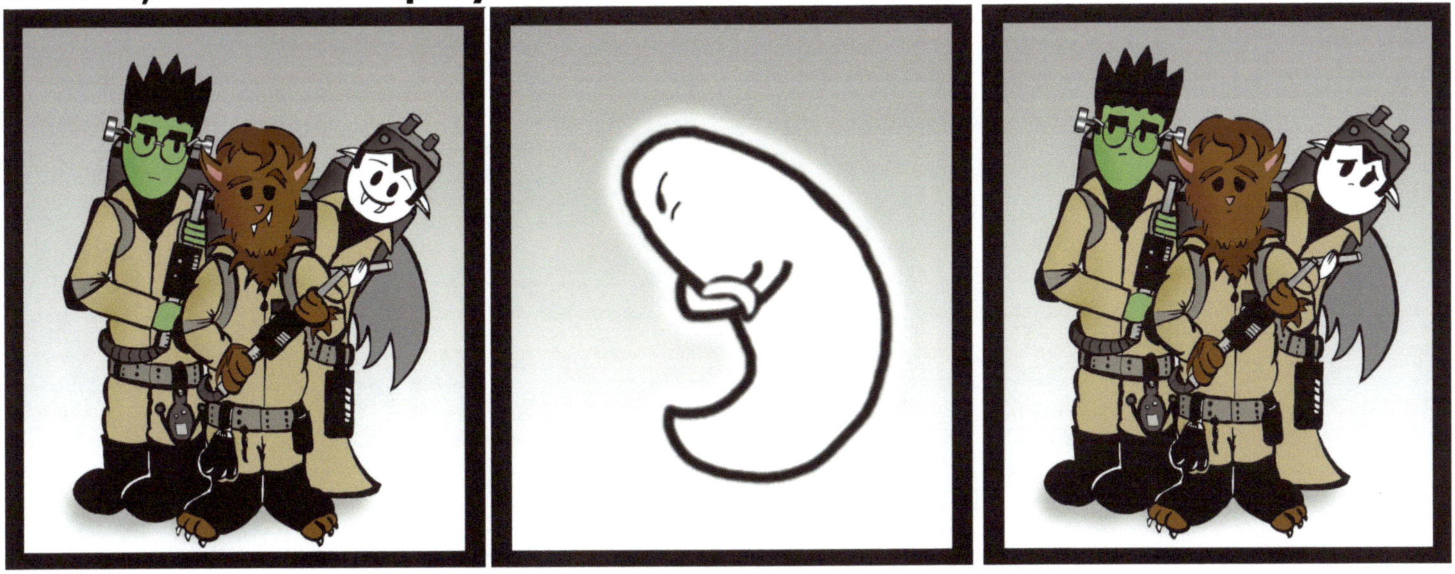

June 9, 2010 • As Seen on TV

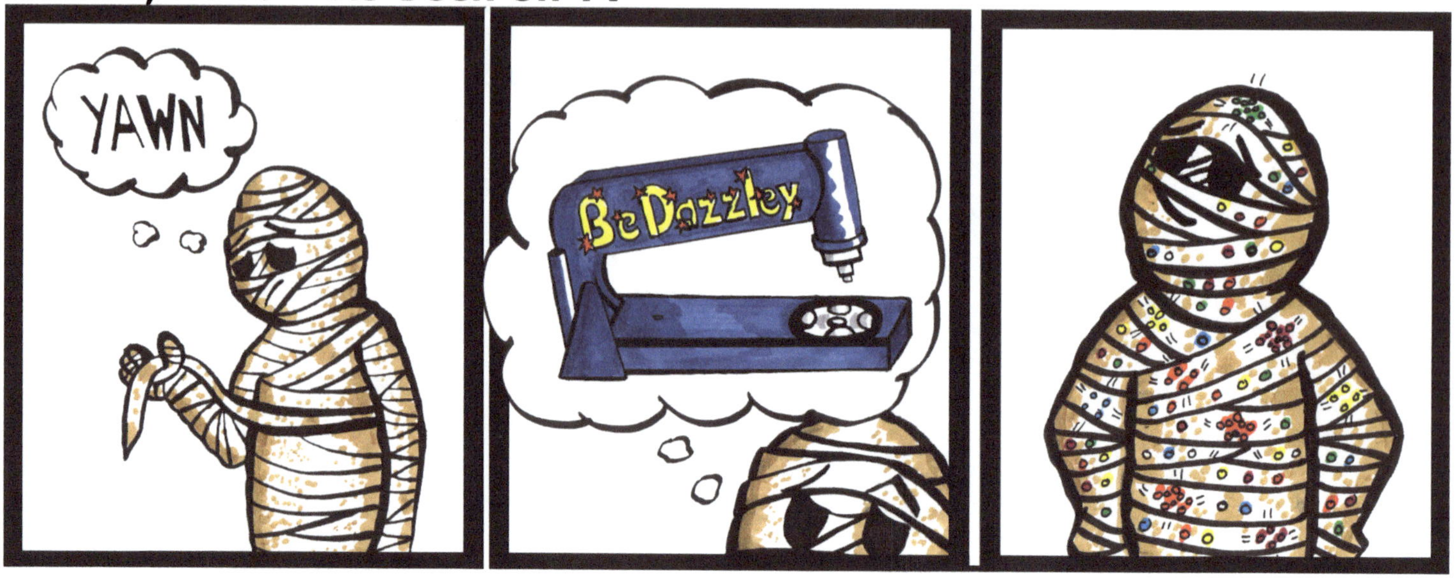
YAWN
BeDazzley

MEET THE CAST

Mumsy felt that he deserved some fun after his holiday giftwrap ordeal. It's not that he's not proud of his wraps. They just get a bit dull after thousands of years.

June 16, 2010 • Camping with Little Bigfoot

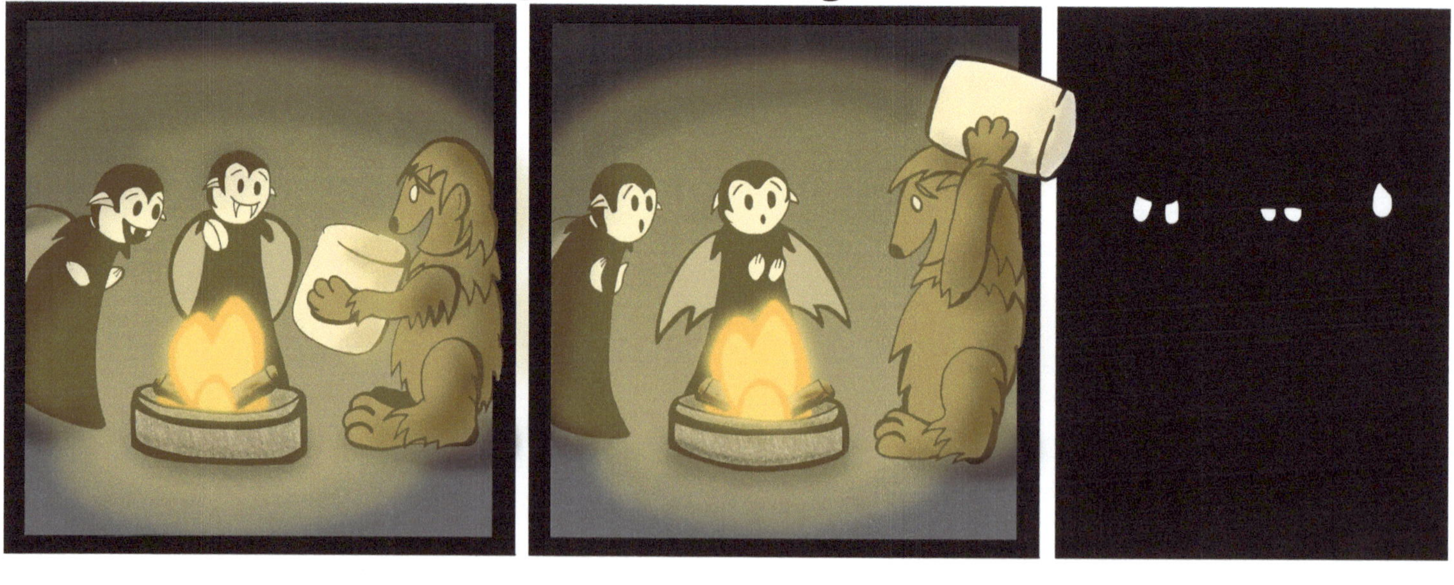

June 23, 2010 • Come Sail Away

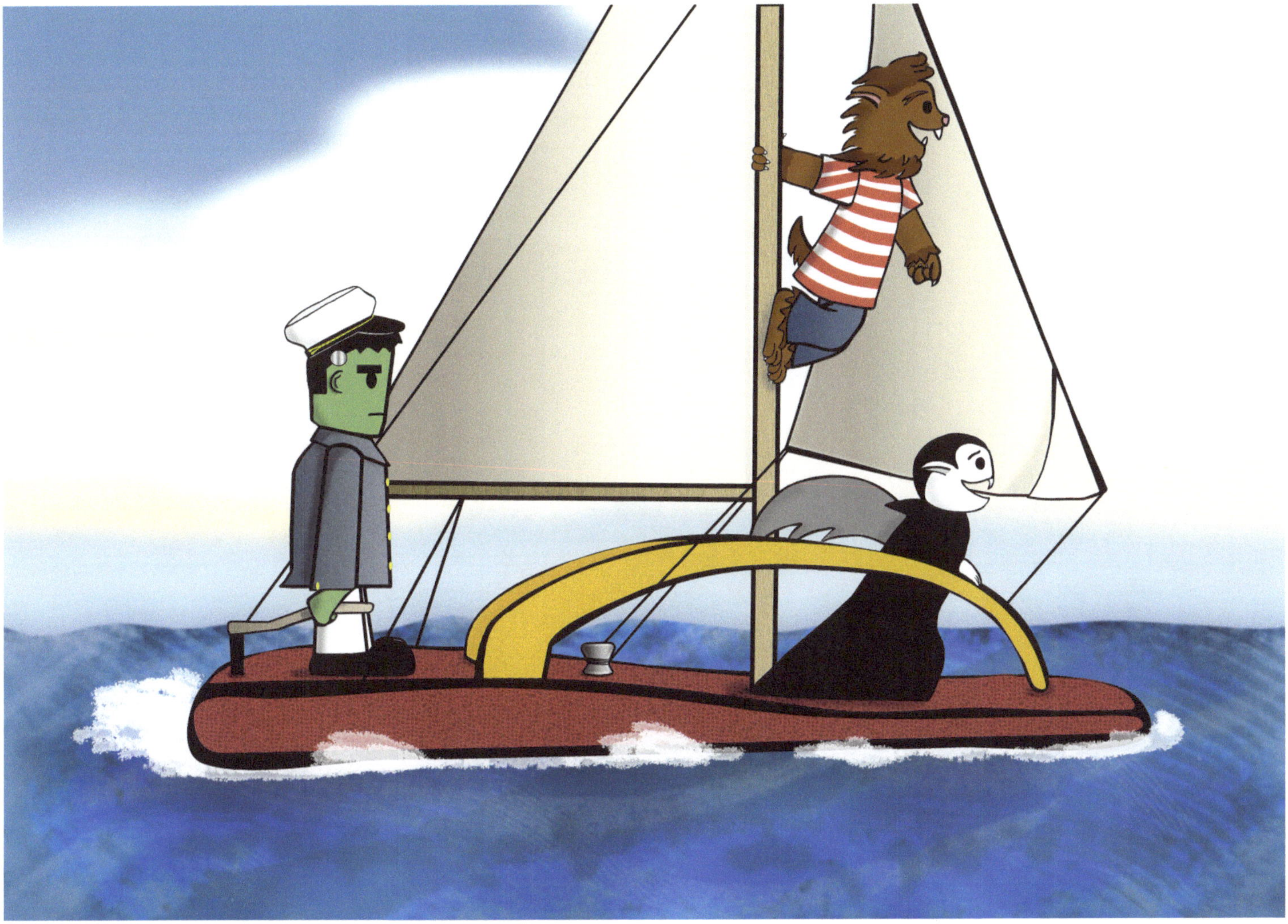

BEHIND THE SCENES

I get so much inspiration from the places I've lived, the places I've traveled to on vacation, and from the places I travel to for conventions. That doesn't mean I don't get a lot of inspiration from my home base, San Diego, California. I love the rich maritime history on display here. The USS Midway Aircraft Carrier Museum and the Maritime Museum with the Star of India, the world's oldest active ship, are two of my favorite places to take friends and family when they visit.

June 30, 2010 • Monster Spirit of '76

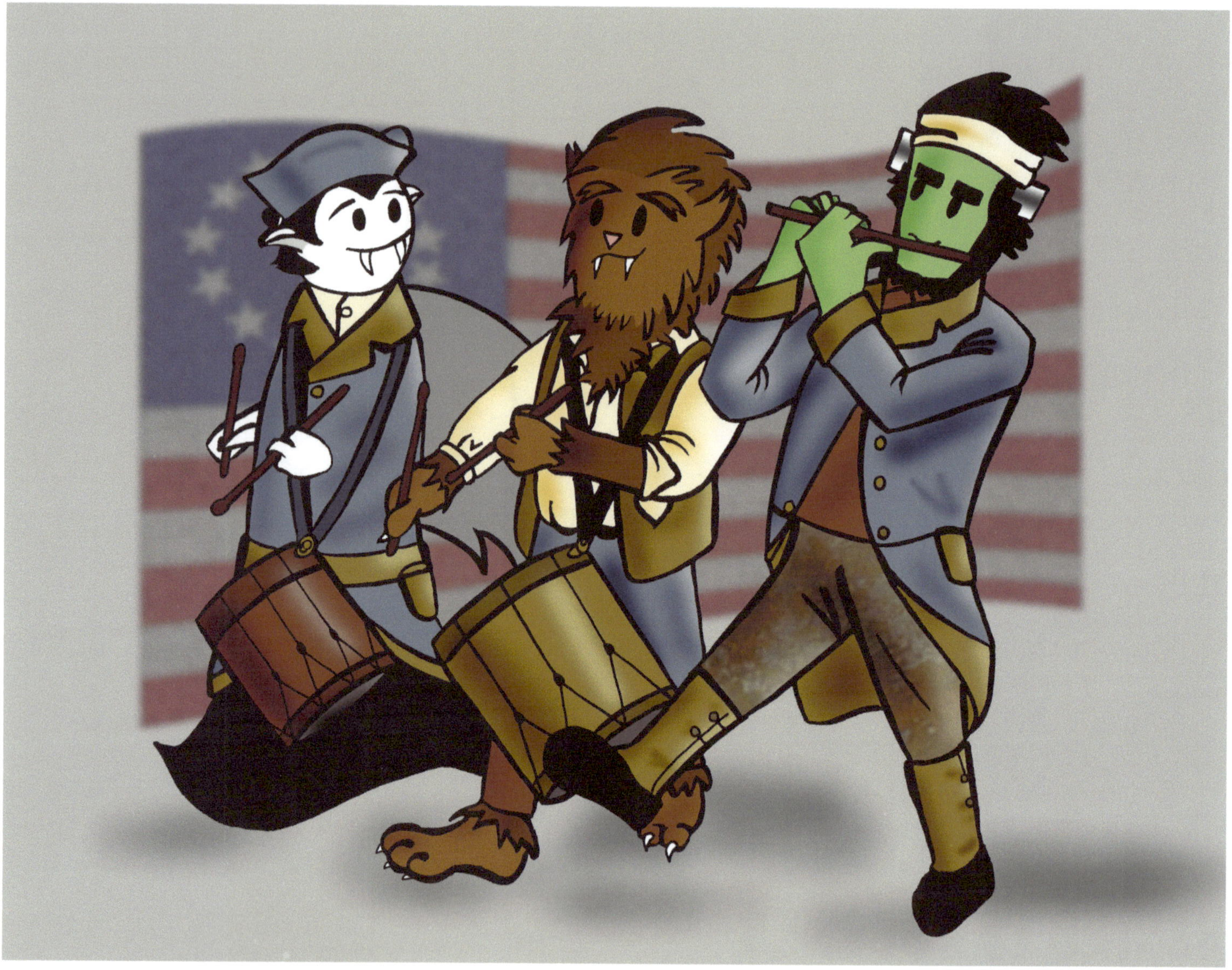

ART DIRECTION

For American Independence Day, I could think of no better painting to monsterize than the iconic *The Spirit of '76* by Archibald MacNeal Willard.

July 7, 2010 • Sparkle Revisited

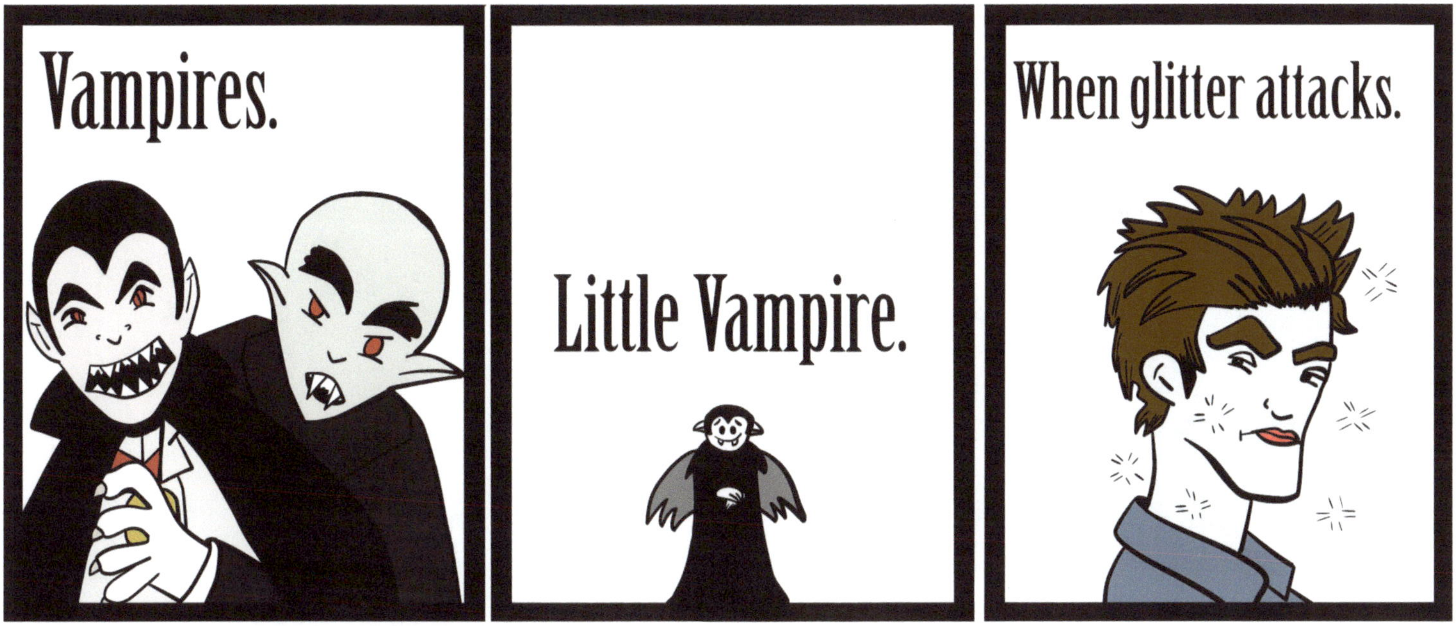
Vampires.
Little Vampire.
When glitter attacks.

BEHIND THE SCENES

I could no longer resist the urge to draw Robert Pattinson's hair, and to poke fun at *Twilight* one more time.

July 14, 2010 • Little Zombie Piñata Party

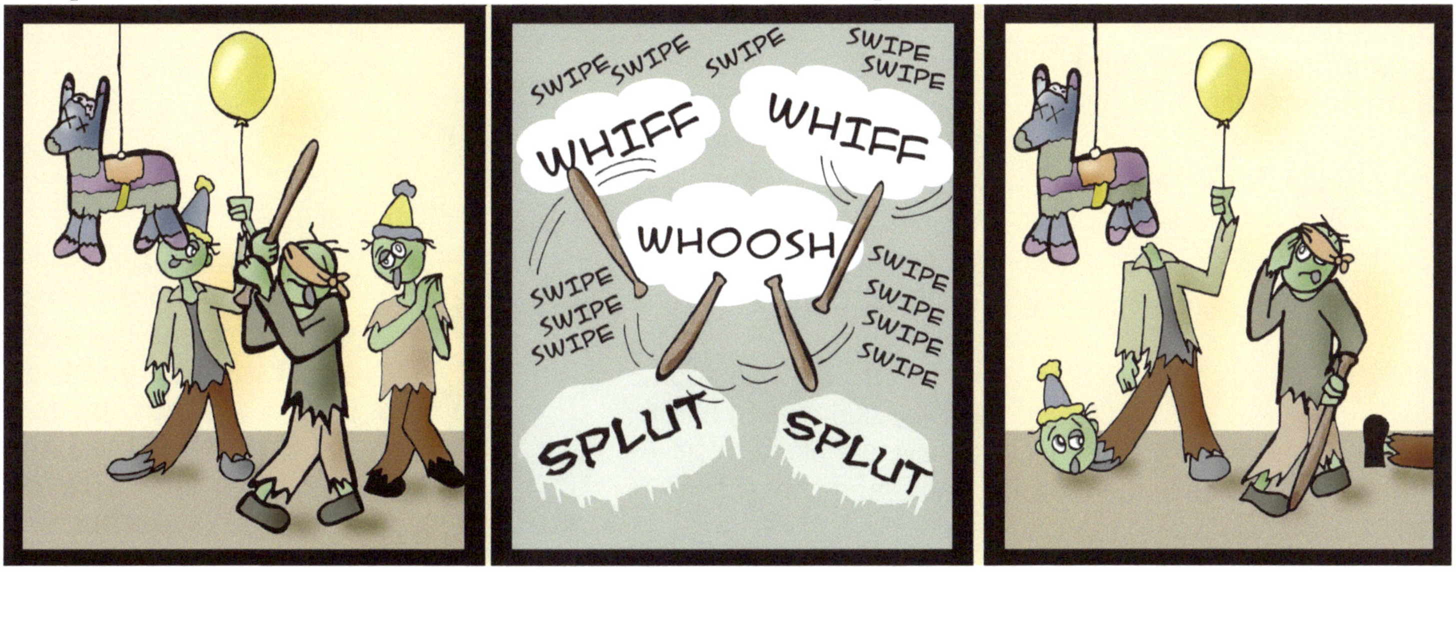
SWIPE SWIPE
SWIPE
SWIPE SWIPE
WHIFF
WHIFF
WHOOSH
SWIPE SWIPE SWIPE
SWIPE SWIPE SWIPE SWIPE
SPLUT
SPLUT

July 28, 2010 • Dreams of Flight

BEHIND THE SCENES

This was the first *Little Vampires* guest comic, drawn by the creator of *Weregeek*, the amazing Alina Pete. Alina and the equally amazing Layne Myhre traveled all the way from Canada to share a booth with us at the mother of all comic conventions, San Diego Comic-Con International. Alina was kind enough to draw this comic, thus allowing me to get some sleep after an exhausting convention.

ON LOCATION

James and I have been attending San Diego Comic-Con since 1994. As a life-long comic book and pop culture fan, I absolutely loved that everything I was passionate about was gathered together under one roof for close to one week.

I still can't believe that I'm now behind a table at Comic-Con. I miss going to panels, and I miss getting sketches from my favorite comic book artists, but I like having a place to sit down and eat lunch in the crowded San Diego convention center during Comic-Con week.

I'm a huge comic book fan, which means the Little Vampires and their friends are too. Batman is the Little Vampires' favorite superhero, of course.

August 4, 2010 • The Gift of Tuna

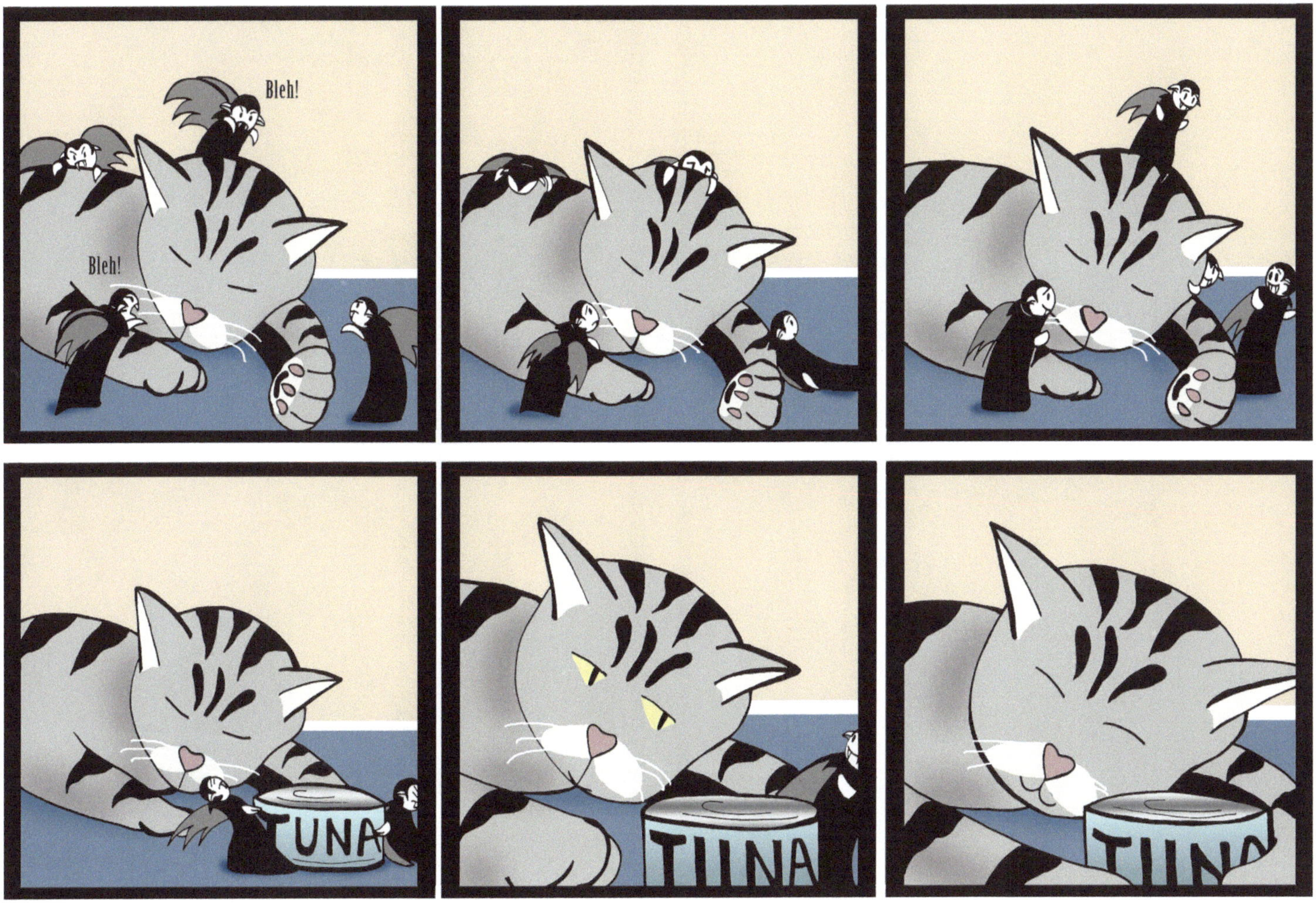
Bleh!
Bleh!
TUNA
TUNA
TUN

BEHIND THE SCENES

Matt the Cat was still valiantly fighting cancer at the time I drew this comic. He was close to 17 years old at this time, but consistently amazed James and I with his strength and his will to live.

We only ever fed Matt food made for cats . . . with one exception. The only "people food" he ever demanded was tuna, and we were more than happy to give him the occassional fishy treat. I decided to give The Cat that same trait. Good thing, too, since the Little Vampires needed some way to show their apprecation for all the times The Cat allowed them to practice being fierce at him.

August 11, 2010 • The Gift of Opened Tuna

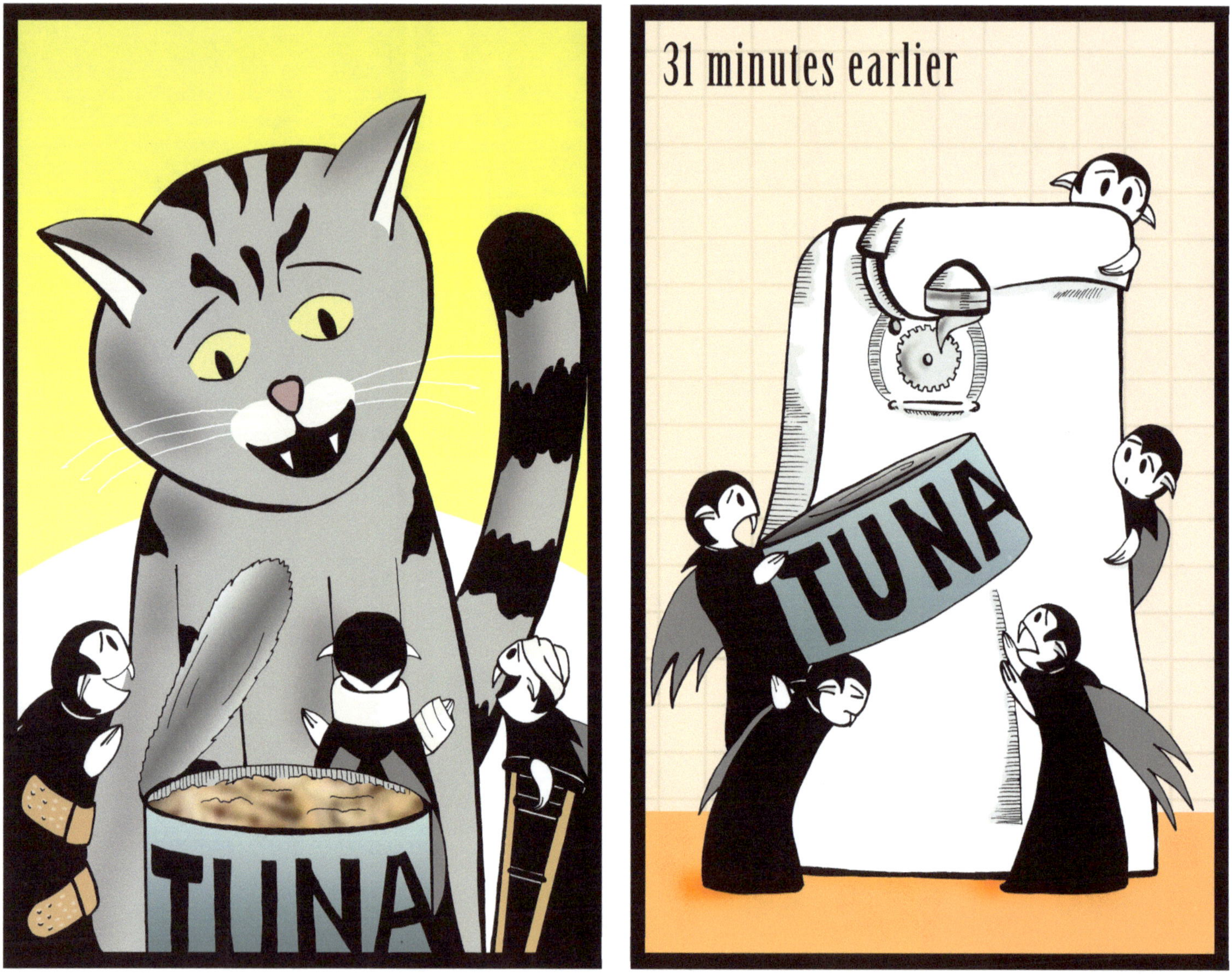
TUNA
31 minutes earlier
TUNA

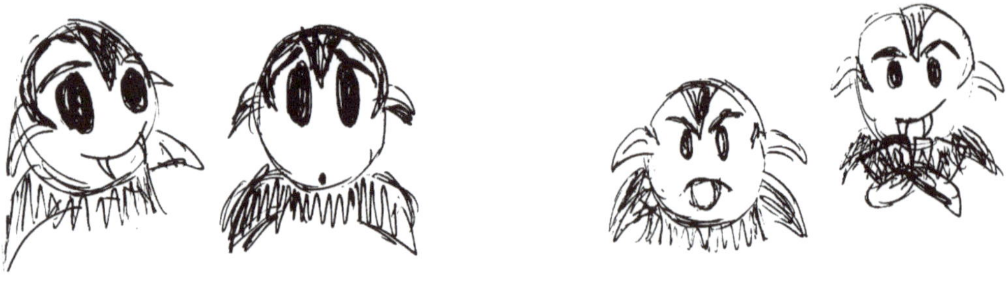

Little Vampires ink sketches from 2007.

August 18, 2010 • Scare Fail

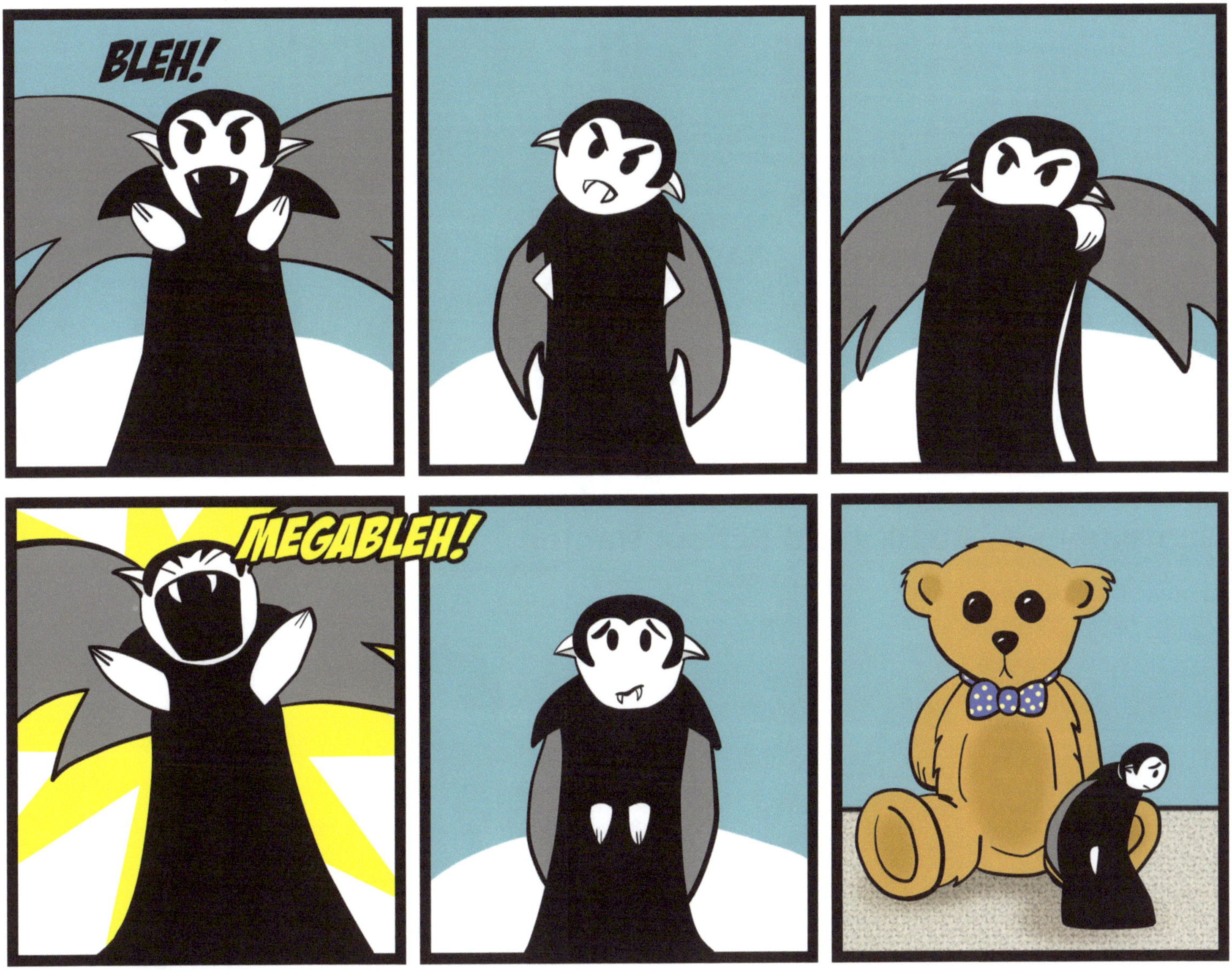
BLEH!
MEGABLEH!

BEHIND THE SCENES

And so began the "blehs." I never intend to let the Little Vampires talk, but I realized that they needed to vocalize in some manner. The idea of there being different types of "blehs" really resonated with readers, so it became a gag that I would revisit often.

August 25, 2010 • Liblehry

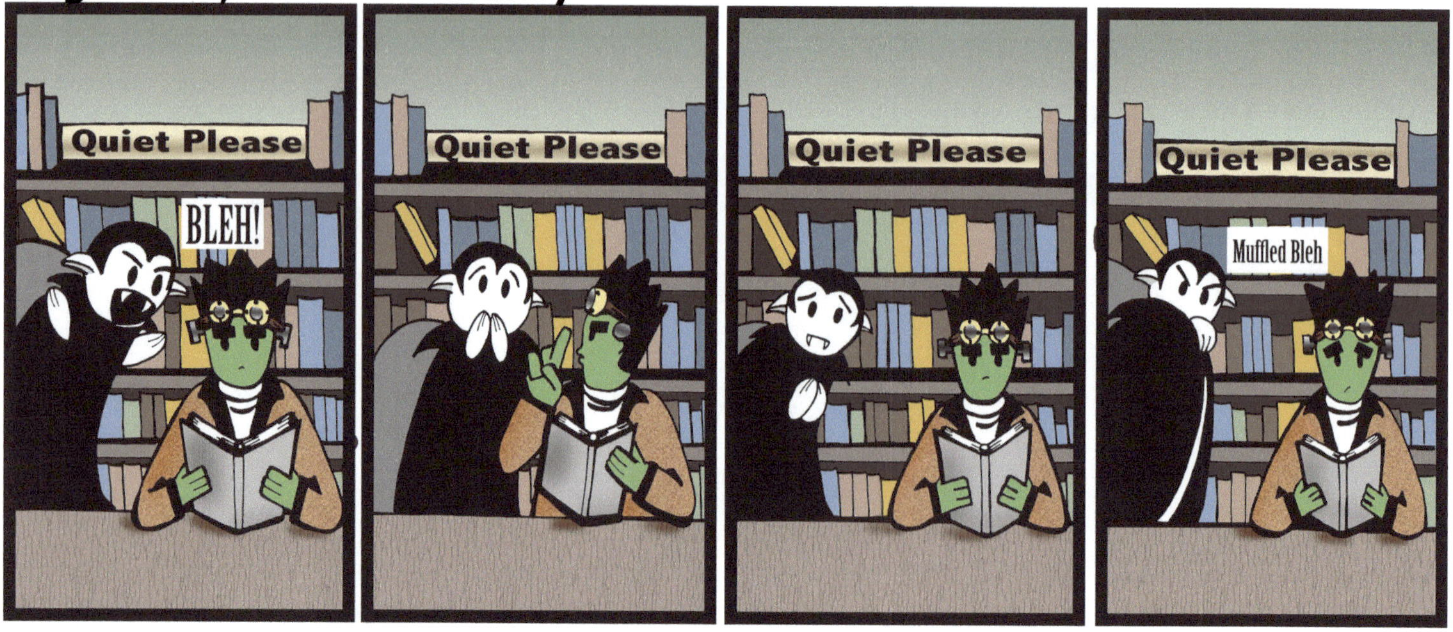
Quiet Please
BLEH!
Quiet Please
Quiet Please
Quiet Please
Muffled Bleh

September 1, 2010 • Old School Gamer

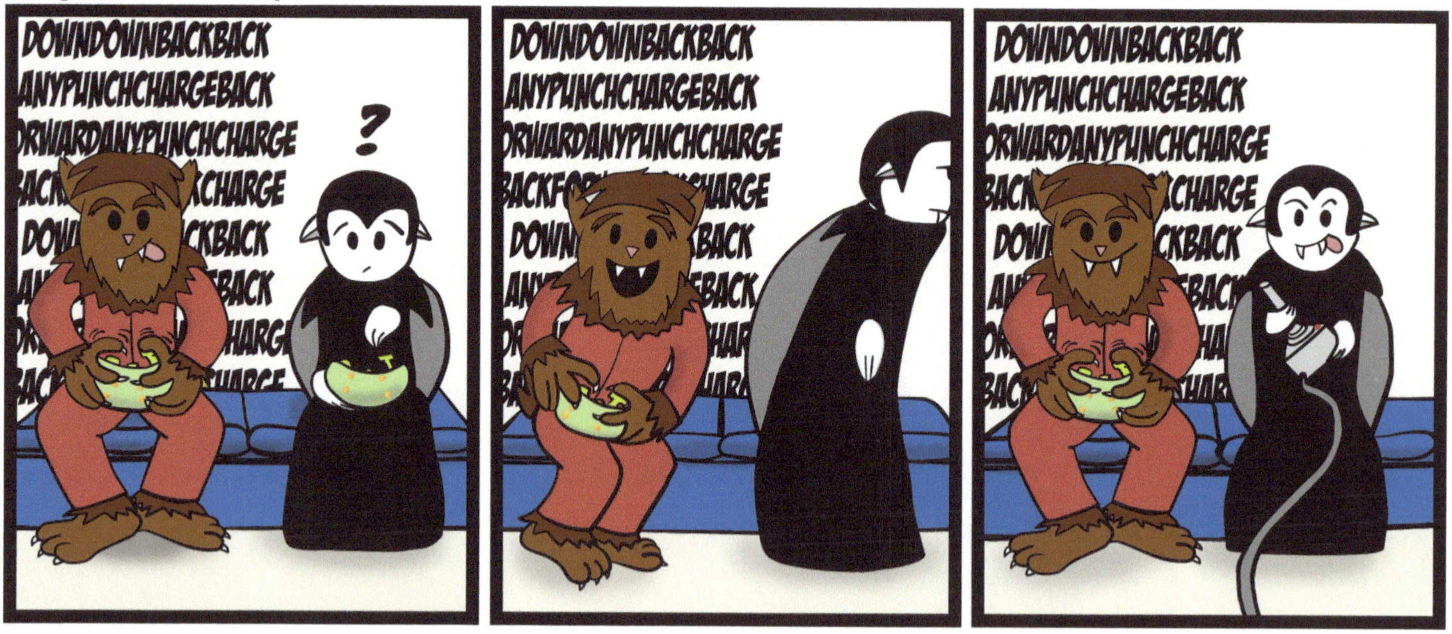
DOWNDOWNBACKBACK
ANYPUNCHCHARGEBACK
?

BEHIND THE SCENES I love modern games, but I'd choose a simple Atari joystick over current controllers any day. Oh, and I still miss the original *Pitfall*, so get off my old gamer lawn, young-un.

September 8, 2010 • Blood Orange Eating 101

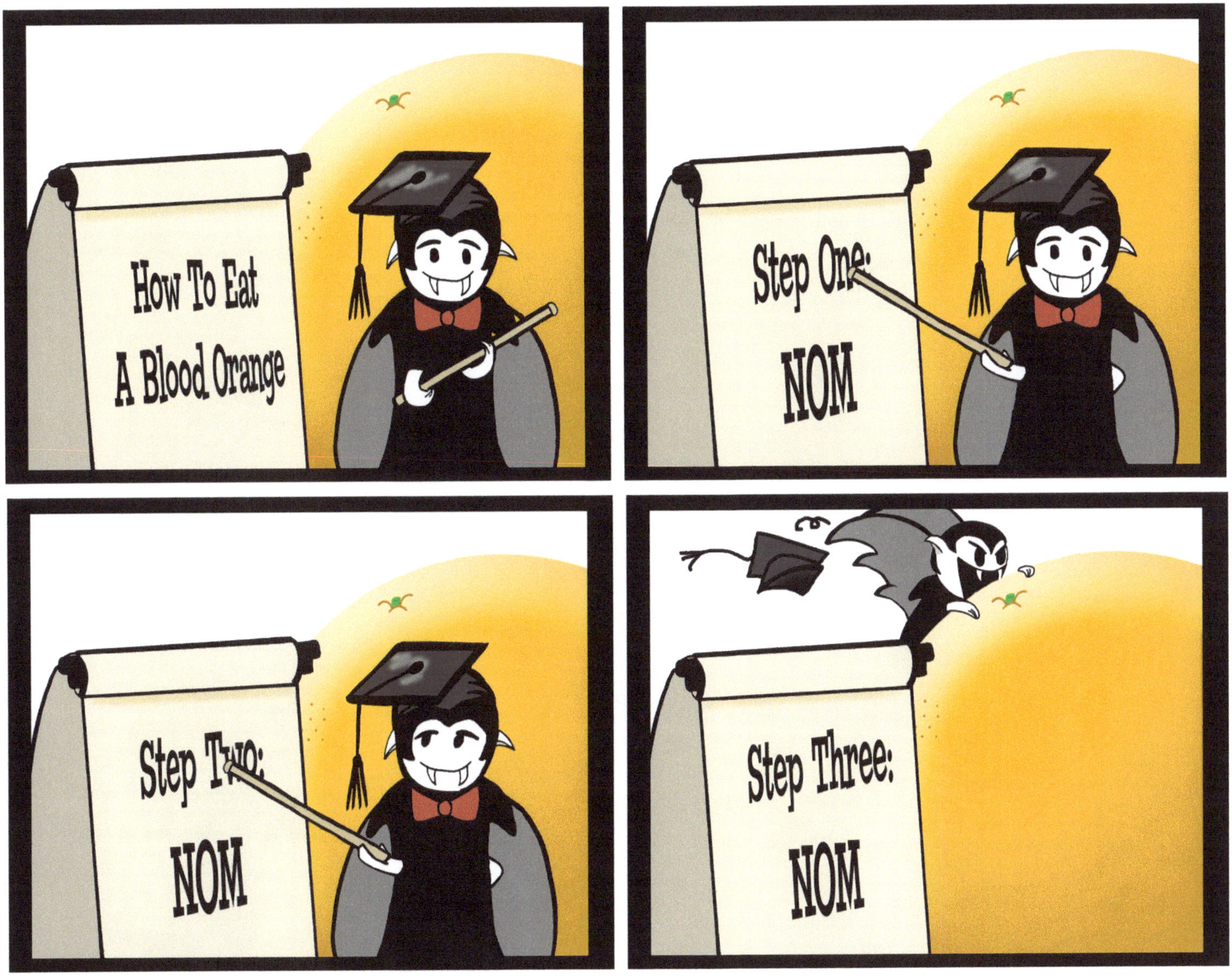

How To Eat
A Blood Orange
Step One:
NOM
Step Two:
NOM
Step Three:
NOM

BEHIND THE SCENES

Blood orange eating techniques were not part of the curriculum when I was a teacher, I'm sorry to say. If they were, I don't think I would have had much trouble enlisting the help of the Little Vampires to demonstrate the proper technique.

September 15, 2010 • Vampirate

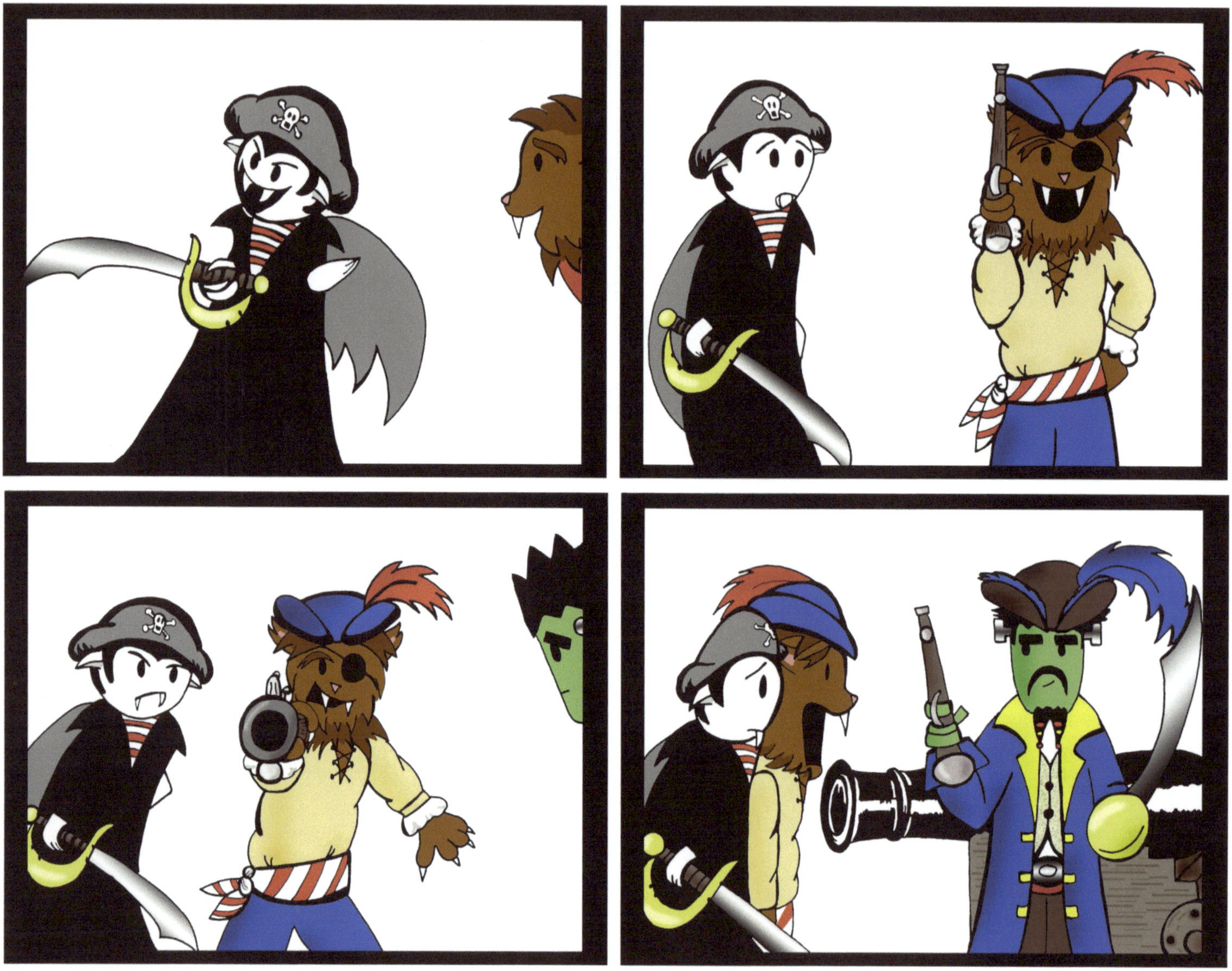

BEHIND THE SCENES

September 19th of each year is International Talk Like a Pirate Day. I'm not making that up. This comic has the friends celebrating in their own unique way. The idea of Frank being into costuming (and awesome prop making) really flowered here from the seed planted in the third comic.

September 22, 2010 • Work of Fang Art

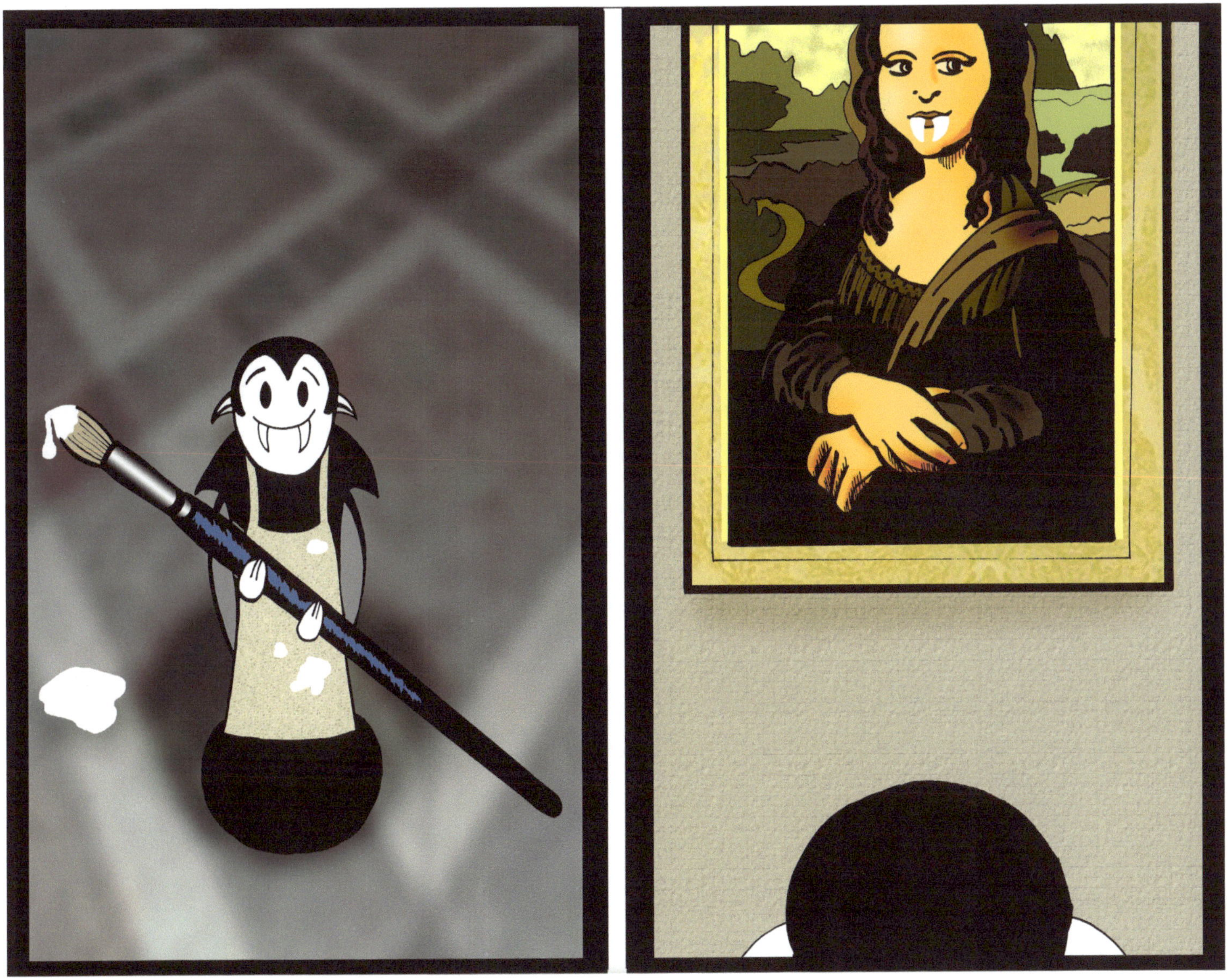

ART DIRECTION

I don't know what made me decide to tackle Da Vinci's *Mona Lisa*, but I did, so there you go. The floor in the first panel is based on a floor pattern in the Louvre.

September 29, 2010 • See No Zombies

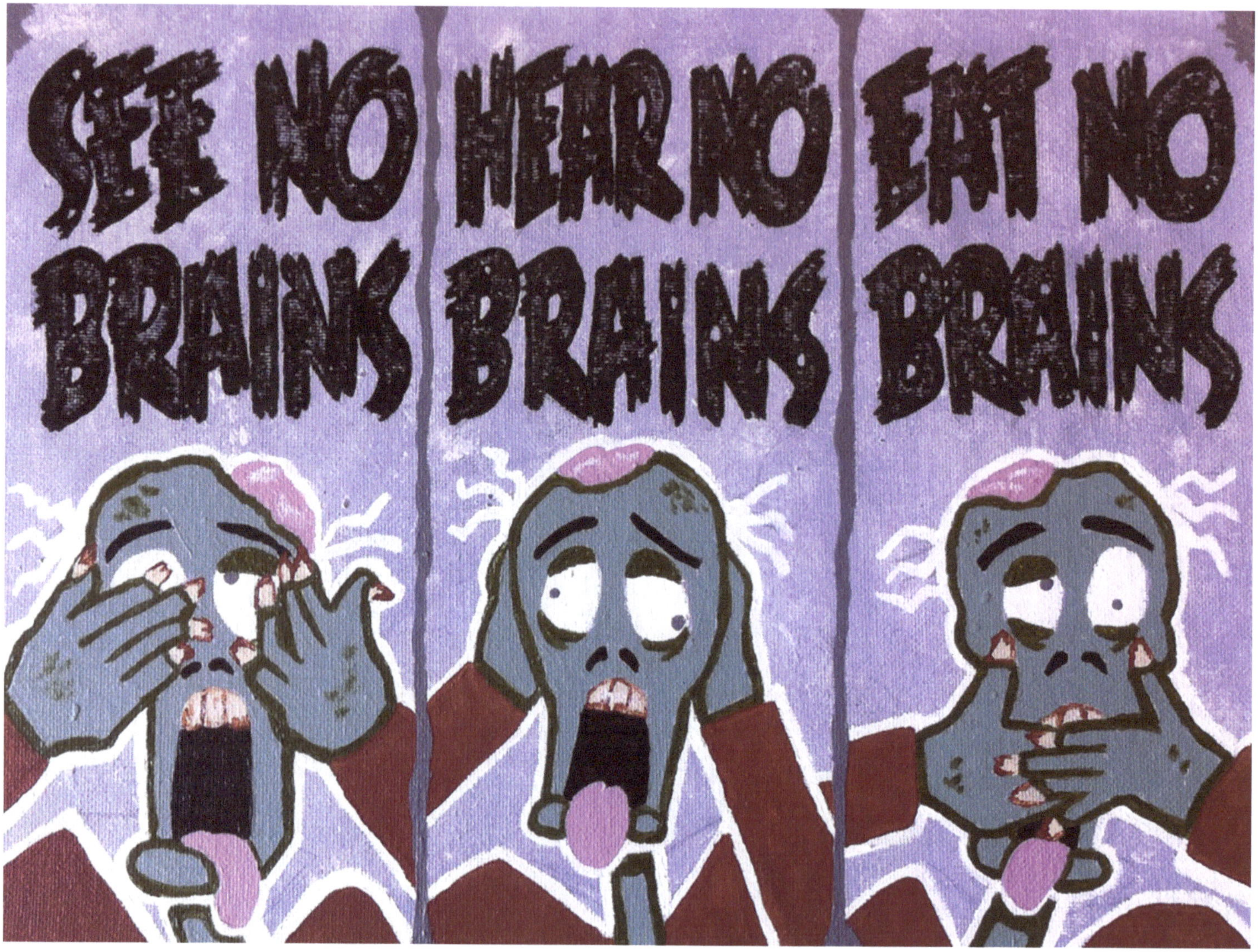
SEE NO BRAINS
HEAR NO BRAINS
EAT NO BRAINS

BEHIND THE SCENES

My friends Jarrett and Norma Crippen run a charity interactive haunted house every fall in Austin, Texas. Their Scare for a Cure haunts raise money for breast cancer research and recovery efforts. In 2010, the haunt's theme was zombies. I auctioned off the original acrylic painting that I did here to help raise money for Scare for a Cure. I used it as that day's comic to help raise awareness for the cause.

October 6, 2010 • All That Evil Piano Jazz

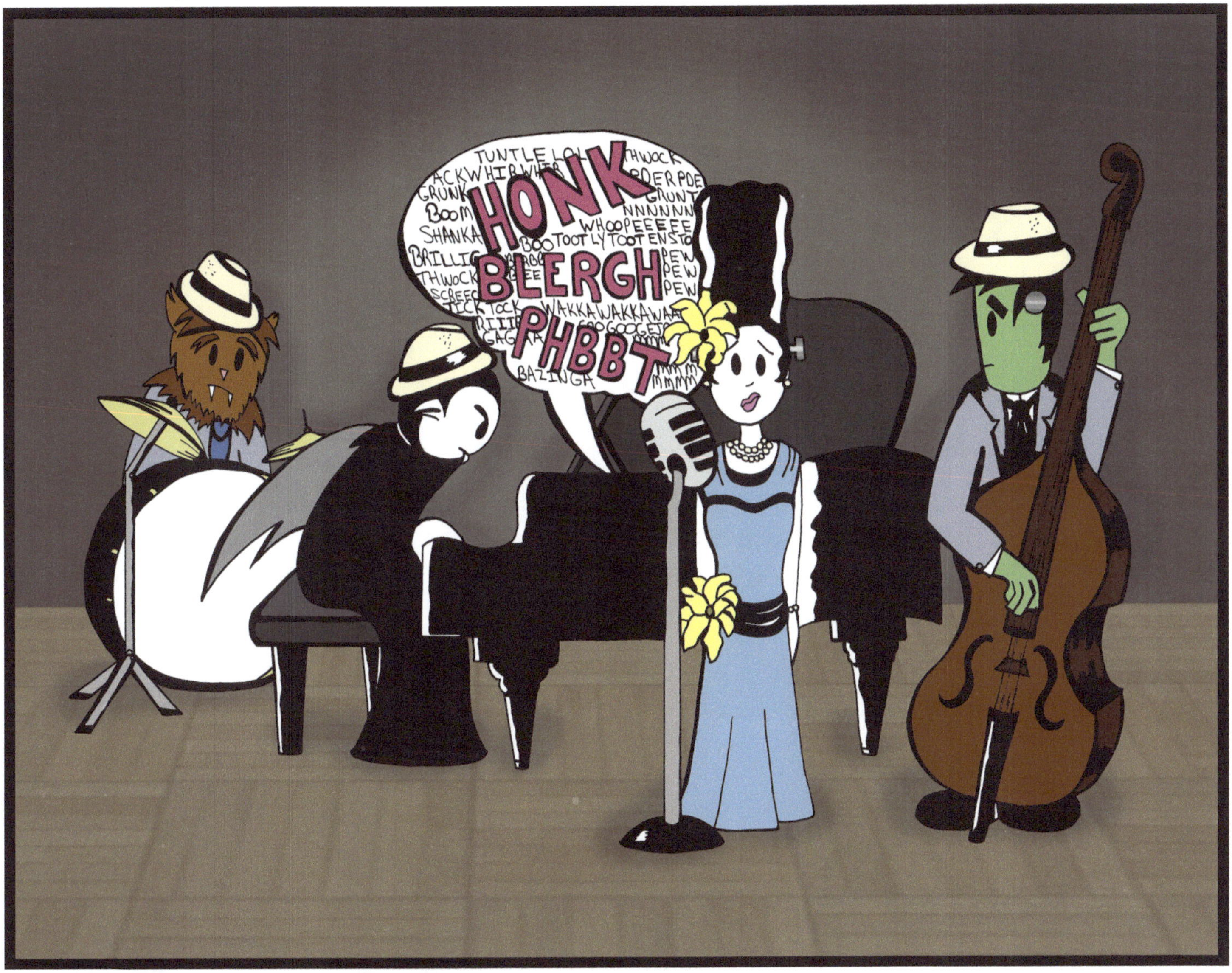
HONK
BLERGH
PHBBT
TUNTLE
GRUNK
BOOM
SHANKA
THWOCK
GRUNT
NNNNNN
WHOOPEEEEE
BOO TOOT LY TOOT
PEW PEW PEW
WAKKAWAKKA
BAZINGA

BEHIND THE SCENES

The return of the piano! This was the 50th Little Vampire webcomic, so I decided to honor the achievement by making a reference to the first comic. Elsa's hair and outfit are based on the signature look of the amazing singer Billie Holiday.

October 13, 2010 • Halloween Costumes: Part One

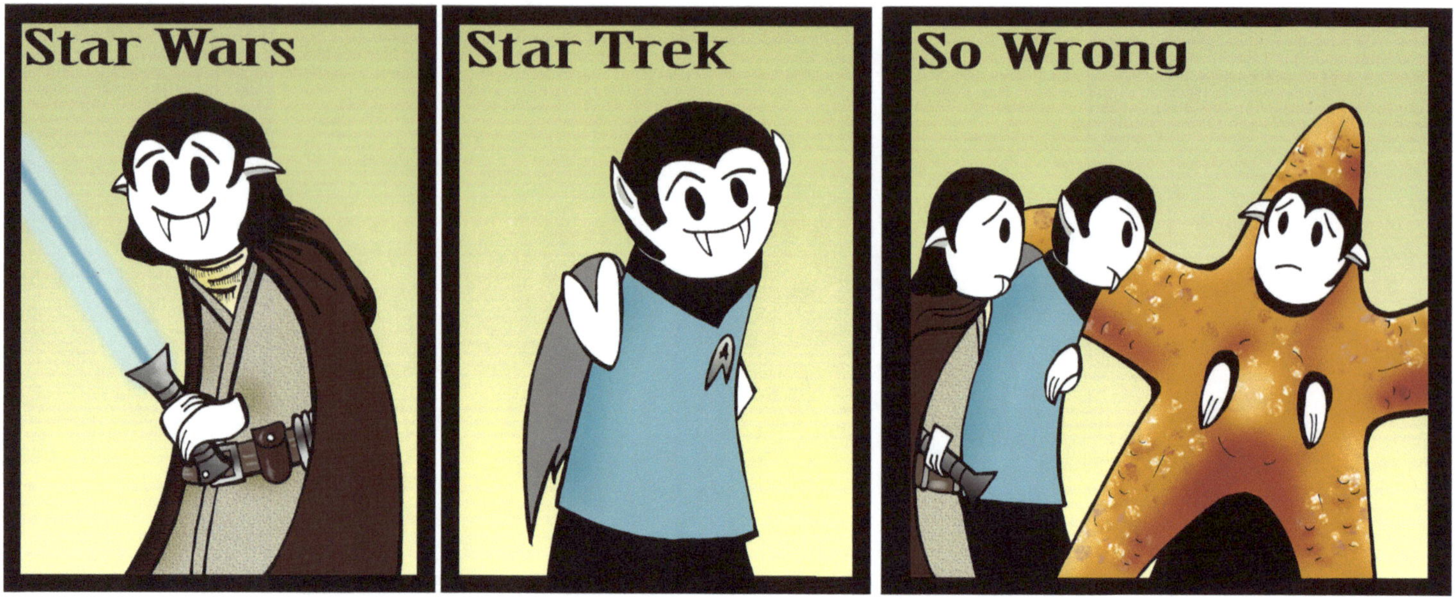
Star Wars
Star Trek
So Wrong

October 20, 2010 • Halloween Costumes: Part Two

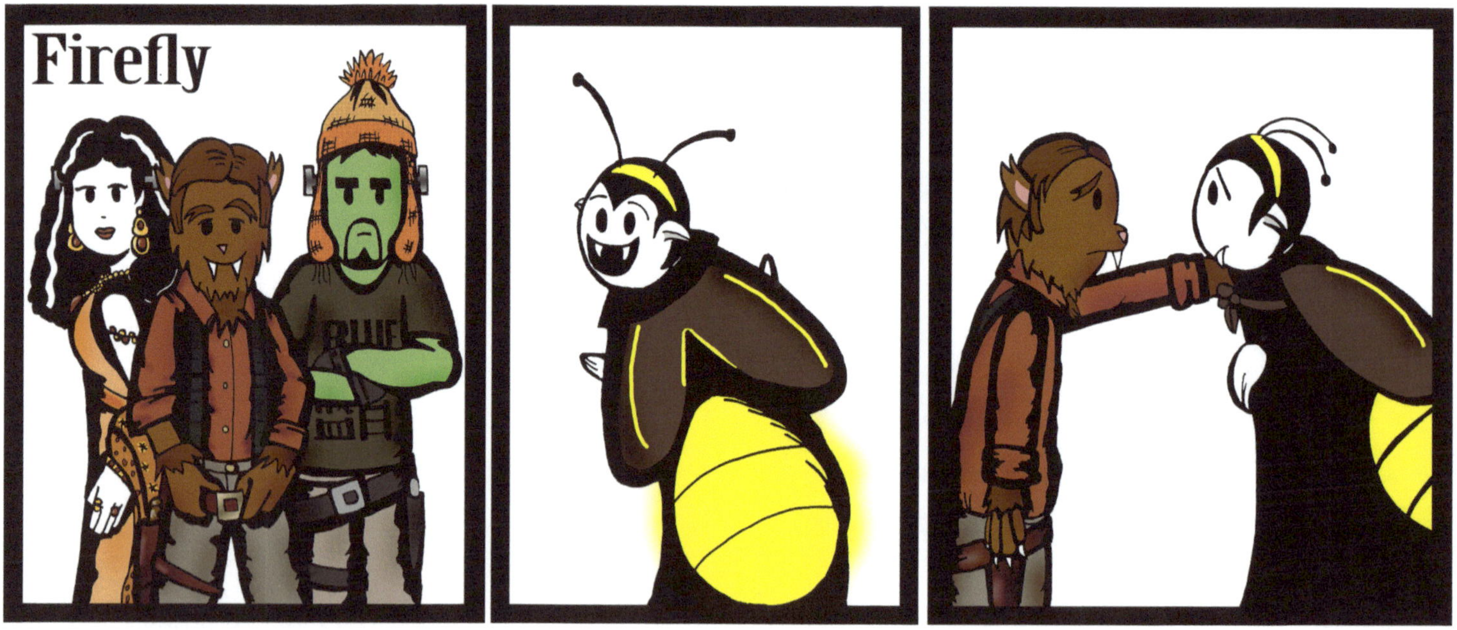
Firefly

BEHIND THE SCENES With Halloween around the corner, I wanted to explore the idea of the friends cosplaying together. Some Little Vampires cosplayed more effectively than others, of course.

October 27, 2010 • Halloween Costumes: Part Three

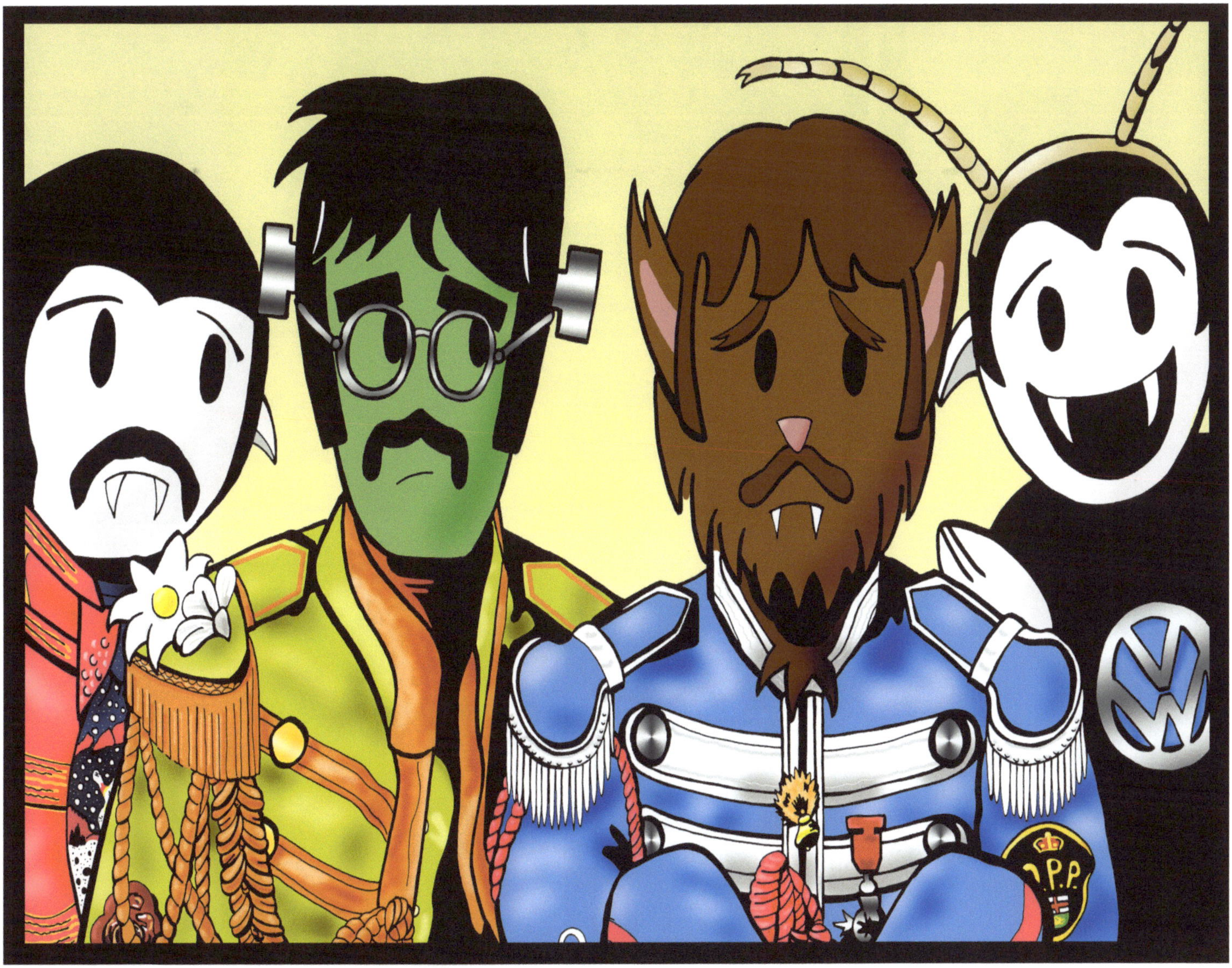

BEHIND THE SCENES

To say I'm a Beatles fan is an understatement. I fell in love with their music when I was just a wee geekling, even though I was born after they broke up. Drawing my characters in the Beatles' *Sgt. Pepper's Lonely Hearts Club Band* costumes was a challenge, but worth every braid-drawing moment.

November 3, 2010 • Fall

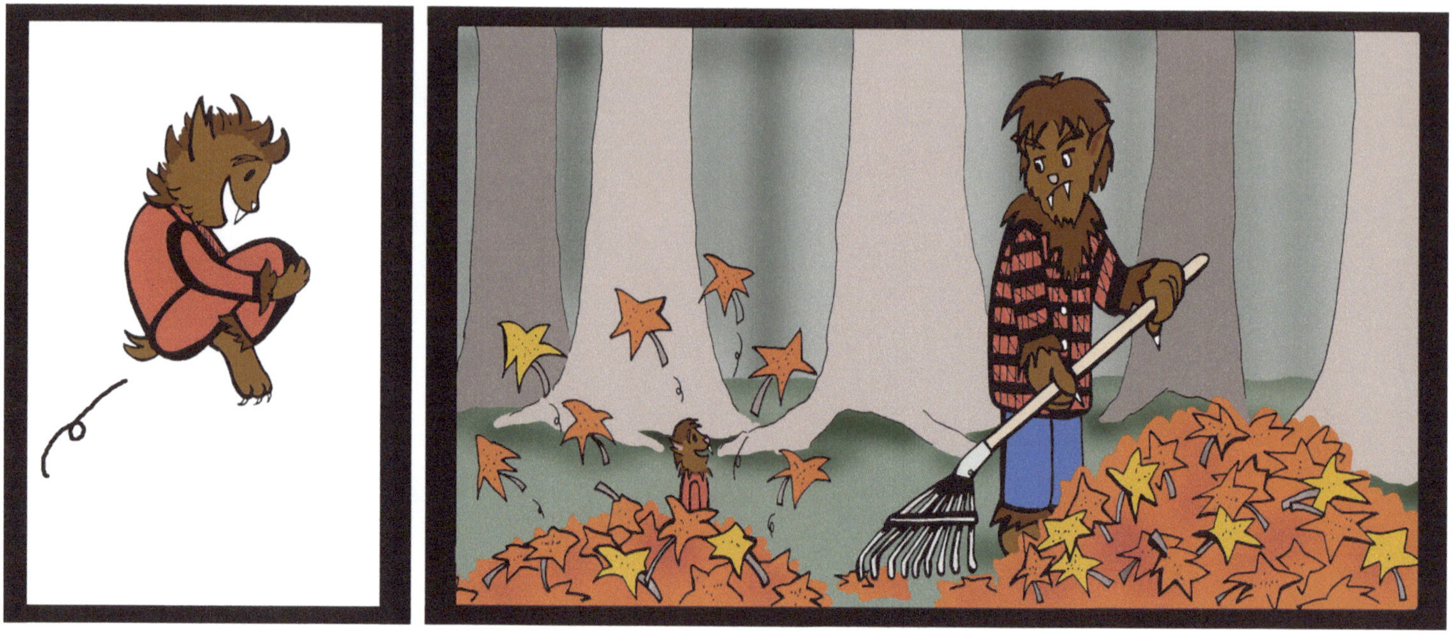

BEHIND THE SCENES

I had already established that the Little Vampires looked up to human-sized vampires as mentors in the first book, but I hadn't touched on that idea in the webcomic. I also hadn't shown the relationship of the other monsters to their larger counterparts. So I began this short arc showing those relationships.

Wolfie looks at larger werewolves more like older brothers than as mentors. And Wolfie would be that pesky but lovable kind of younger brother, as shown in this comic.

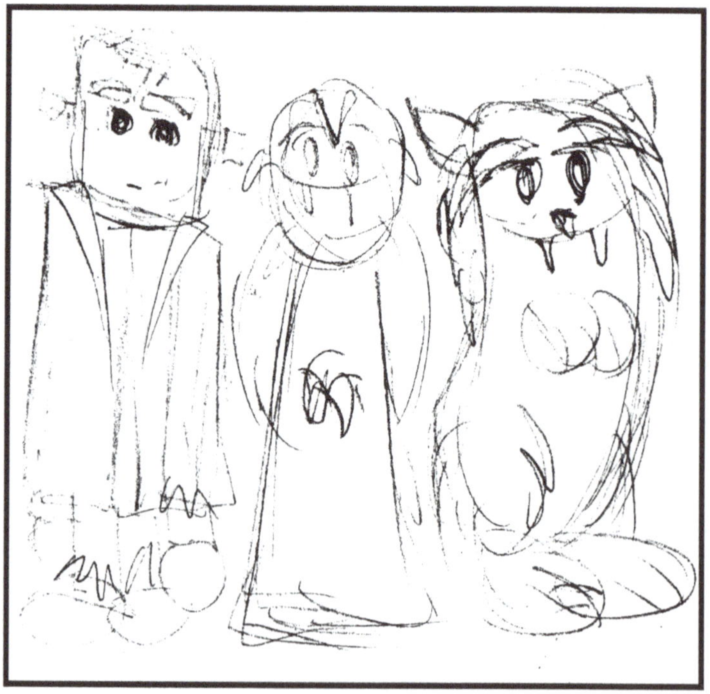

Early sketch of the bestest of friends.

November 10, 2010 • Role Model

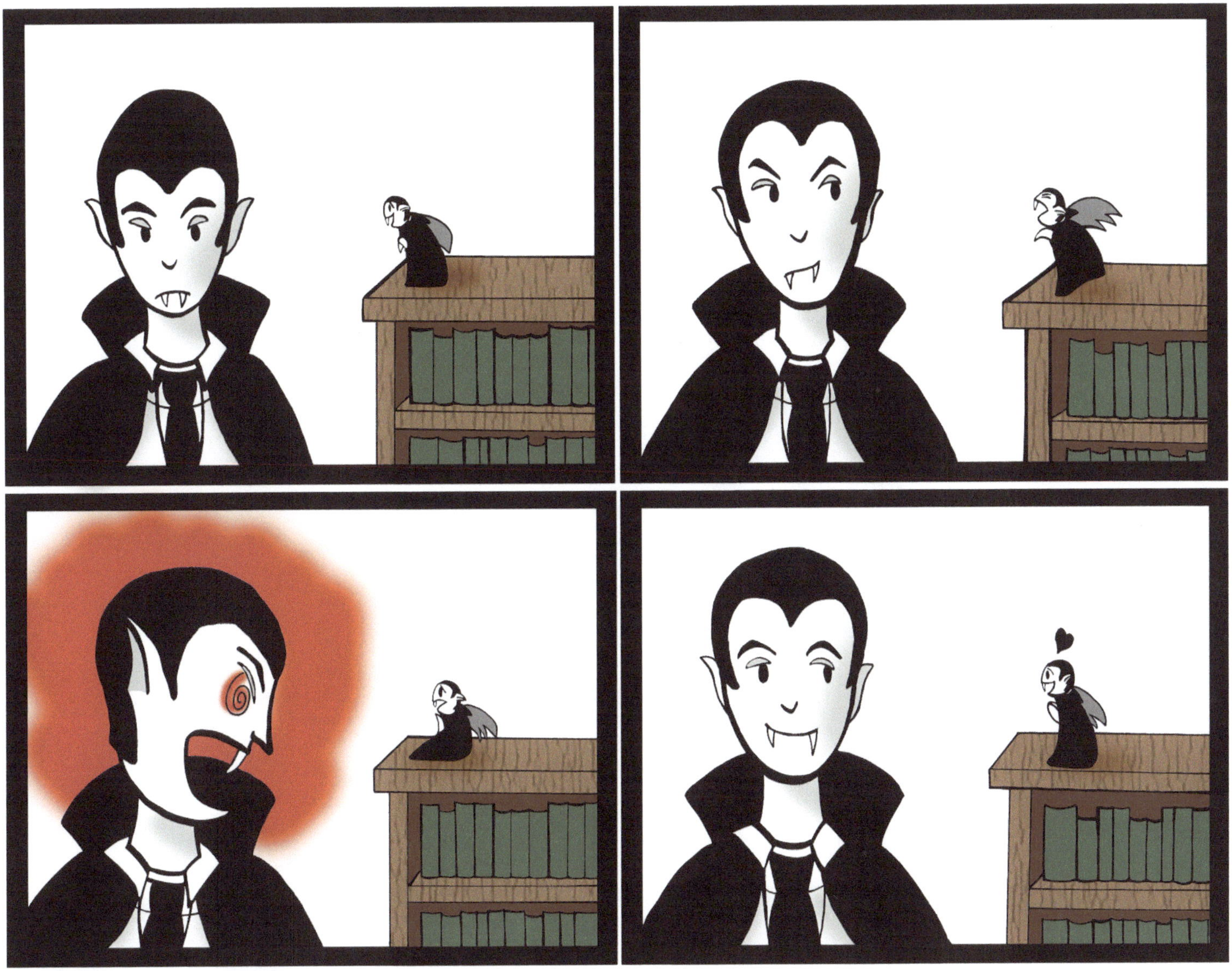

BEHIND THE SCENES

The Little Vampires want to be like their larger cousins because, well, they're fans of human-sized vampires. I liked the idea that the big vampires are amused by the little guys, and actually enjoy mentoring them in the art of being big and fierce.

November 17, 2010 • Bonsai

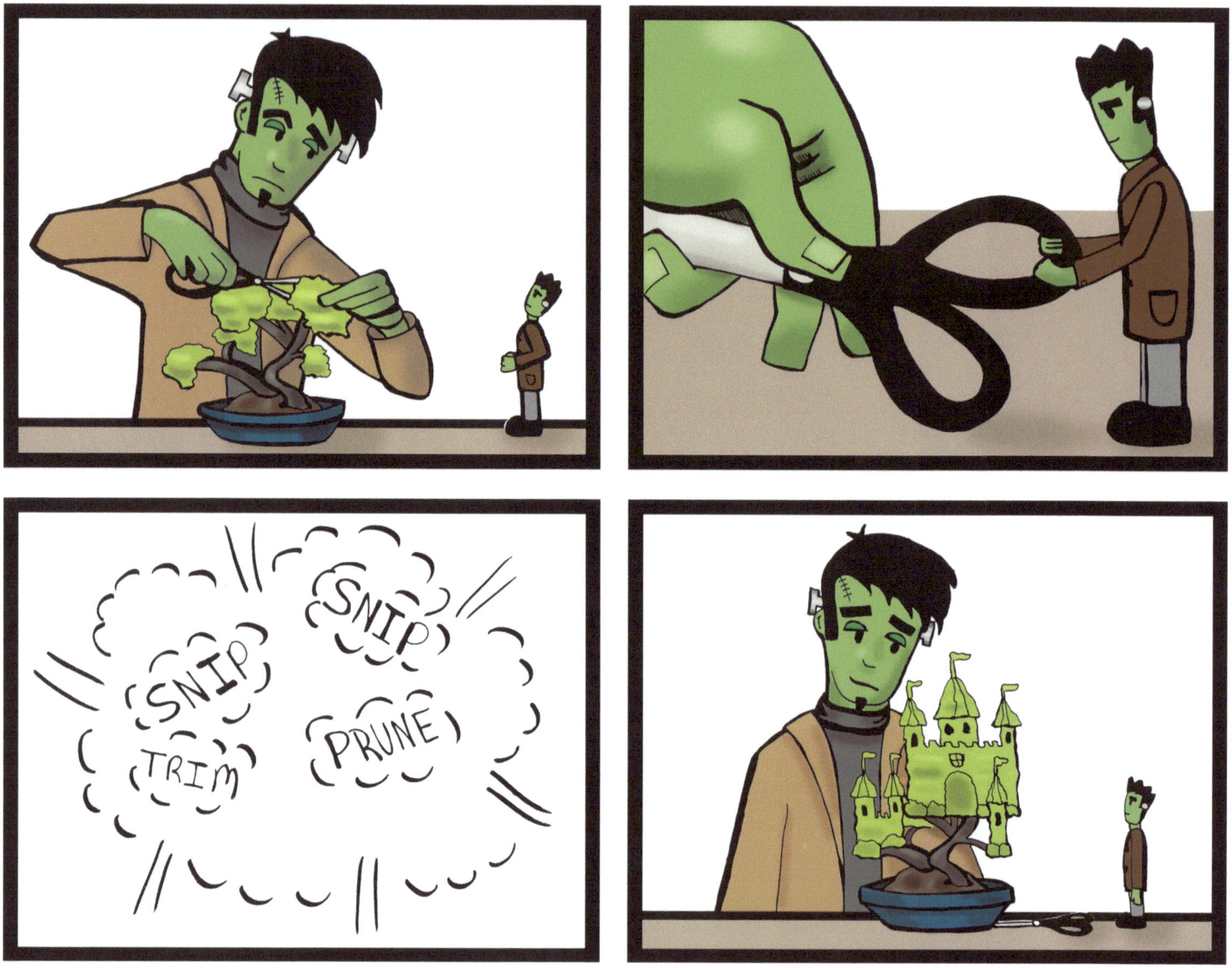
SNIP
SNIP
TRIM
PRUNE

BEHIND THE SCENES

Unlike the Little Vampires, Frank does not try to be like his larger counterpart, Frankenstein's Monster. He admires him, and they do share similar interests. But Frank is his own reanimated man, and actually has a thing or two to teach FM, at least in regards to the gardening arts.

November 24, 2010 • Happy Turkey Day

Frank's hand turkey
Wolfie's hand turkey
GOBBLE
GOBBLE
TOUCHDOWN!
A Little Vampire's... attempt...
at a hand turkey like something.

ART DIRECTION

When I was a kid, there were certain arts and crafts projects that could be found in almost all elementary schools throughout the United States. These projects often coincided with holidays. One was the macaroni necklace, which could be used as a great Christmas gift for moms lacking jewelry made from pasta. Another was the paper snowflake, popular because even Little-Timmy-Uses-Safety-Scissors-Like-They-Were-A-Chainsaw could cut up a folded piece of paper in such a way as to form a vague snowflake shape when it was unfolded. And yet another was the Thanksgiving hand turkey. The Thanksgiving hand turkey could make anyone, even a Little Vampire, feel that they were a fine artist.

An early color study for Frank. His final design is very close to the original concept I had for him.

December 1, 2010 • Happy Hanukkah

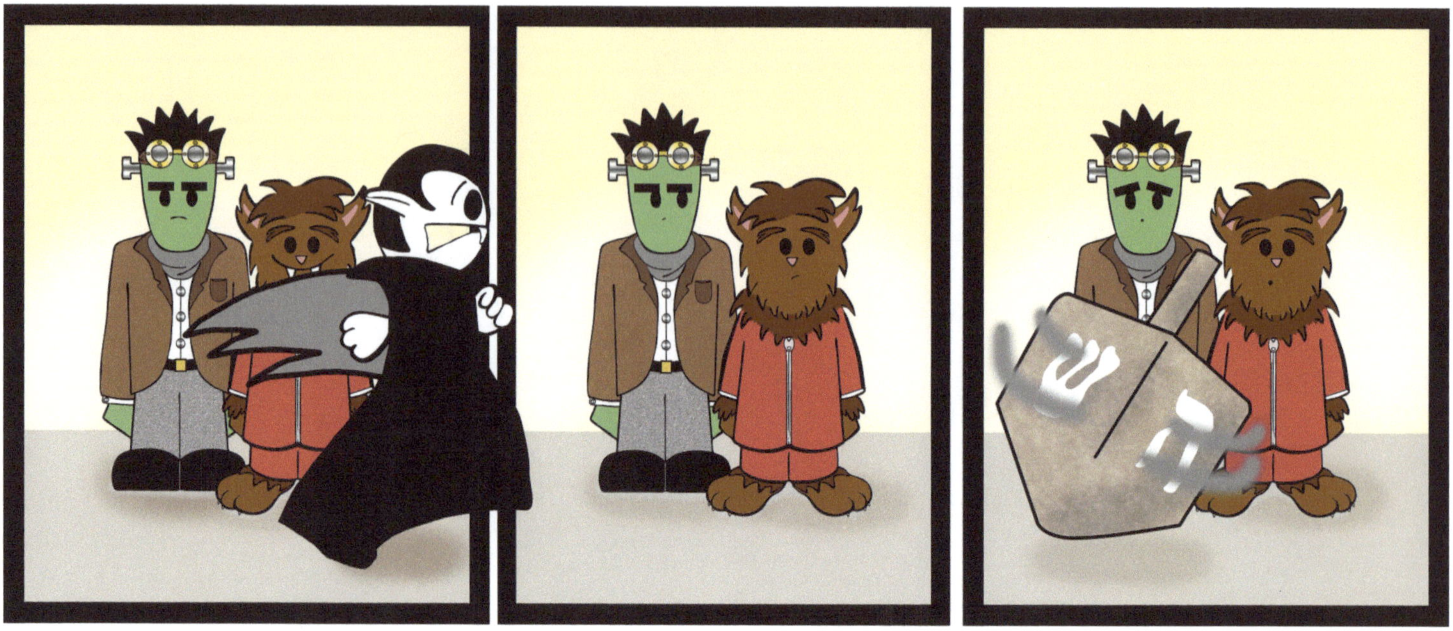

BEHIND THE SCENES

Like the piano in the first, second, and fiftieth comics, I imagined that a dreidel would have a personality all its own. This dreidel has no problem being spun, but does not tolerate being "blehed" at and gnawed on by little fangs.

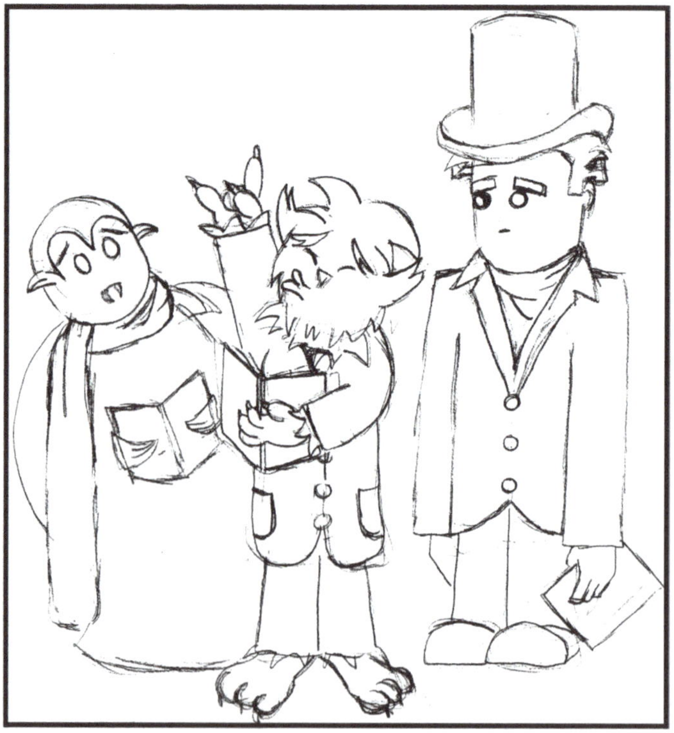

This sketch became the fan Christmas card for 2008.

December 8, 2010 • Gingerbread House

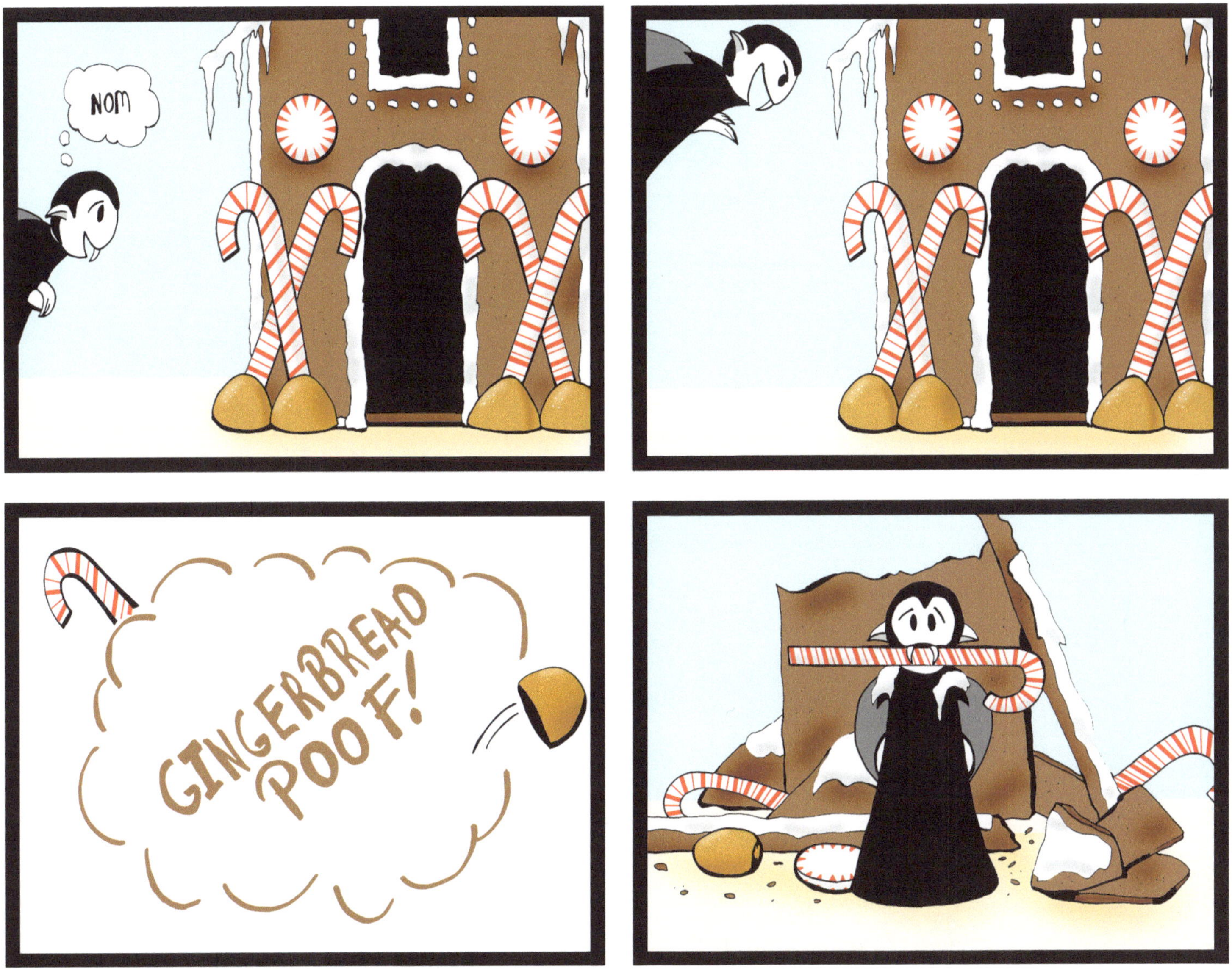
NOM
GINGERBREAD POOF!

BEHIND THE SCENES

There are so many Little Vampire sized Christmas objects that the little guys could get into trouble with. Tree ornaments, toy trains, even bows on gifts would give them ample opportunity for interaction. I chose a gingerbread house as the object of a Little Vampire's unintentionally destructive attention for this comic.

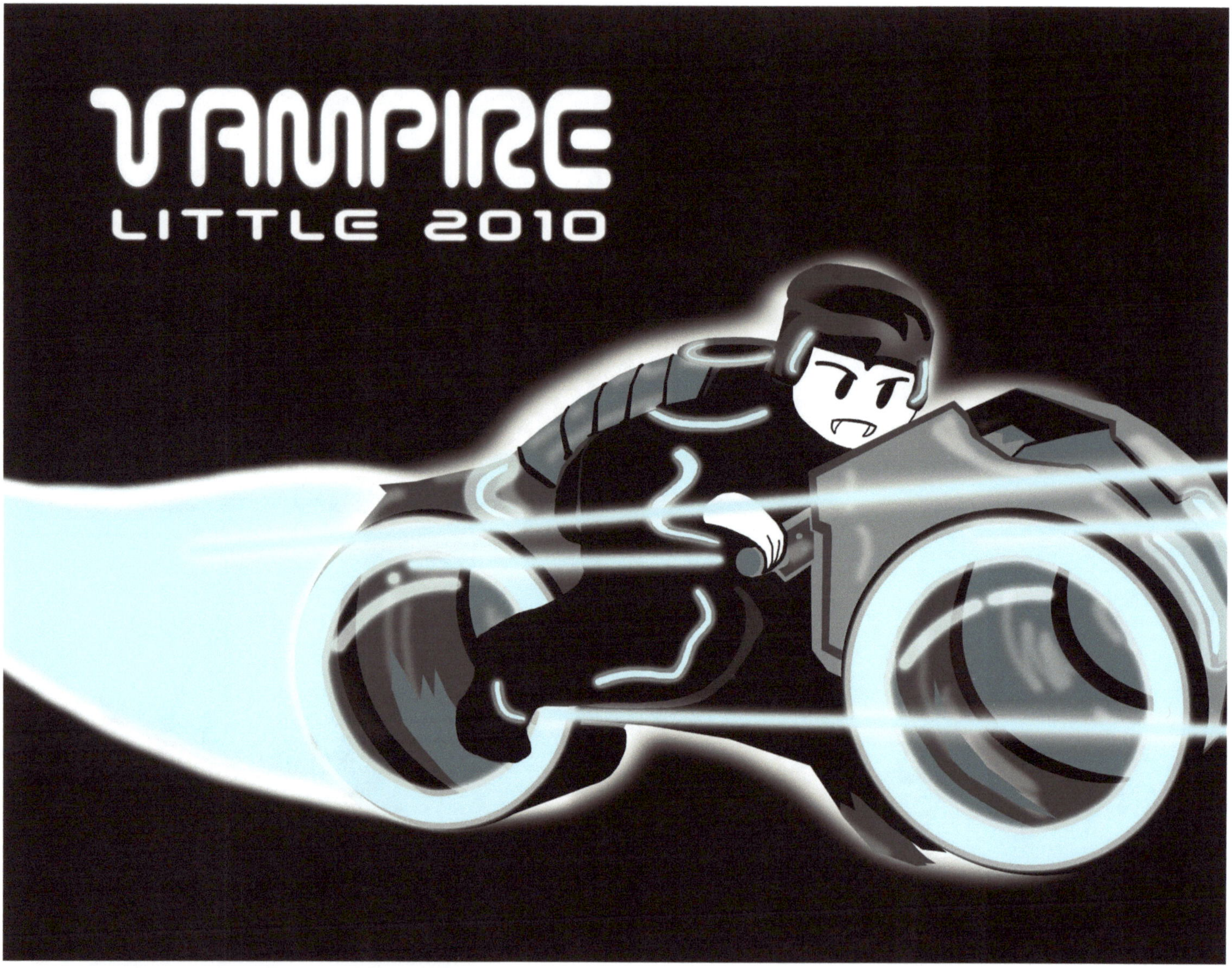
VAMPIRE
LITTLE 2010

BEHIND THE SCENES

Though I didn't get to see it in the theater when it was originally released, I enjoyed the first *Tron* movie when I finally saw it on television. James and I were excited about the release of *Tron: Legacy*, so I challenged myself to draw this Little Vampire on a light cycle.

December 22, 2010 • Sugar Plum Vampire

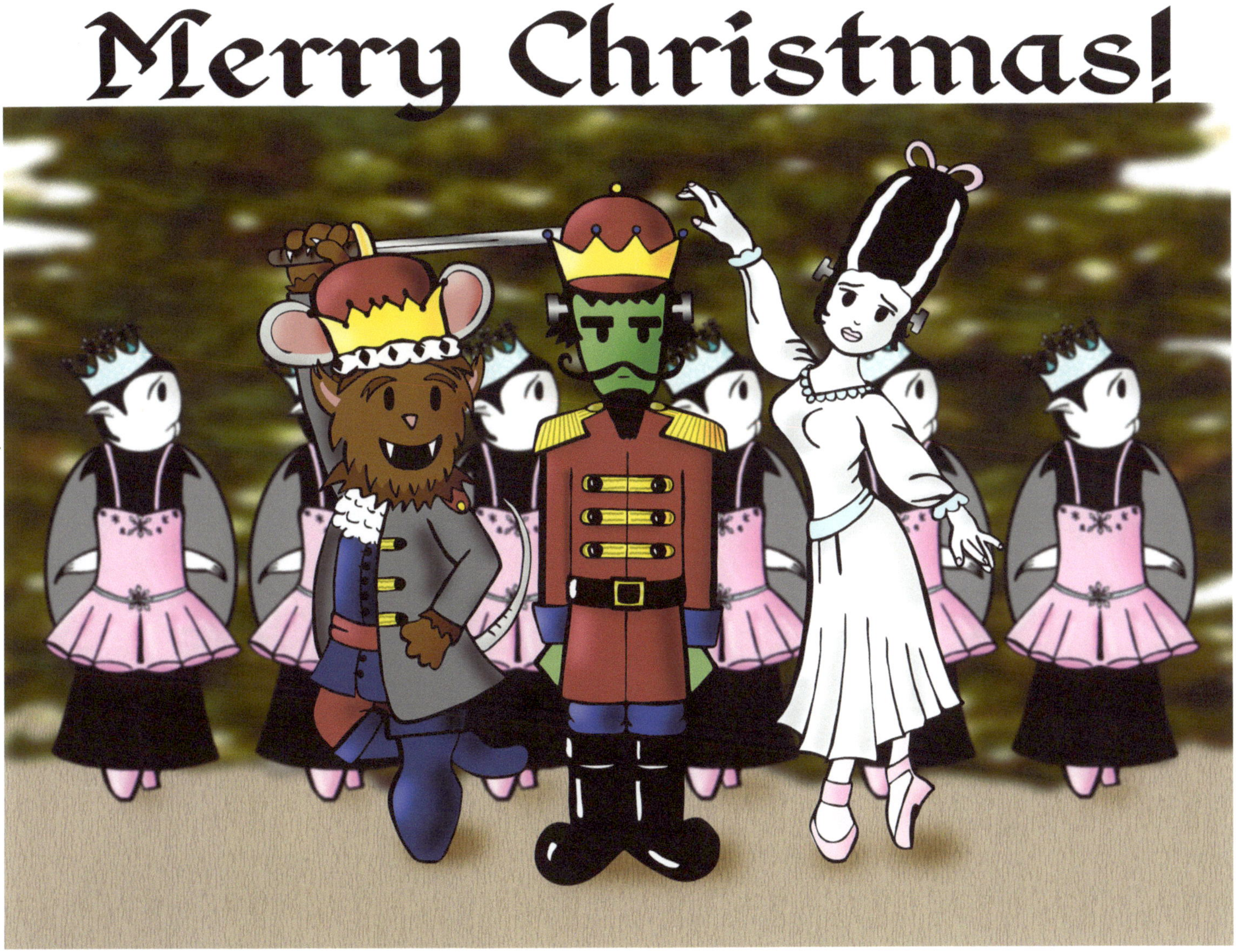
Merry Christmas!

BEHIND THE SCENES

This was the art for the 2010 fan Christmas card. I didn't realize it when I drew it, but my cousin's lovely daughter Alexa had a part in her ballet class's performance of *The Nutcracker*. She thought I made the card just for her, an idea that I retroactively declare as truth.

December 29, 2010 • Happy New Year 2011

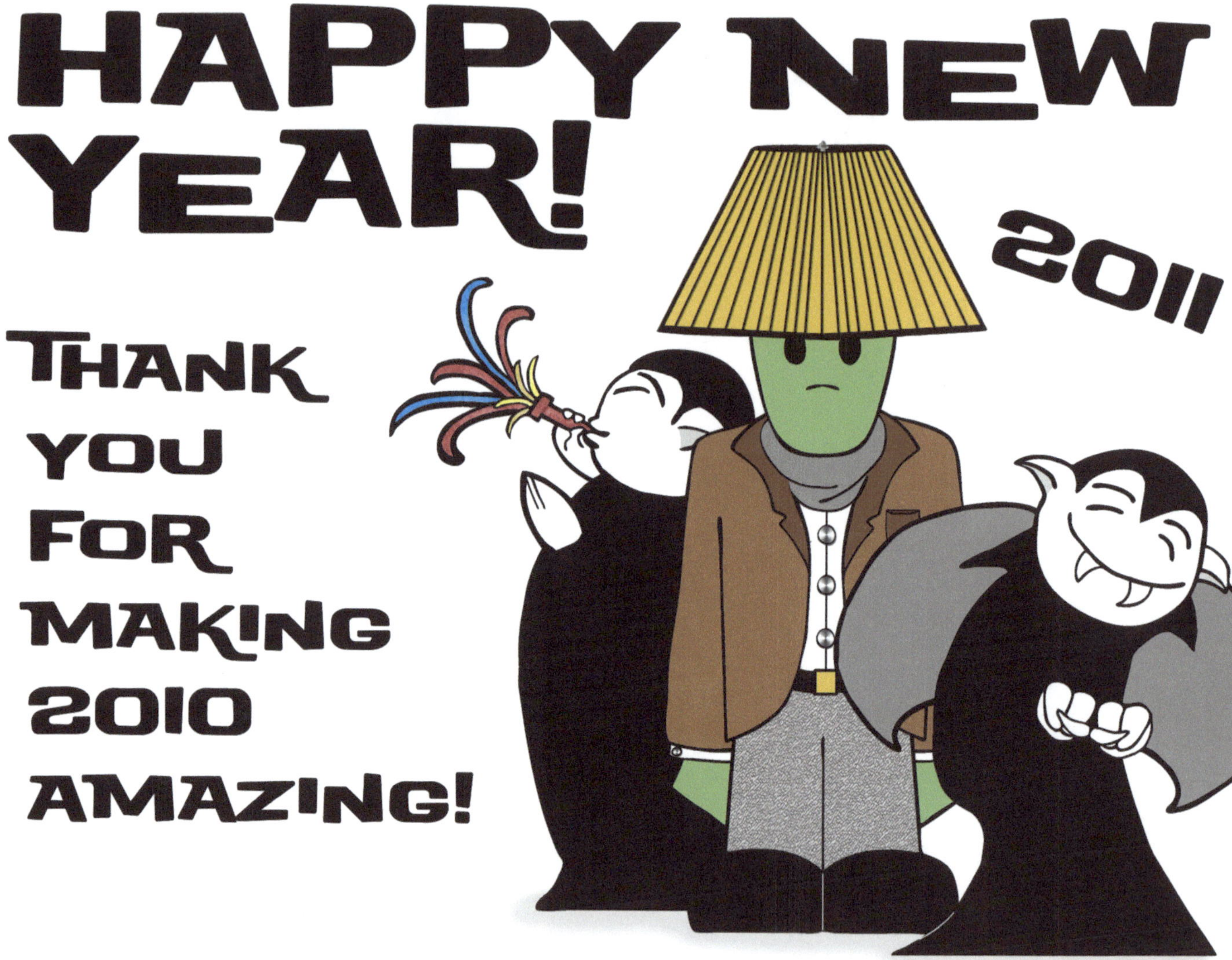
HAPPY NEW YEAR!
2011
THANK YOU FOR MAKING 2010 AMAZING!

BEHIND THE SCENES

There is no way for me to effectively convey how much fan support has meant to me over the years. I can't find the right words or drawings to adequately describe that emotion. That doesn't keep me from trying to express my appreciation, as I tried to do in this comic.

SKETCHBOOK-Character Development

San Jose Super-Con, June 2007

I was promoting my comic book at the 2007 Super-Con, but I had reached the point where I couldn't stop thinking about the Little Vampires. During slow moments at the convention, I focused on pulling all my random ideas about the characters together to form a narrative.

It was from these sketches and notes that the first Little Vampires book really came together. And though I wouldn't revisit the idea until I began the webcomic many years later, the concept of Little Vampire Girls began here.

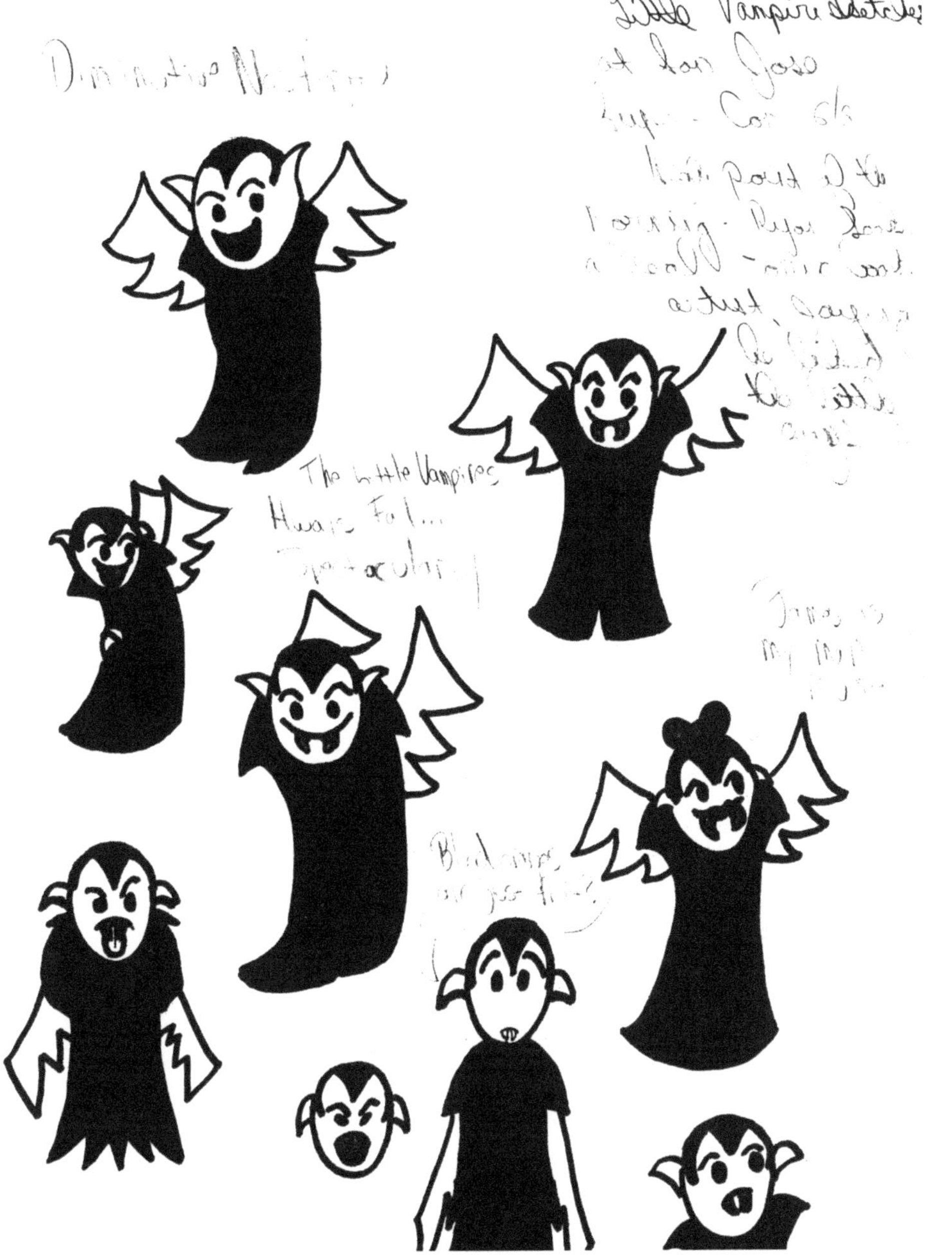

Little Vampire Sketches
at San Jose
The Little Vampires

SKETCHBOOK-Character Development

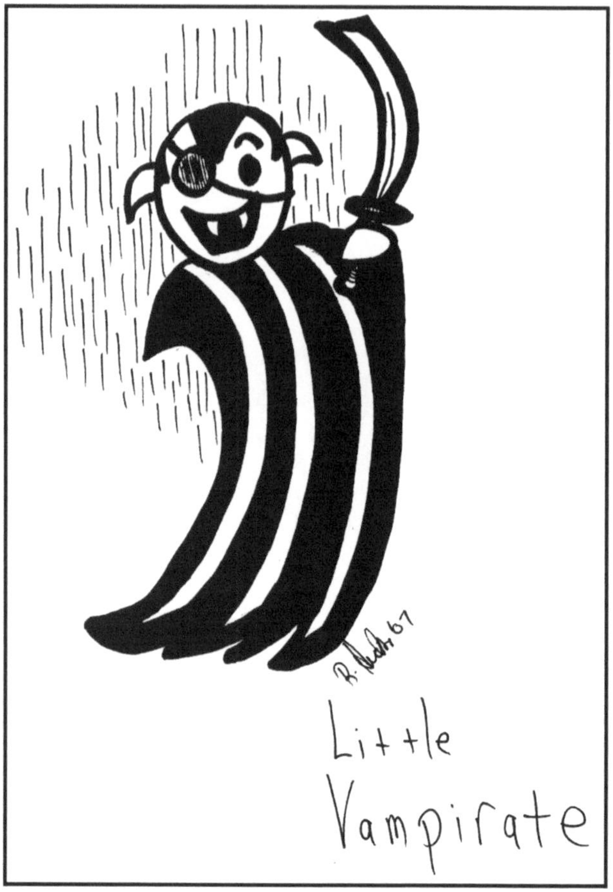
R. [illegible] '07
Little Vampirate

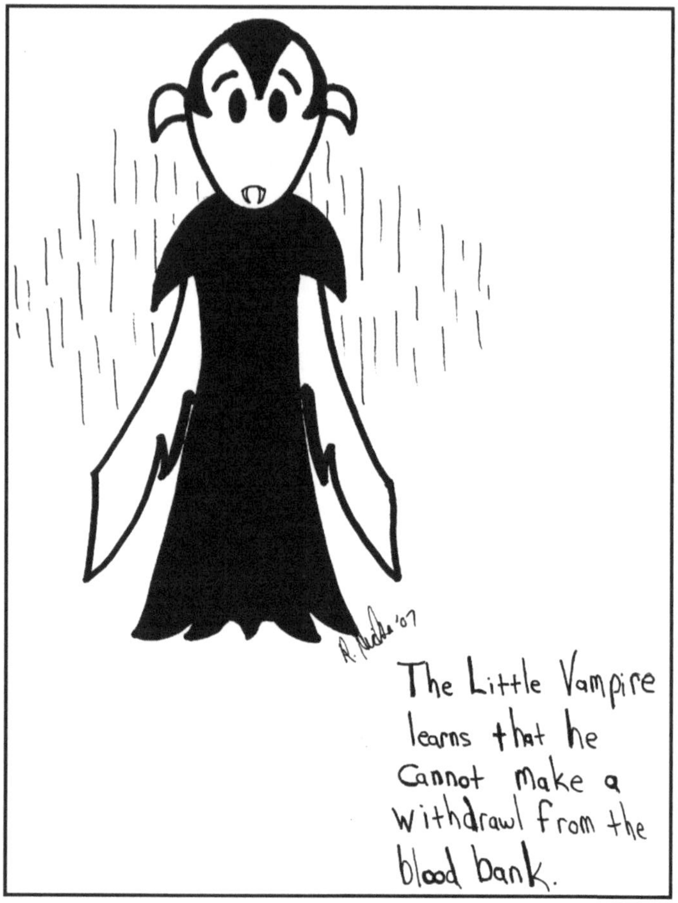
The Little Vampire learns that he cannot make a withdrawl from the blood bank.

Our artist alley table at Super-Con happened to be next to the table of comic book artist Ryan Sook, who is best known for his amazing cover art. Ryan did not even have to acknowledge my existence, but he talked to me as if I was an artistic peer. He was incredibly encouraging and supportive, and was the first person to ever buy a piece of Little Vampire art. I wanted to give him a sketch for free, but he insisted on paying for it.

"Your art has value," he explained.

Those words have stayed with me, and I pass Ryan's wisdom on to everyone that needs to hear it.

SKETCHBOOK-Art Prints

The modern vampire was developed in the Victorian era, and Frankenstein's monster is a product of Victorian literature, so drawing the Little Vampires and their friends in Victorian clothing seemed like a good idea.

This sketch was later developed into one of the first Little Vampire art prints, which featured the friends in Victorian garb. That print became a favorite of steampunk fans.

Introduction to Little Vampires and Friends

The first Little Vampires book premiered at the 2007 San Diego Comic-Con. One of the first fans of the book was Jess Miller (thank you forever, Jess). She enthused about the book to her friend Margaret Mannatt, and it was Margaret who invited us to do a book signing at her book store in Sacramento. Margaret has been our patron goddess ever since, encouraging us to continue to create. Her husband, Phil, also encouraged us to continue creating, but did so in a very different way than his wife.

A follow-up to the Little Vampires book was forming in my mind soon after we got the first book printed in hardcover. I knew that the sequel would involve the friendship between the Little Vampires and some other creatures, at the very least a werewolf and Frankenstein's monster. Phil was especially enthusiastic about the idea of including a "little wolfman," so much so that he would greet me at conventions with "Hi. Little wolfman." He would inject "little wolfman" into conversations with me. We could be discussing where to eat dinner, and he would say, "You know, you should draw a little wolfman."

Before he was fully formed, Wolfie had a fan.

The second book, *Little Vampires and Friends*, was dedicated to Margaret and Phil.

Little Vampires and Friends

By Rebecca Hicks

Being a Little Vampire
is exhausting work.

There are house cats to
be terrorized…

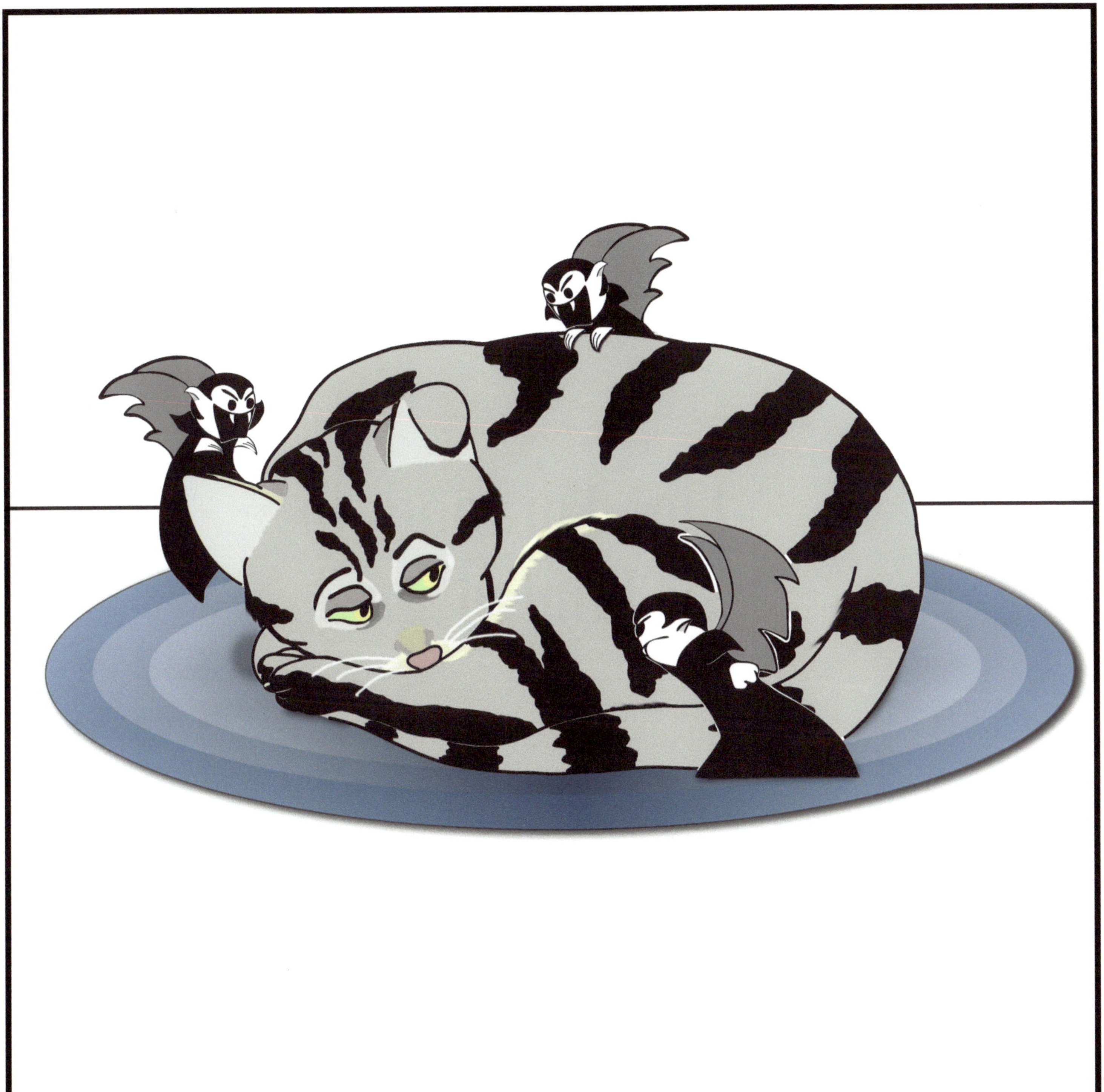

…blood oranges to
be hunted…

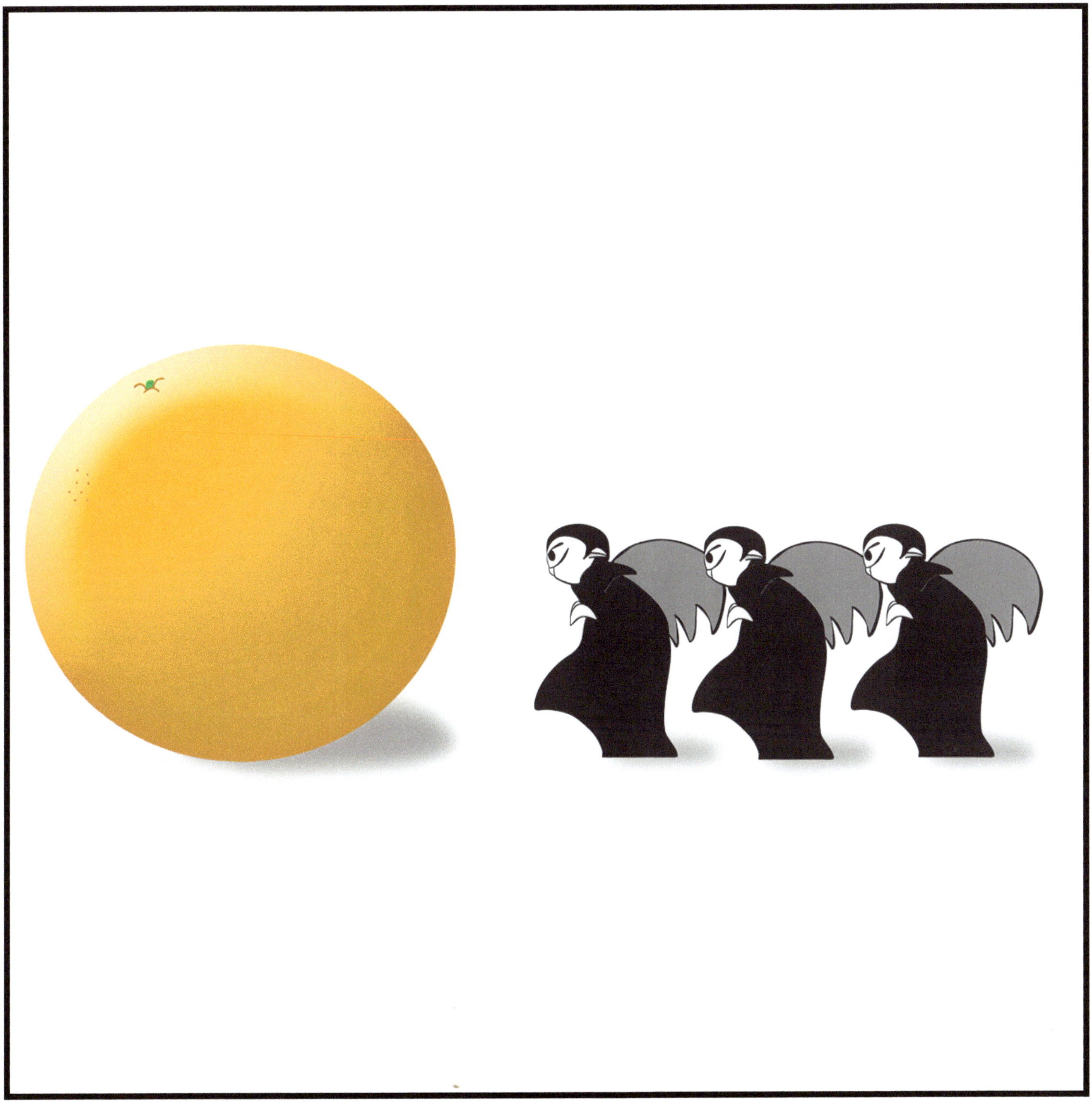

...and fierce poses
to be practiced.

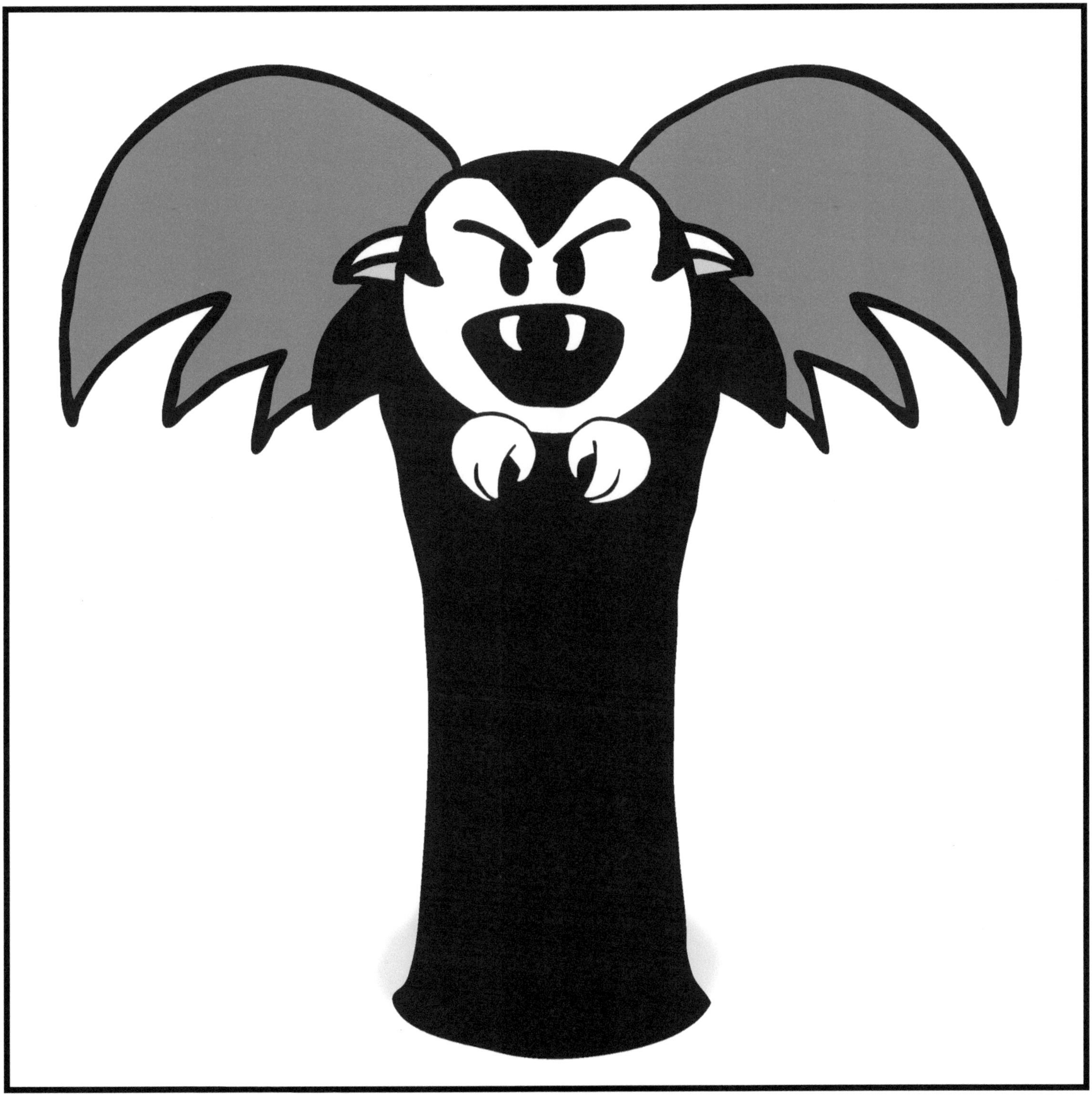

But all work and no play
makes dull Little Vampires.

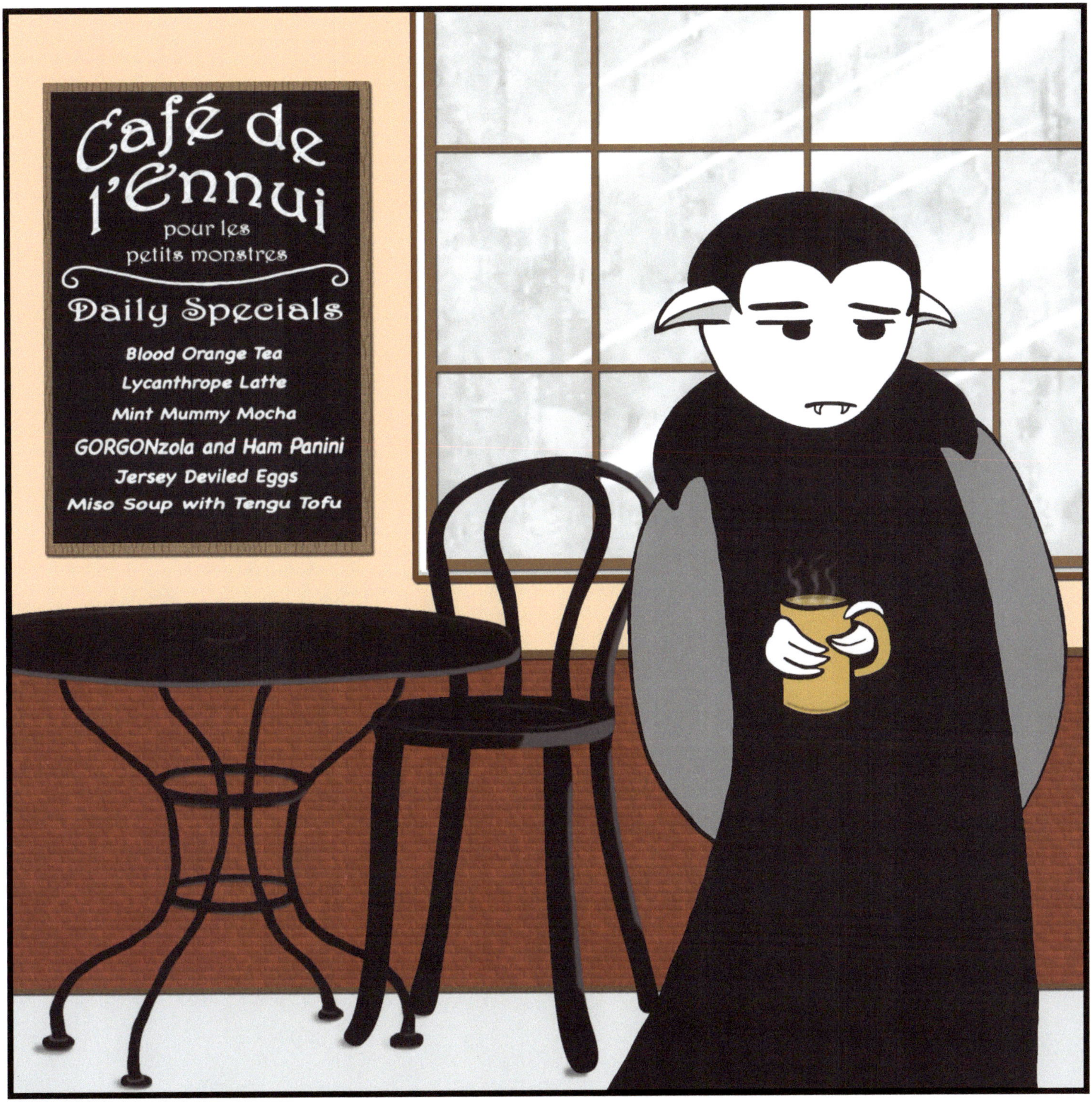
Café de l'Ennui
pour les petits monstres
Daily Specials
Blood Orange Tea
Lycanthrope Latte
Mint Mummy Mocha
GORGONzola and Ham Panini
Jersey Deviled Eggs
Miso Soup with Tengu Tofu

So they play.

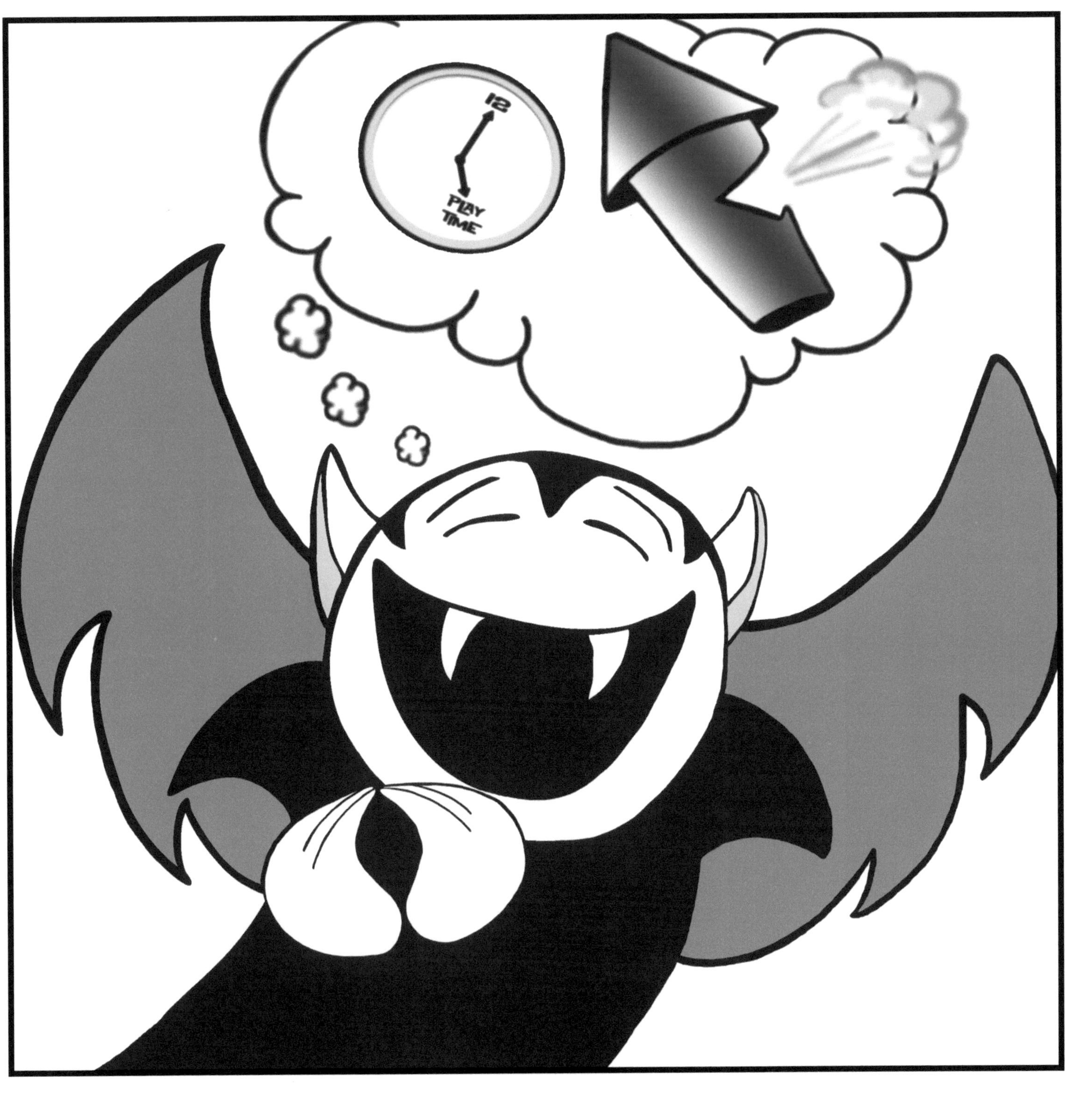
12
PLAY TIME

They like to play
with their friend Frank.

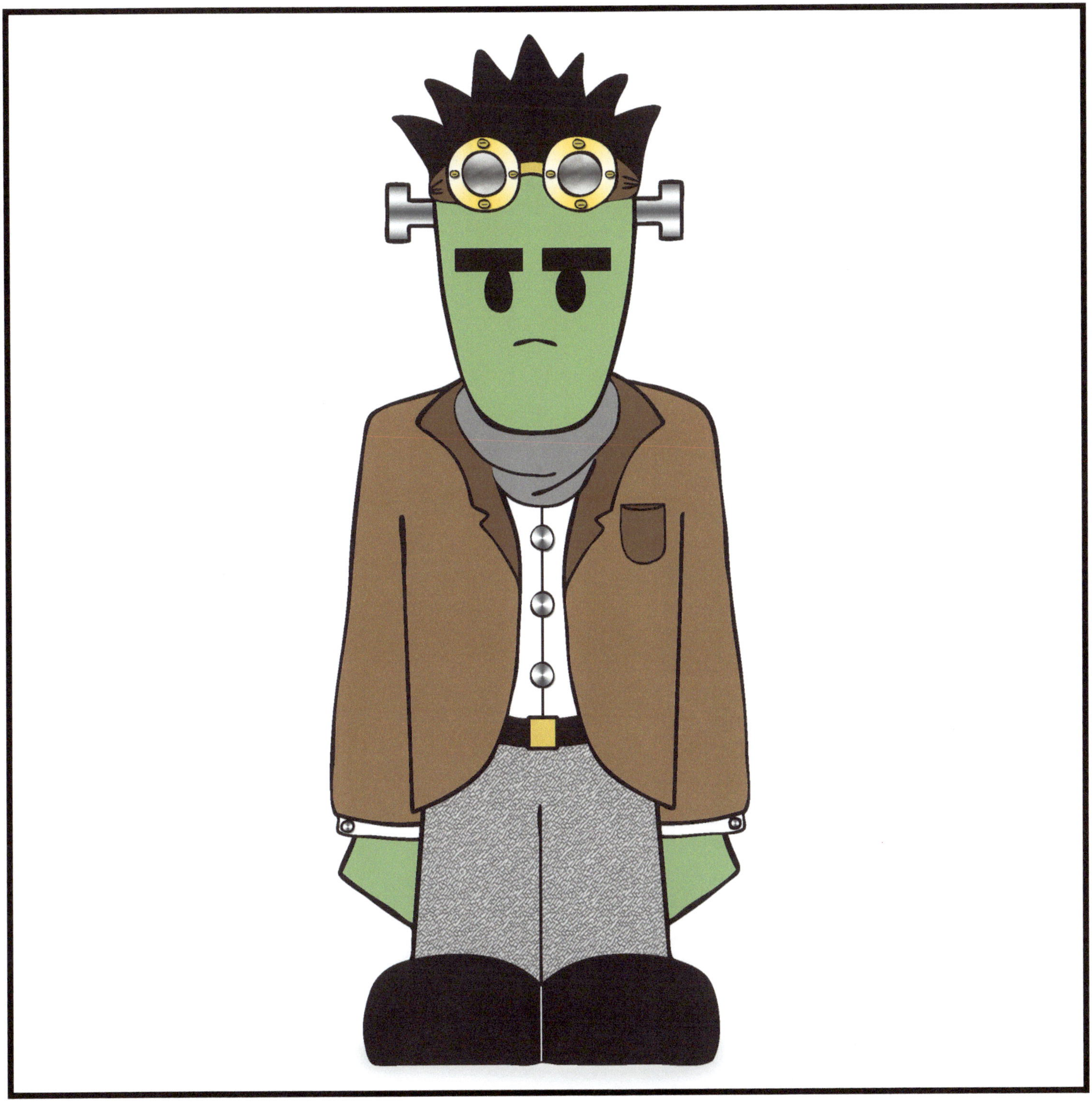

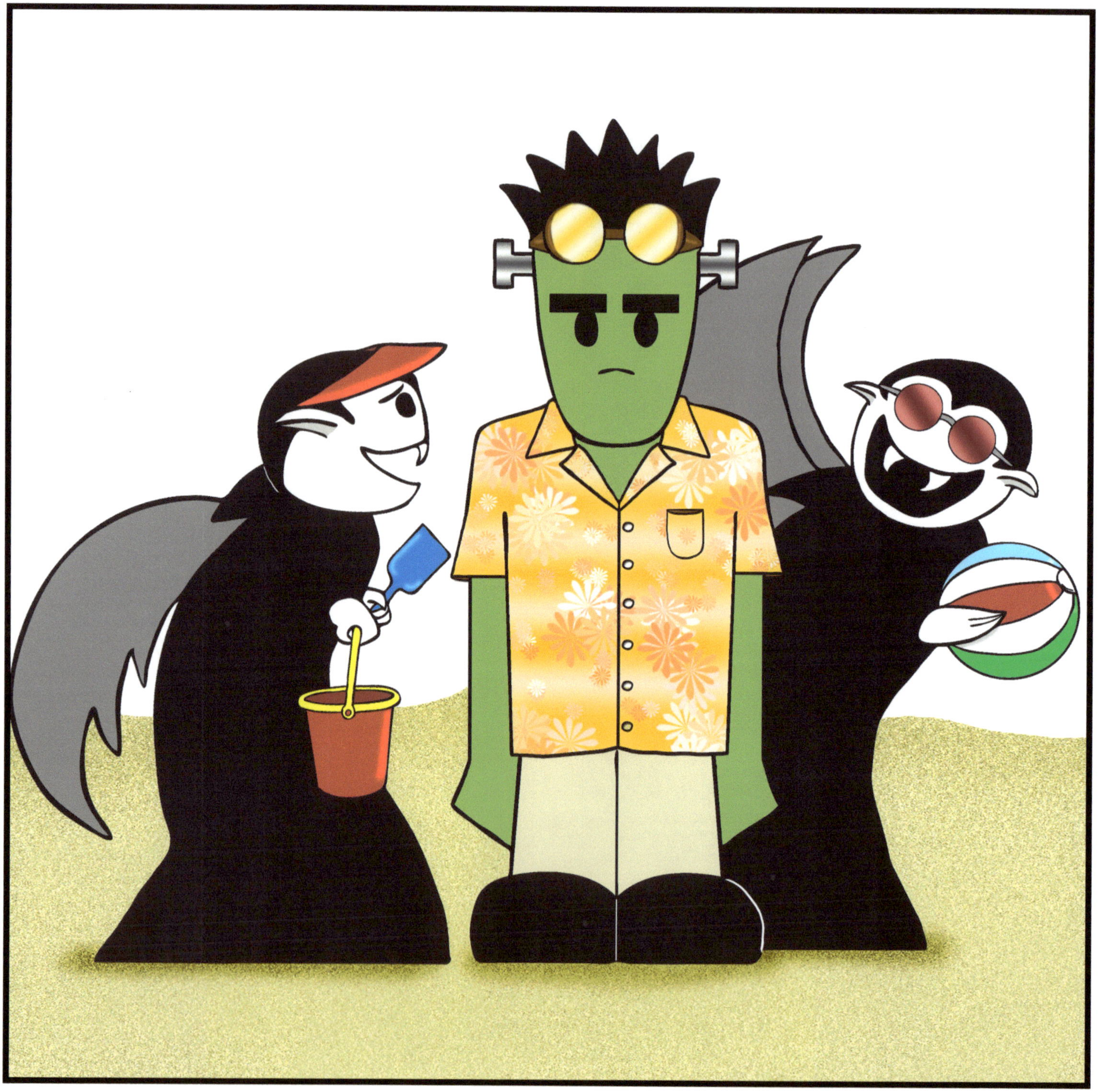

But Frank can
be a little…

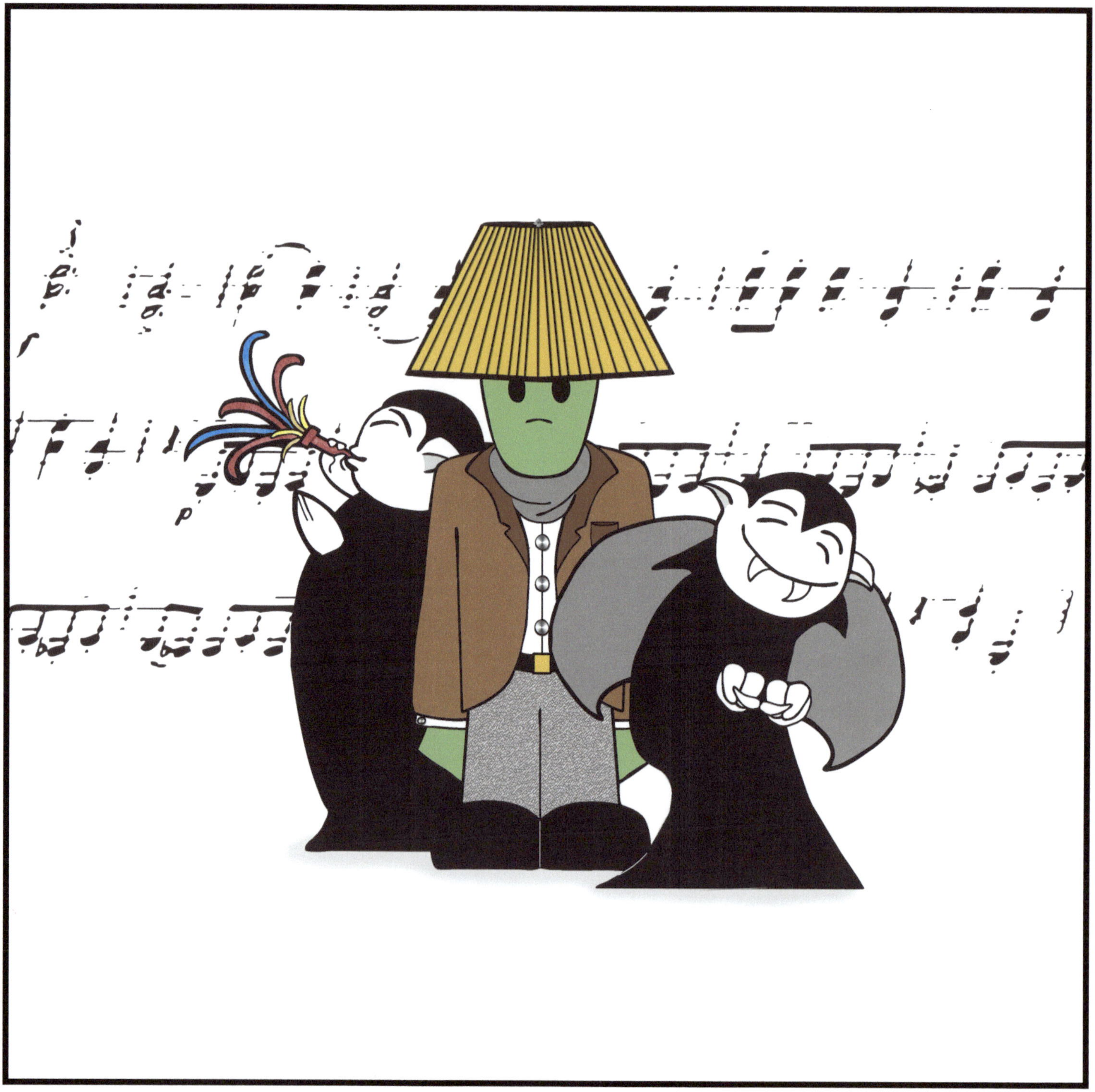

...boring.

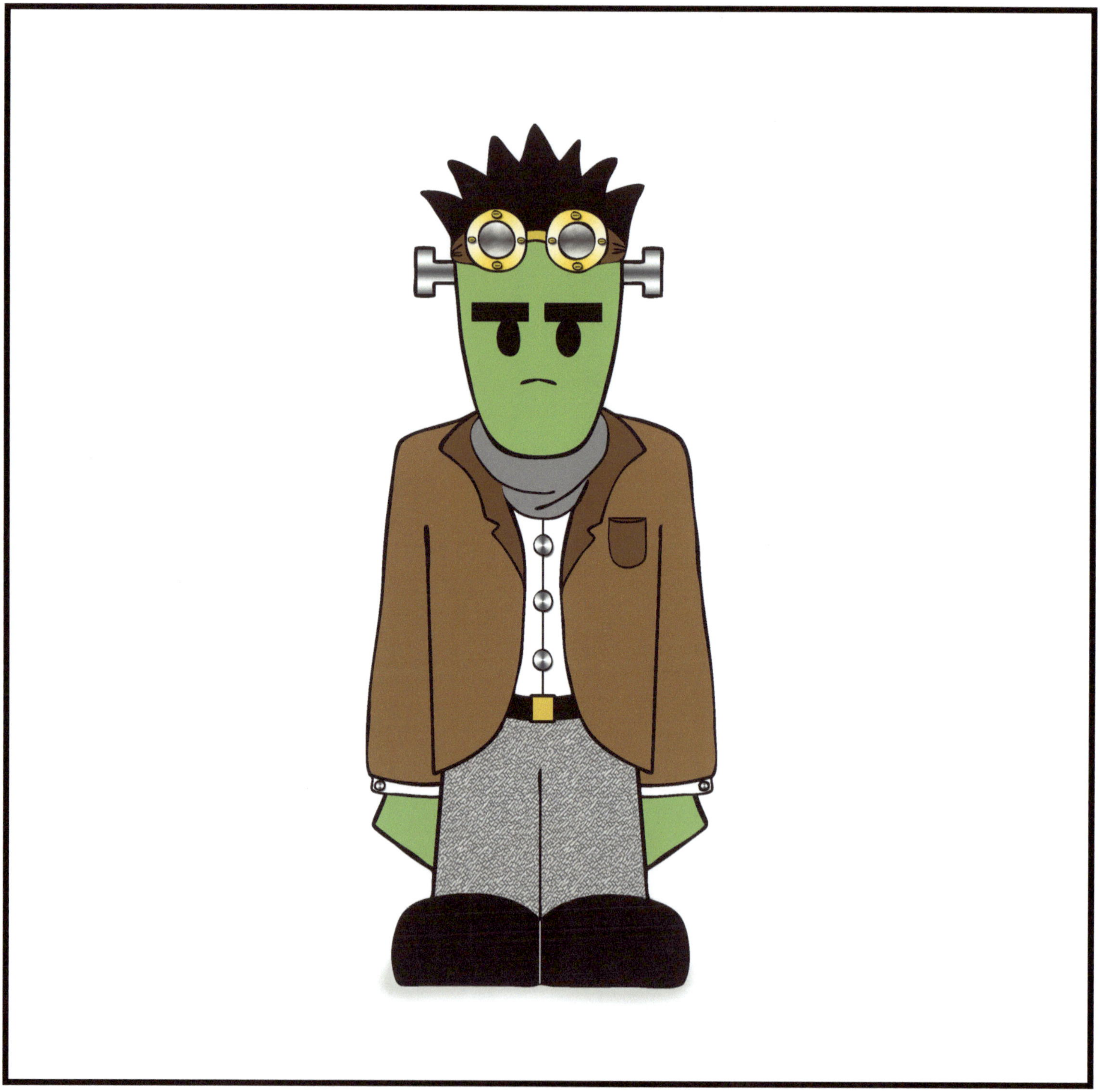

The Little Vampires
love him anyway.

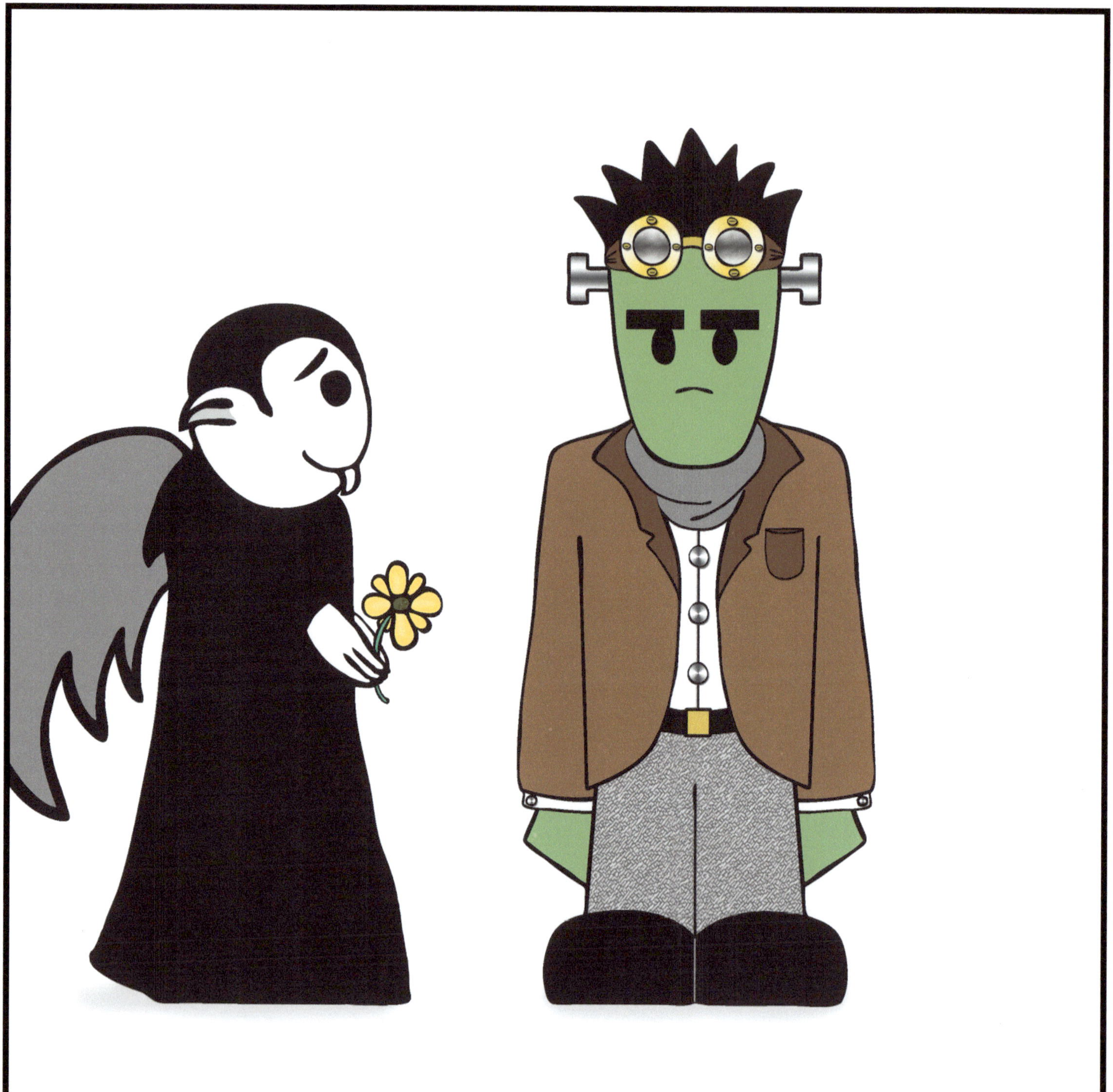

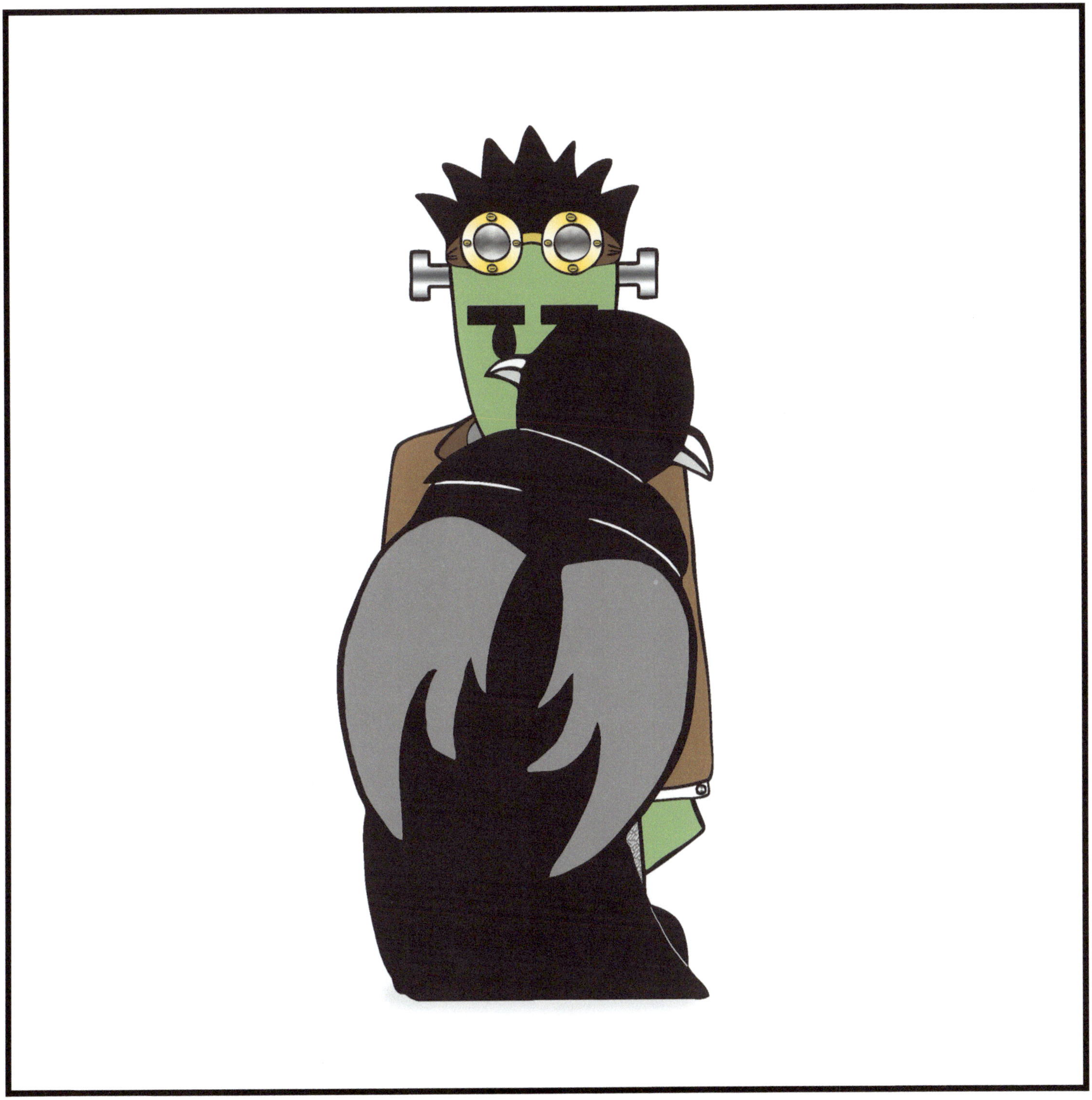

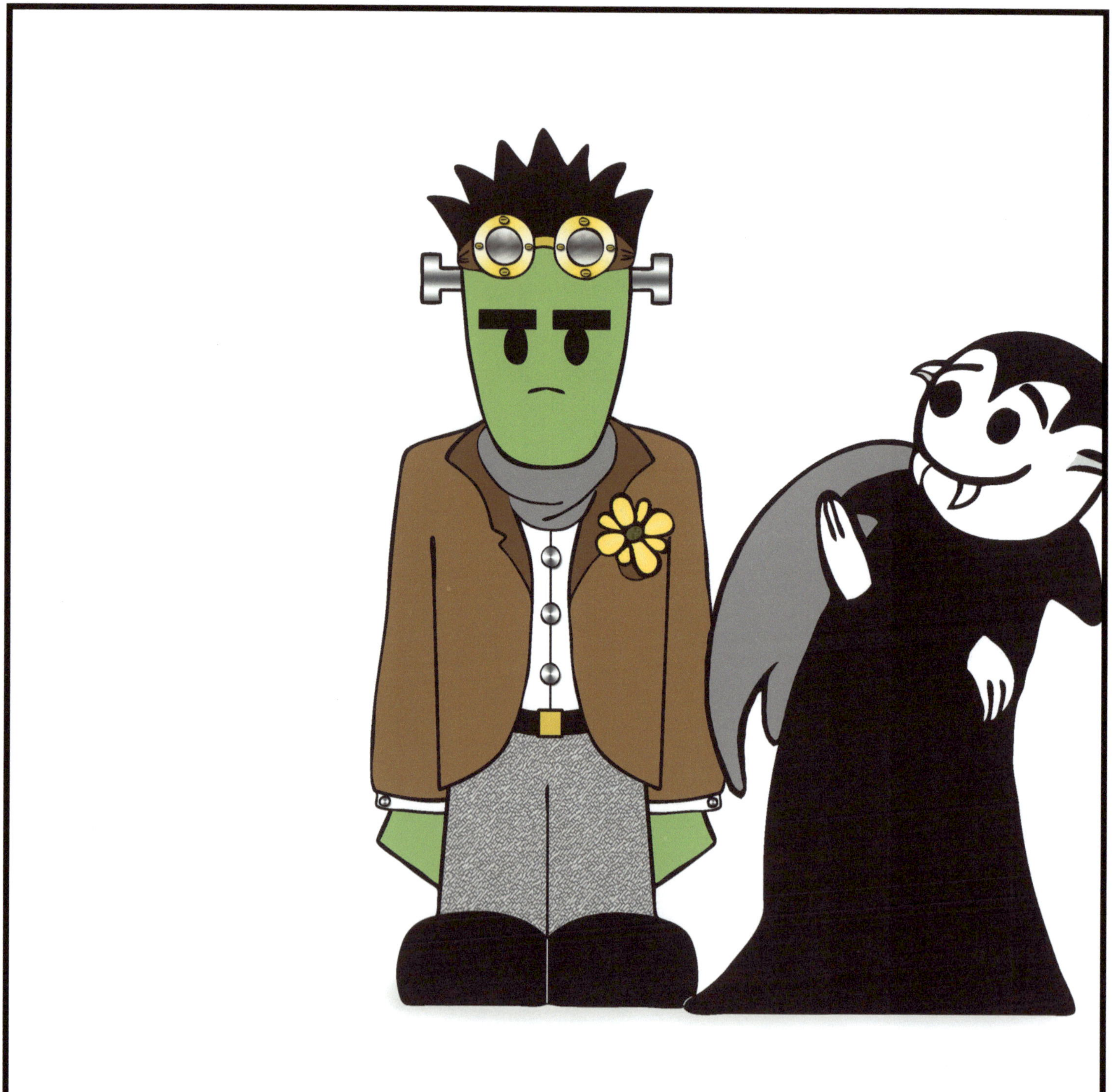

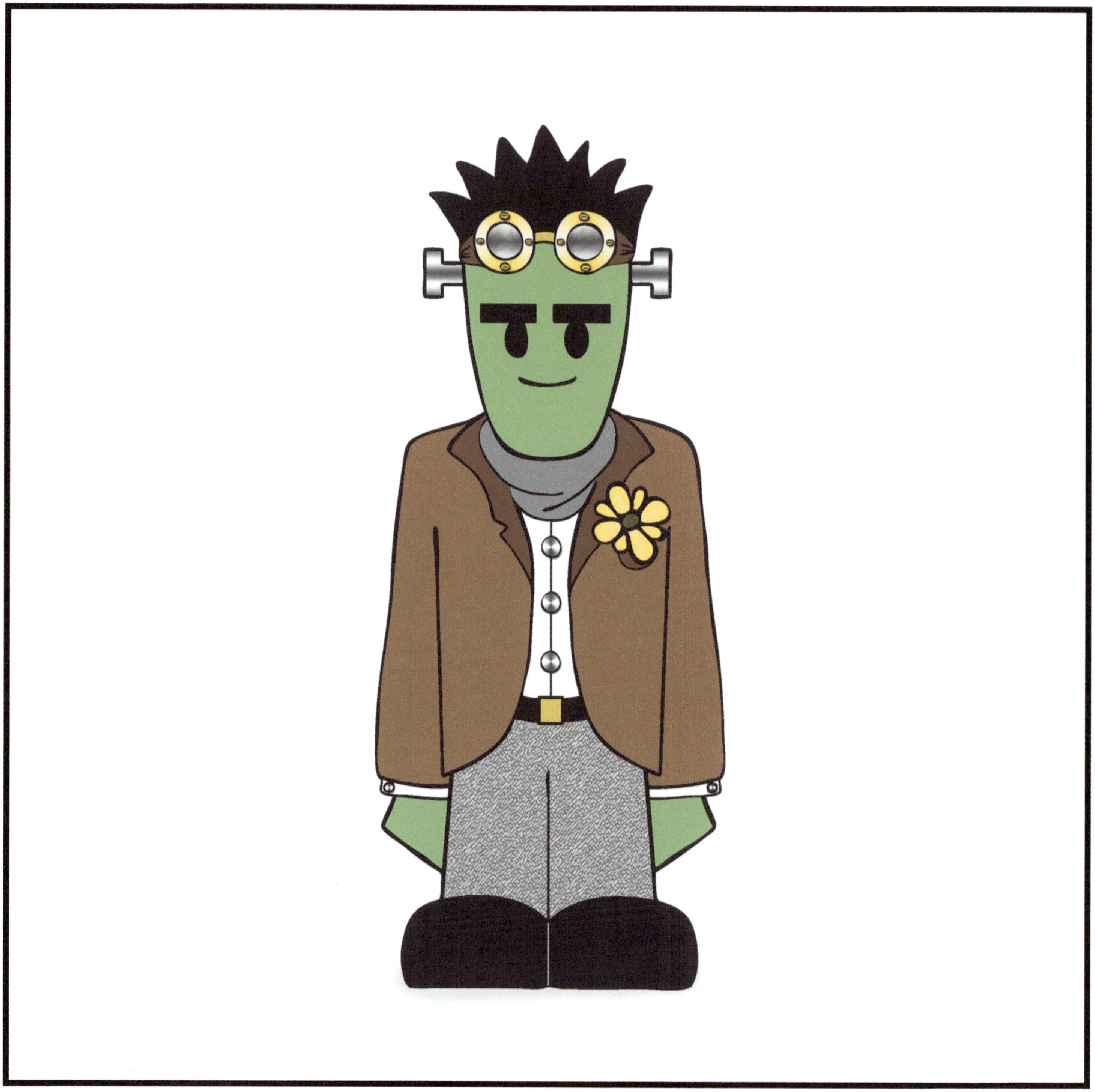

They also like to play with their friend Wolfie.

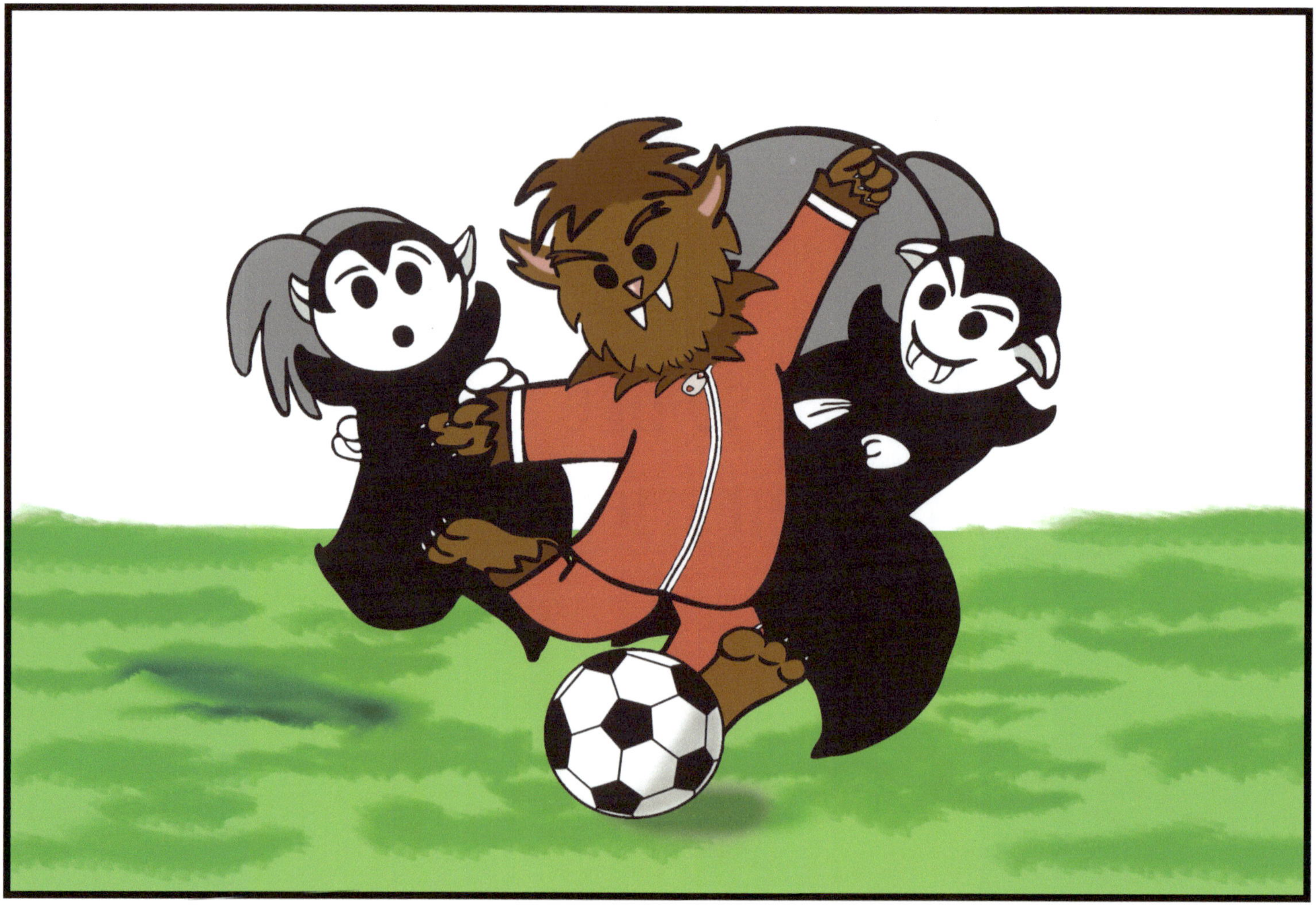

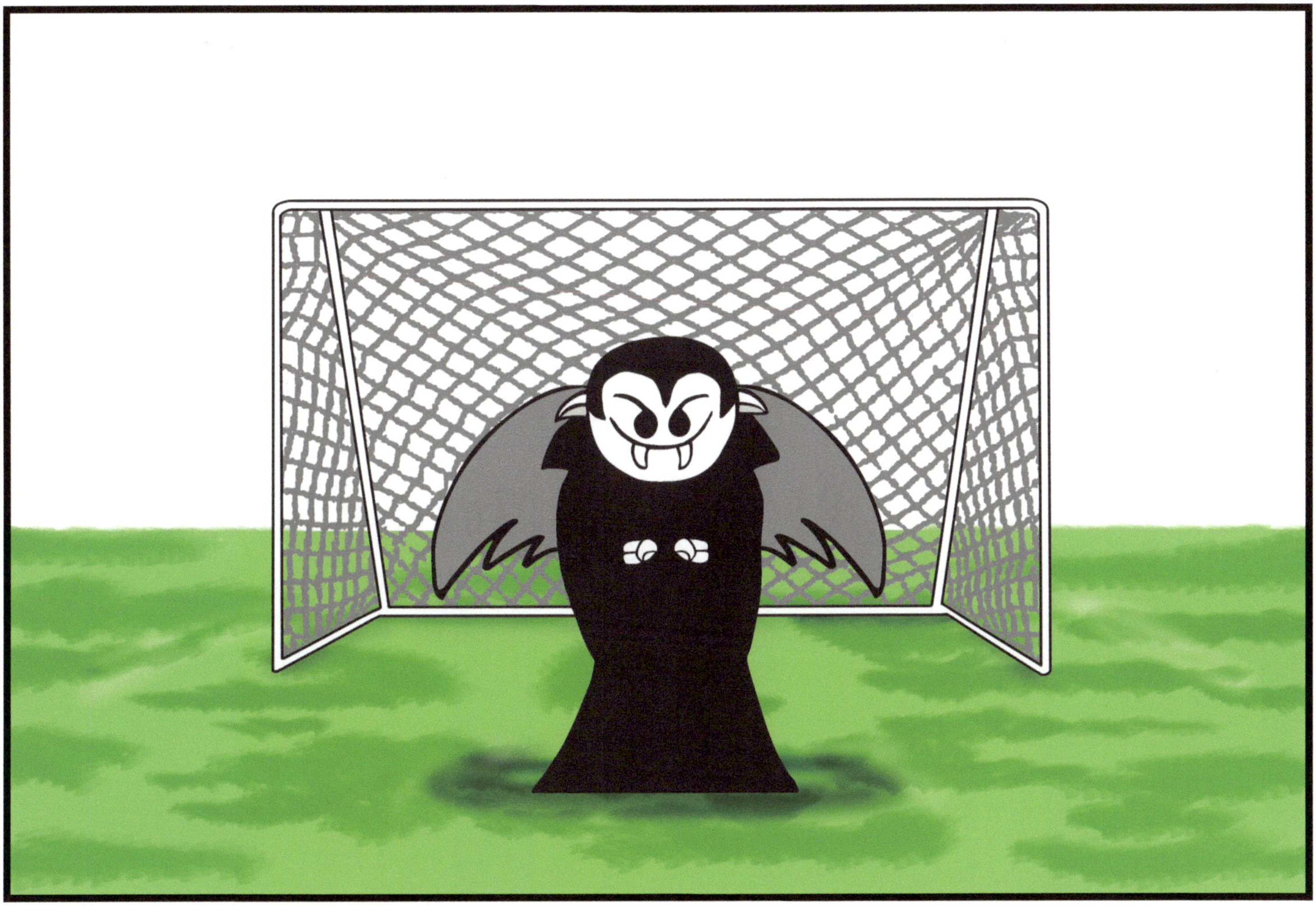

But Wolfie can be a little
too energetic sometimes.

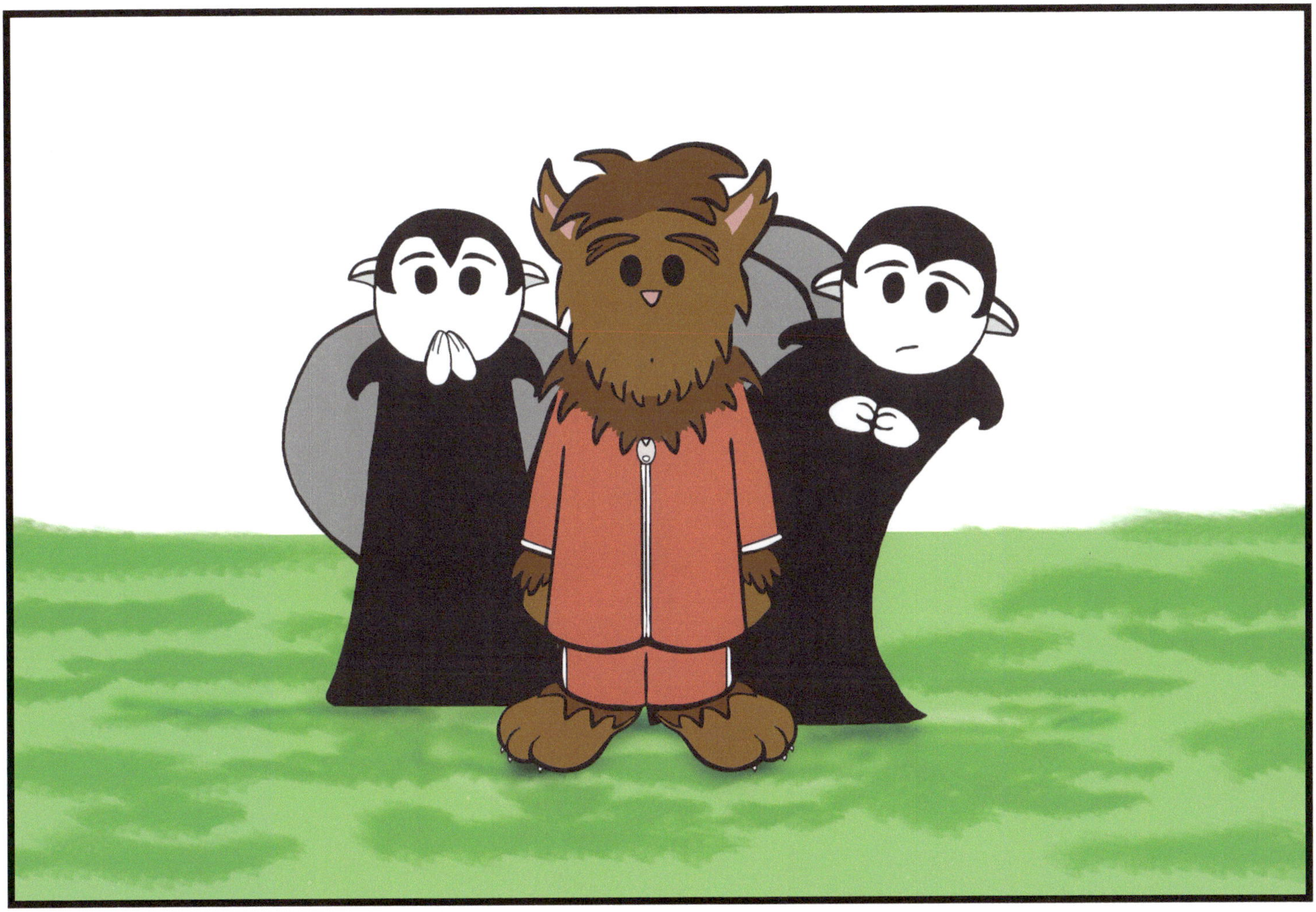

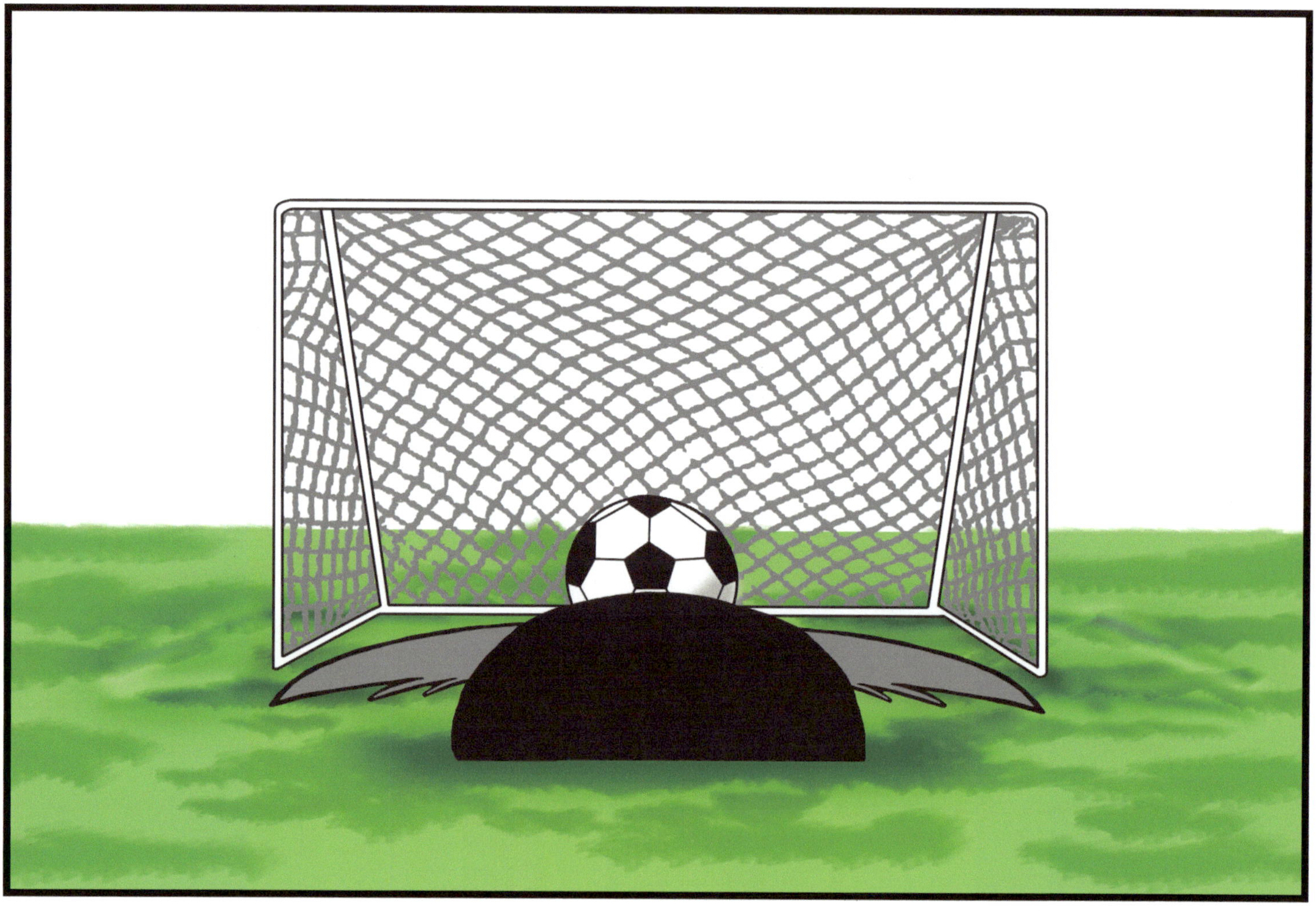

...

The Little Vampires
love him anyway.

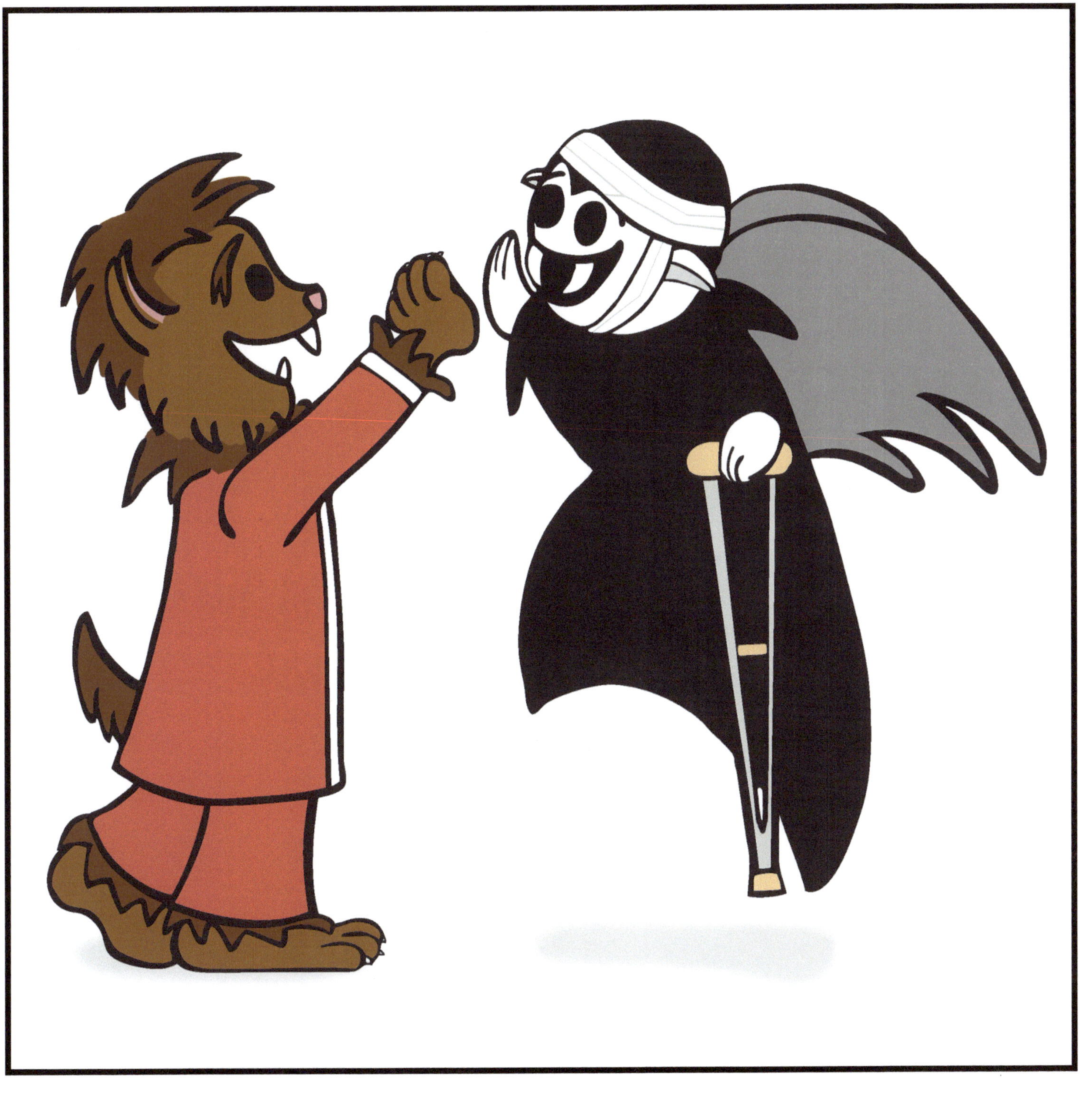

If Frank is too busy being boring, and if Wolfie is too busy being energetic, the Little Vampires ask their larger cousins if they can play.

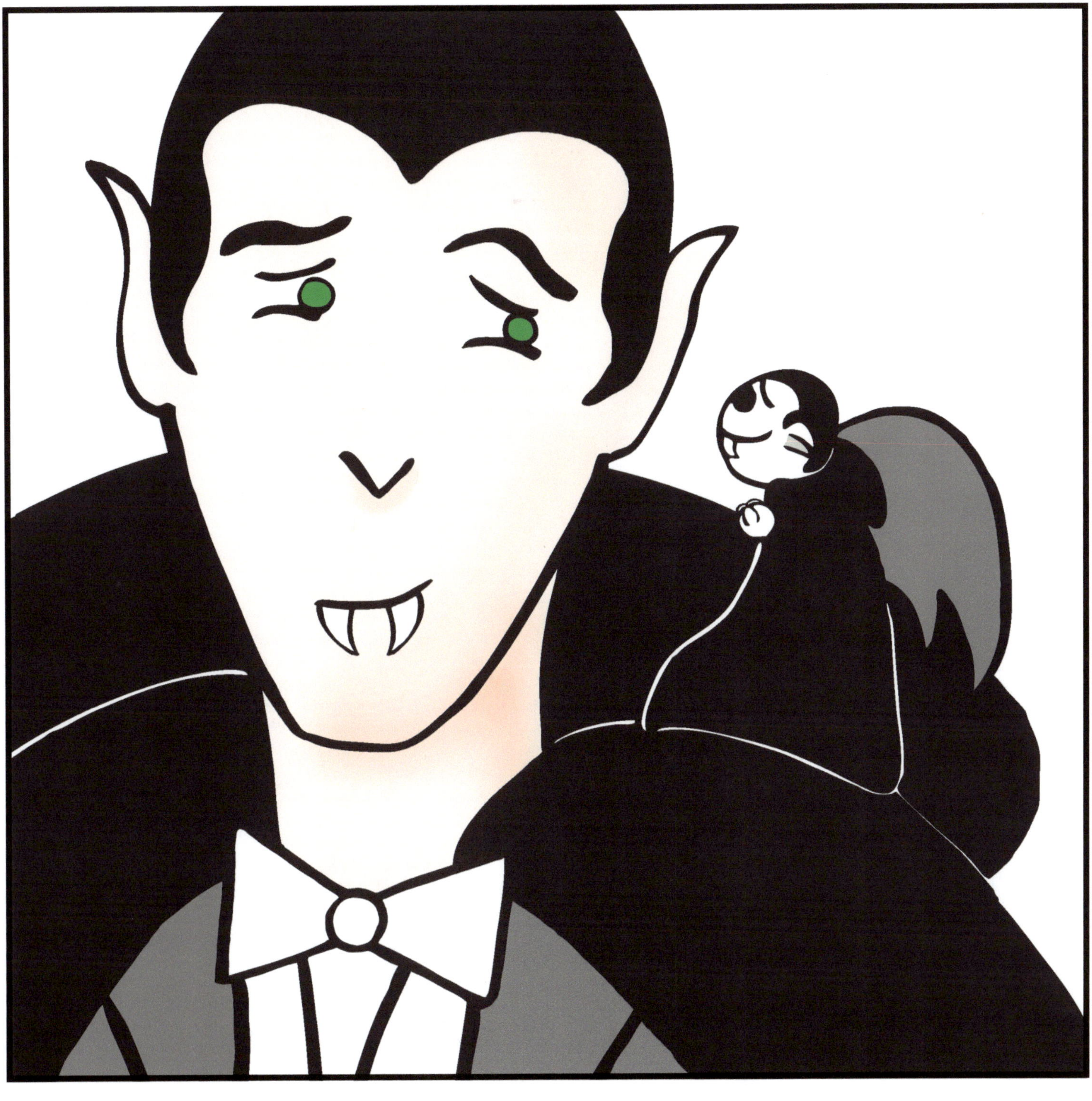

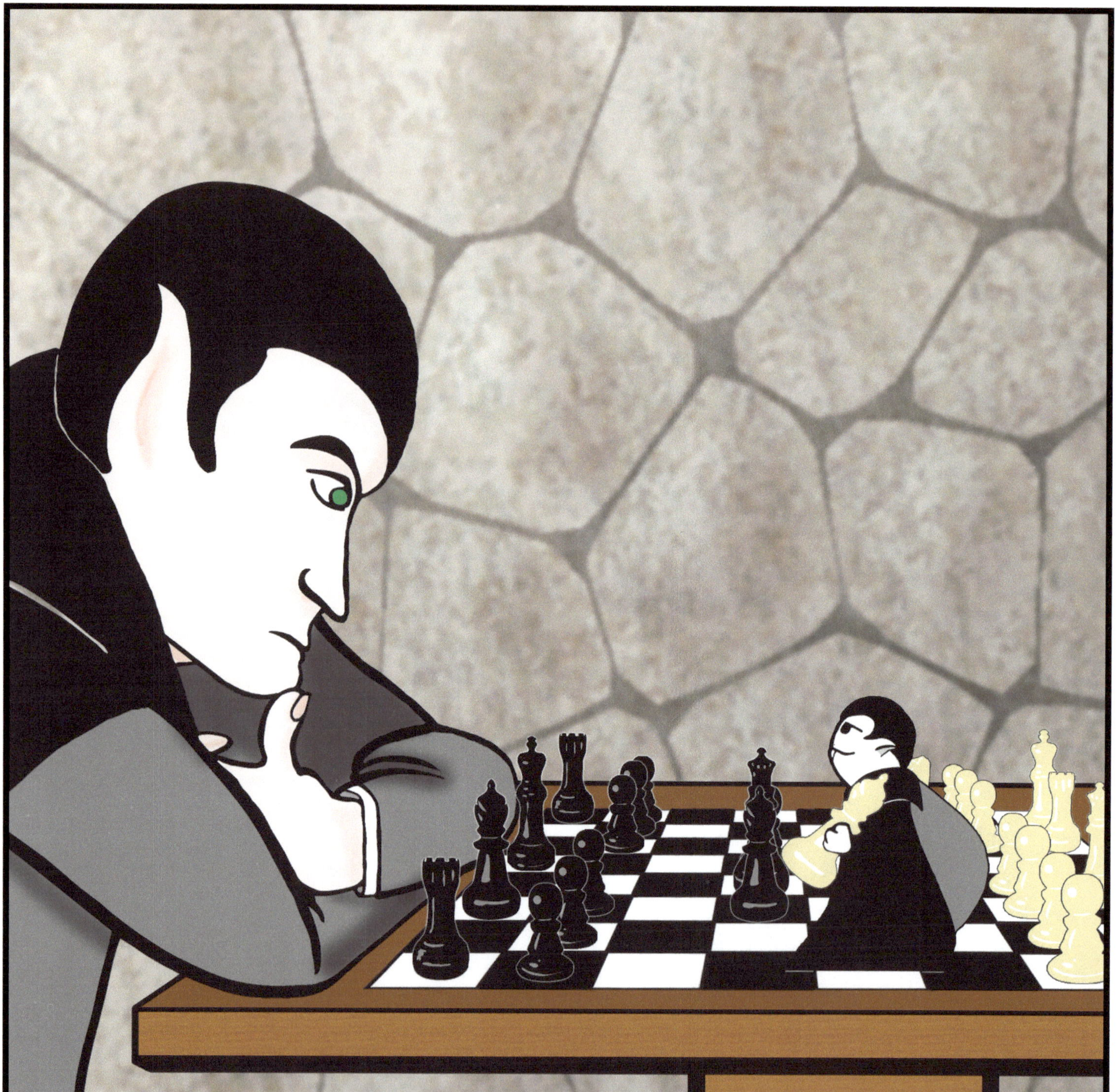

But all play and no work means
no blood oranges for the
Little Vampires.

So back to work they go.

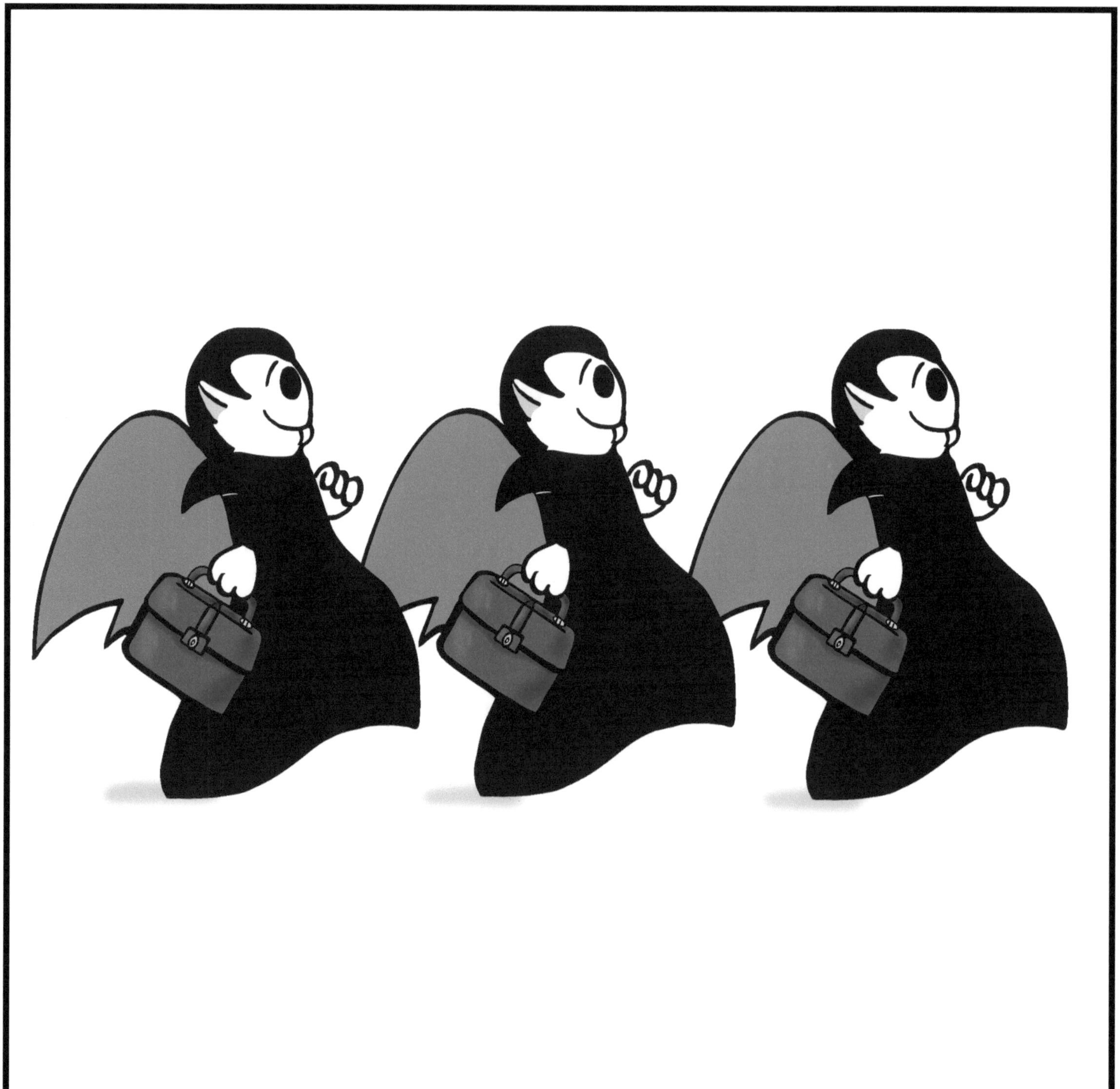

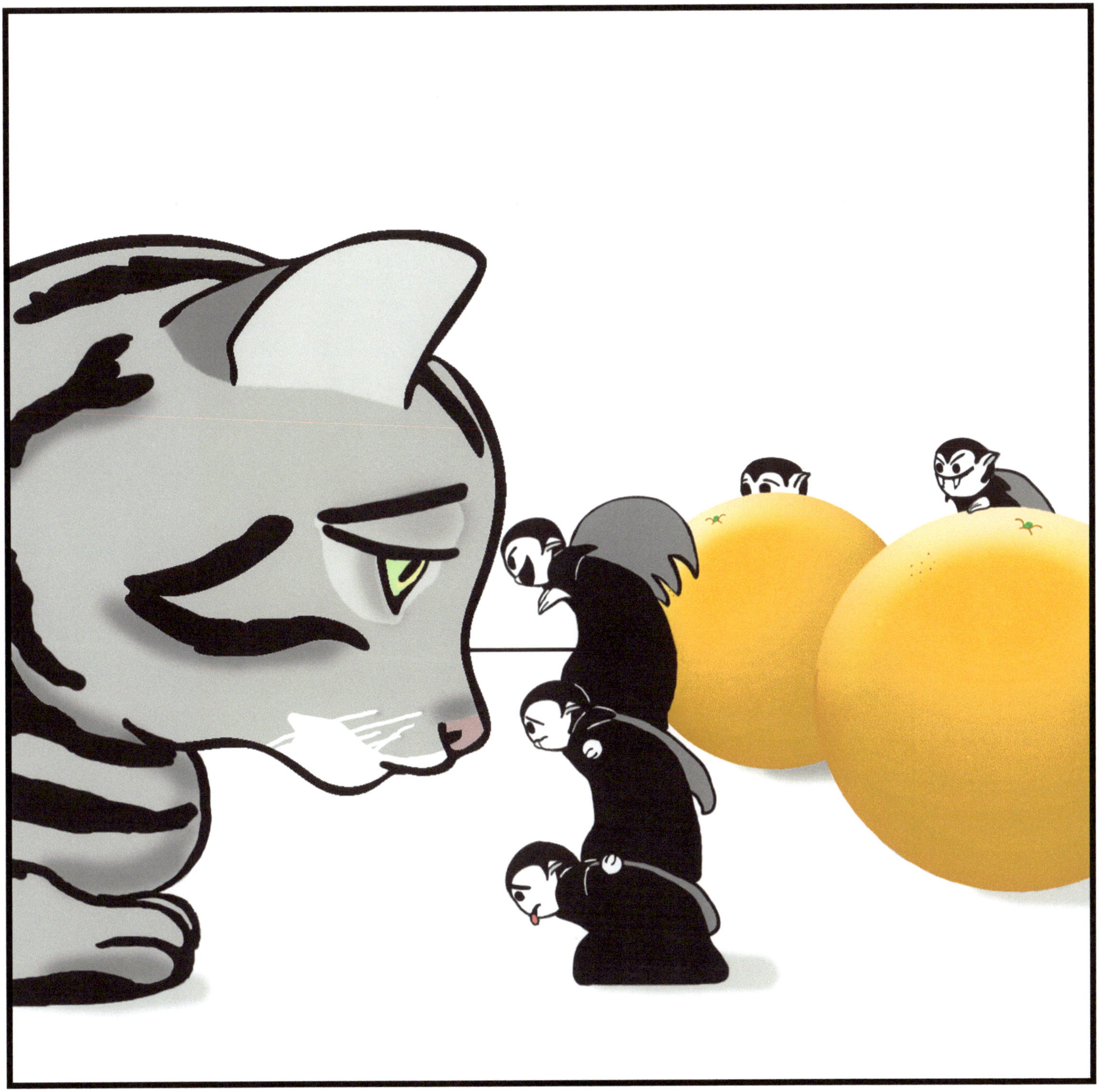

SKETCHBOOK - *Little Vampires and Friends*

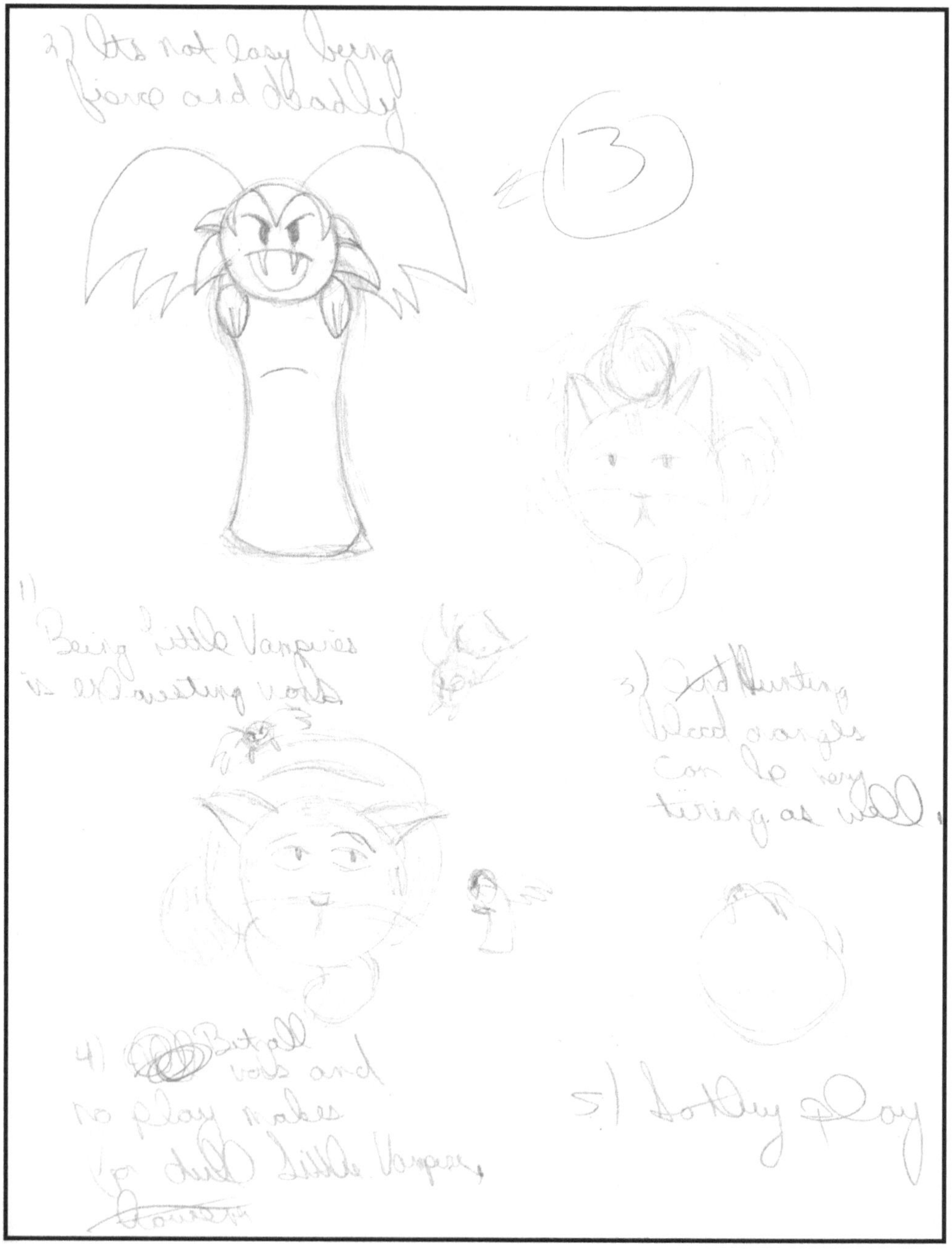
2) Its not easy being fierce and deadly
13
1) Being Little Vampires is exhausting work
4) But all work and no play makes for dull Little Vampires.

SKETCHBOOK - *Little Vampires and Friends*

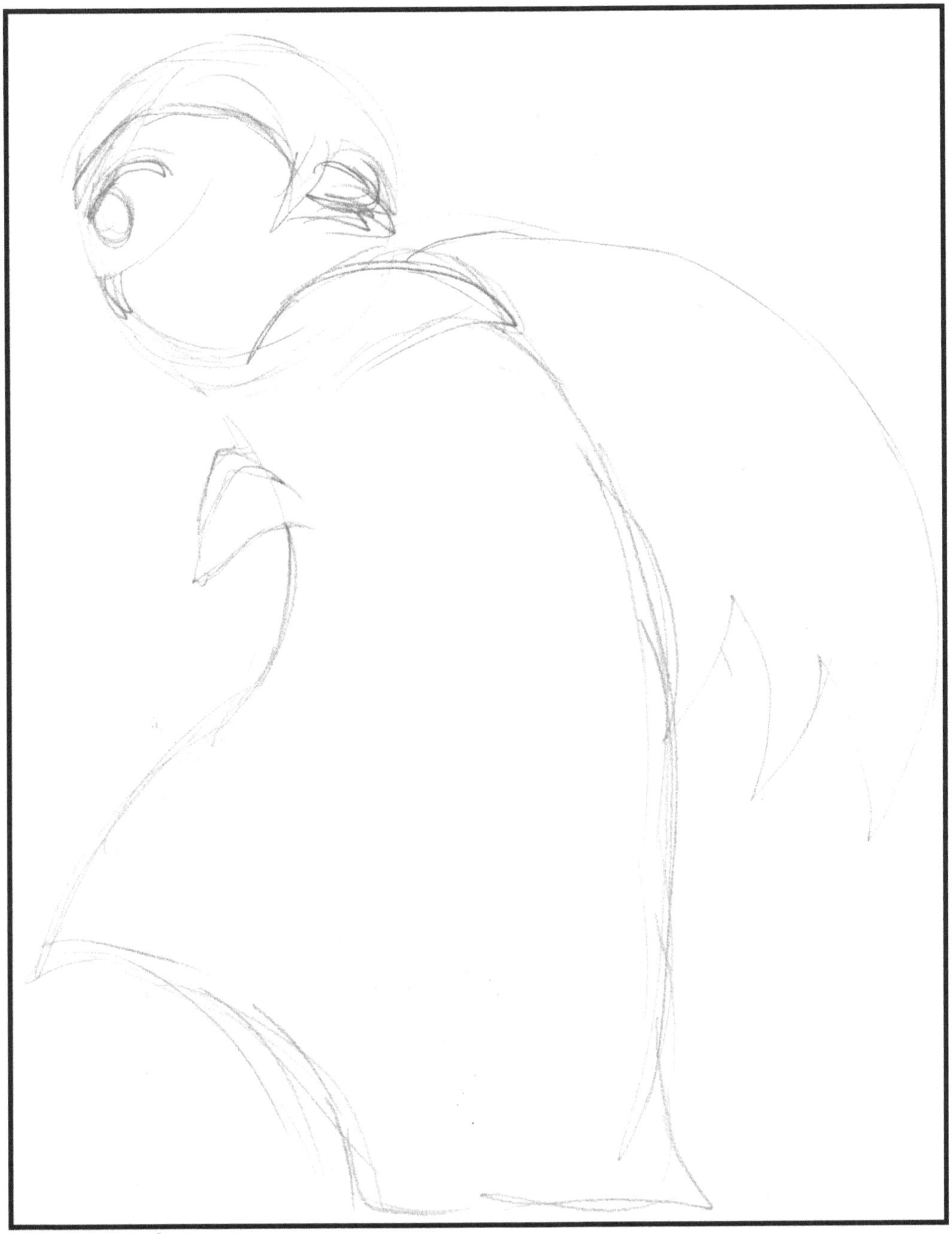

SKETCHBOOK - *Little Vampires and Friends*

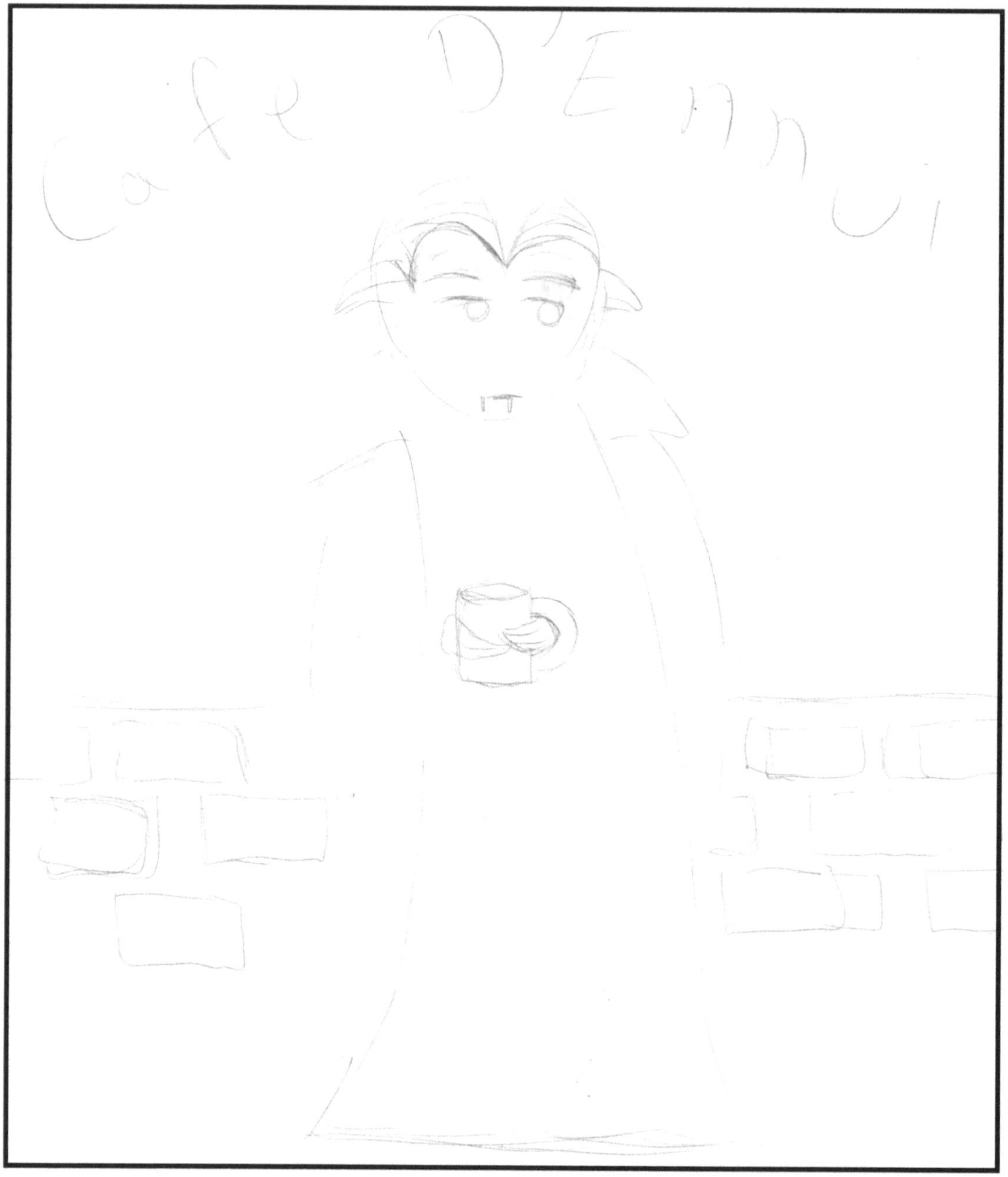
Cafe D'Ennui

SKETCHBOOK - *Little Vampires and Friends*

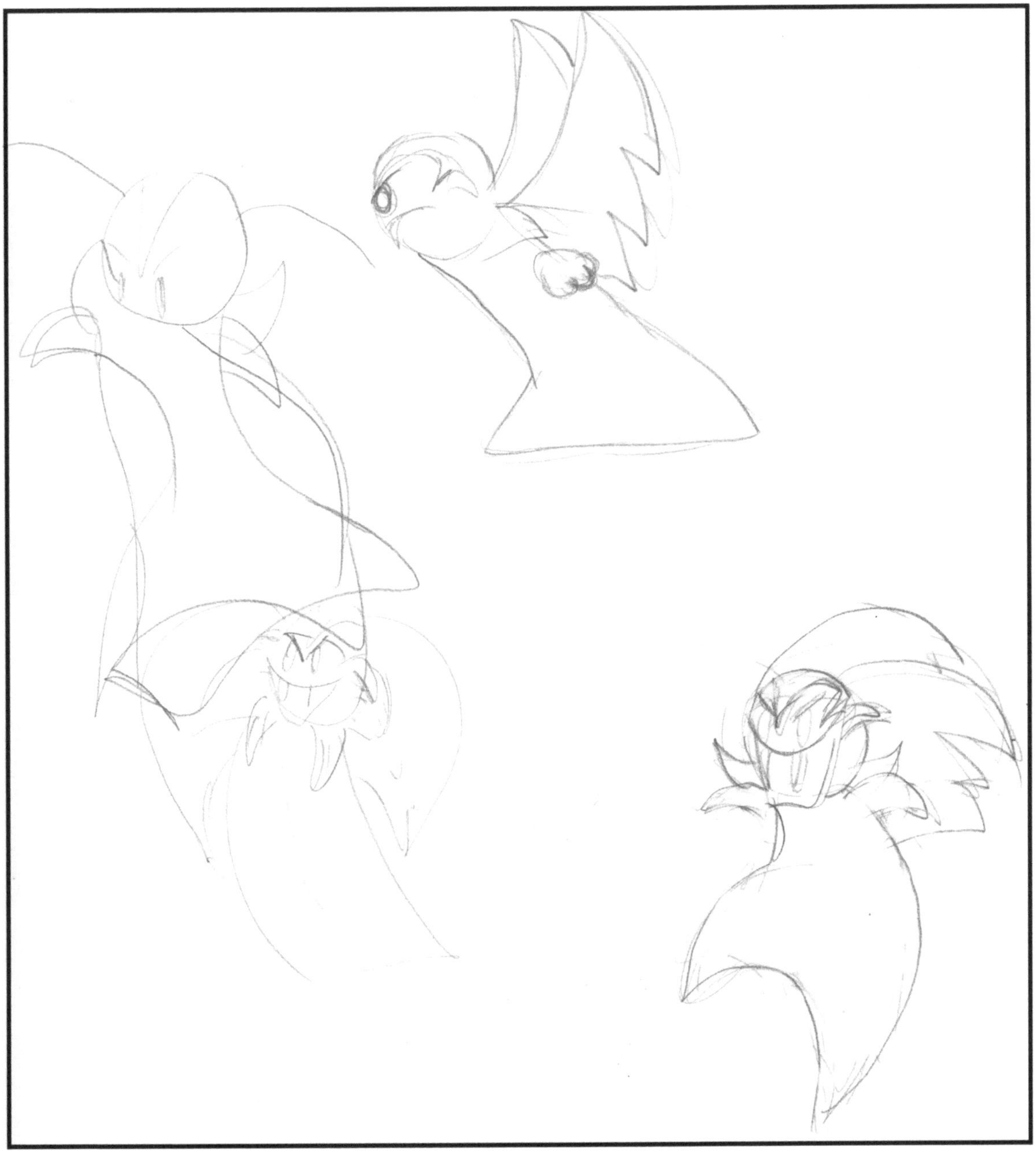

ABOUT THE ARTIST

I grew up in Brooklyn, New York, where I spent many hours seated at the kitchen table, drawing pictures of people on the front of paper, and writing stories about them on the back. I filled notebooks with original stories, as well as sequels to my favorite books and movies. I continued to fill up notebooks when my family moved to Stanton, a small town in Kentucky.

As editor-in-chief of the Powell County High School newspaper, and later as an intern at the local newspaper, *The Clay City Times*, I learned the graphic design and typography skills that would later help me begin my independent publishing career. I majored in English and minored in journalism at the University of Kentucky, with an emphasis in education.

I married James Hicks and moved to San Diego, California, where I continued my college education at San Diego State University. There I changed my minor from journalism to art.

I specialize in pencil and ink illustrations and cartooning. I color digitally, but use Copic markers for commissions and sketch cards. I have dabbled in acrylic painting, and love paper craft like decoupage. I'm inspired by my interests, which are geeky and varied. They include mythology and folklore, Shakespeare, Tolkien and Lewis, *Star Wars* and *Star Trek*, Victorian literature, Abbot and Costello and Laurel and Hardy, the Beatles, comic books, Charles Schulz, Charles Addams, Edward Gorey, and the Muppets.

www.ingramcontent.com/pod-product-compliance
Lightning Source LLC
Chambersburg PA
CBHW040311190426
43198CB00048B/51

It was only then that the Little Monster New Year Celebration Planning Committee realized that making the countdown ball look like a blood orange was not the best of ideas.

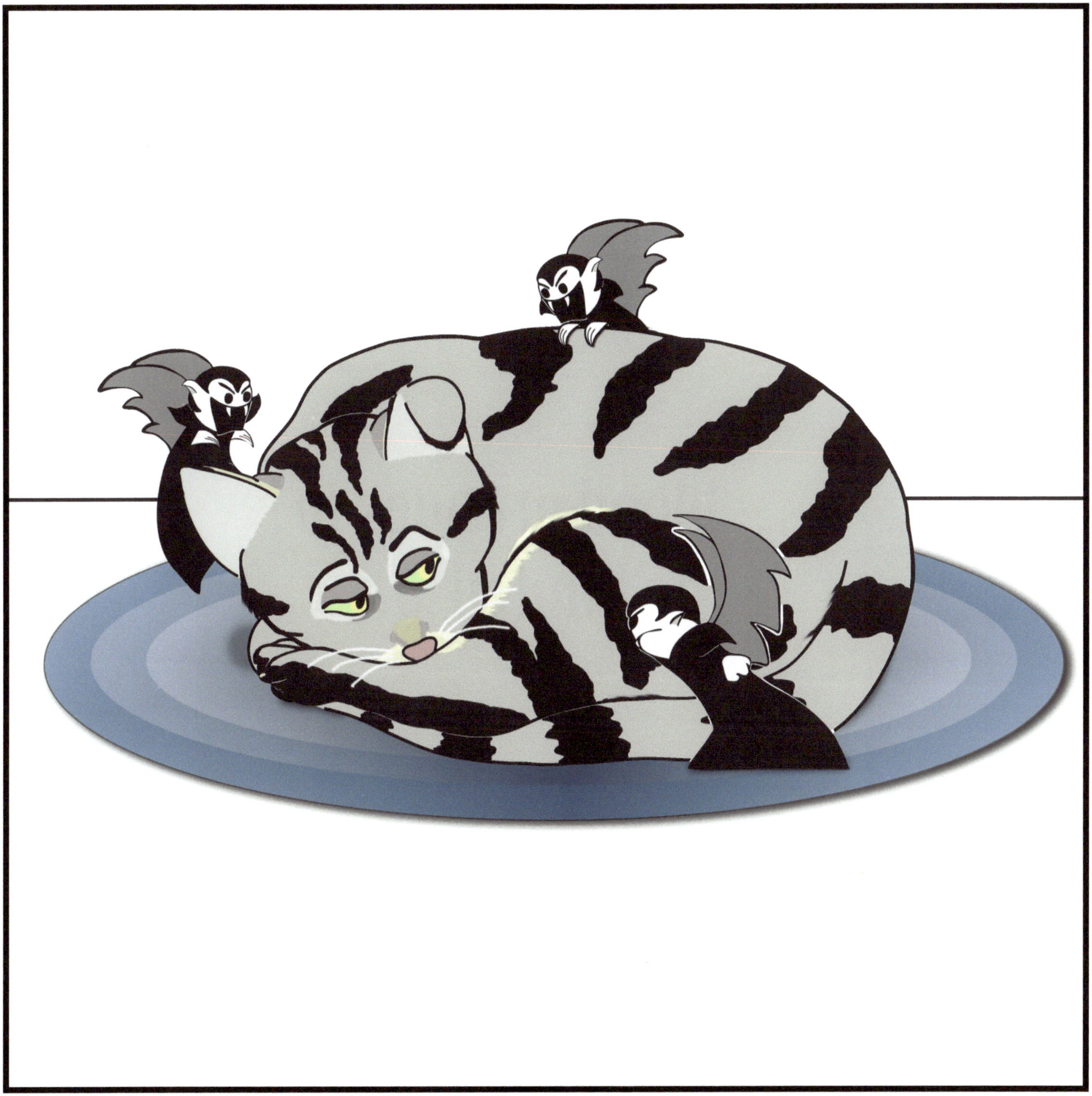

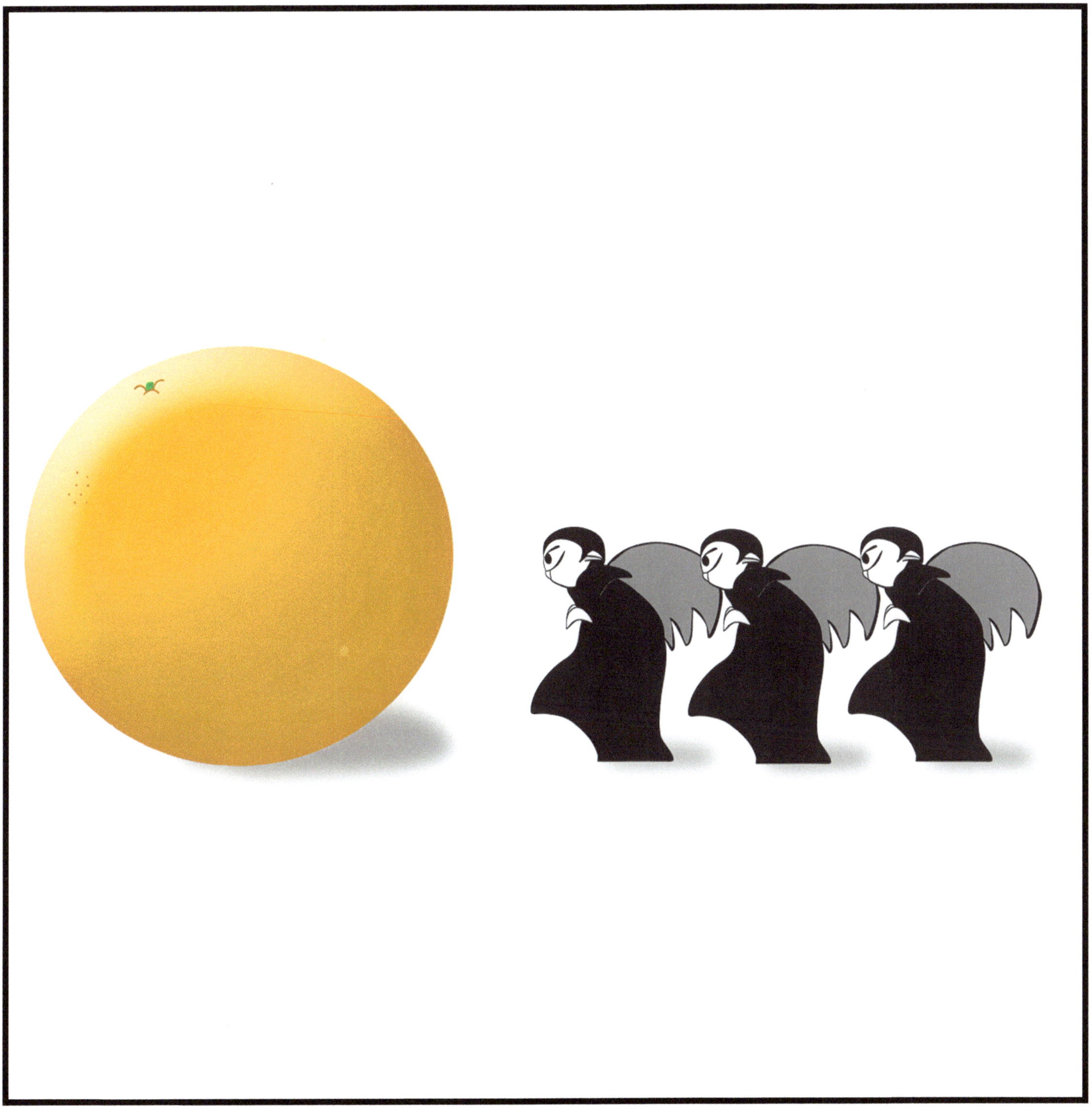

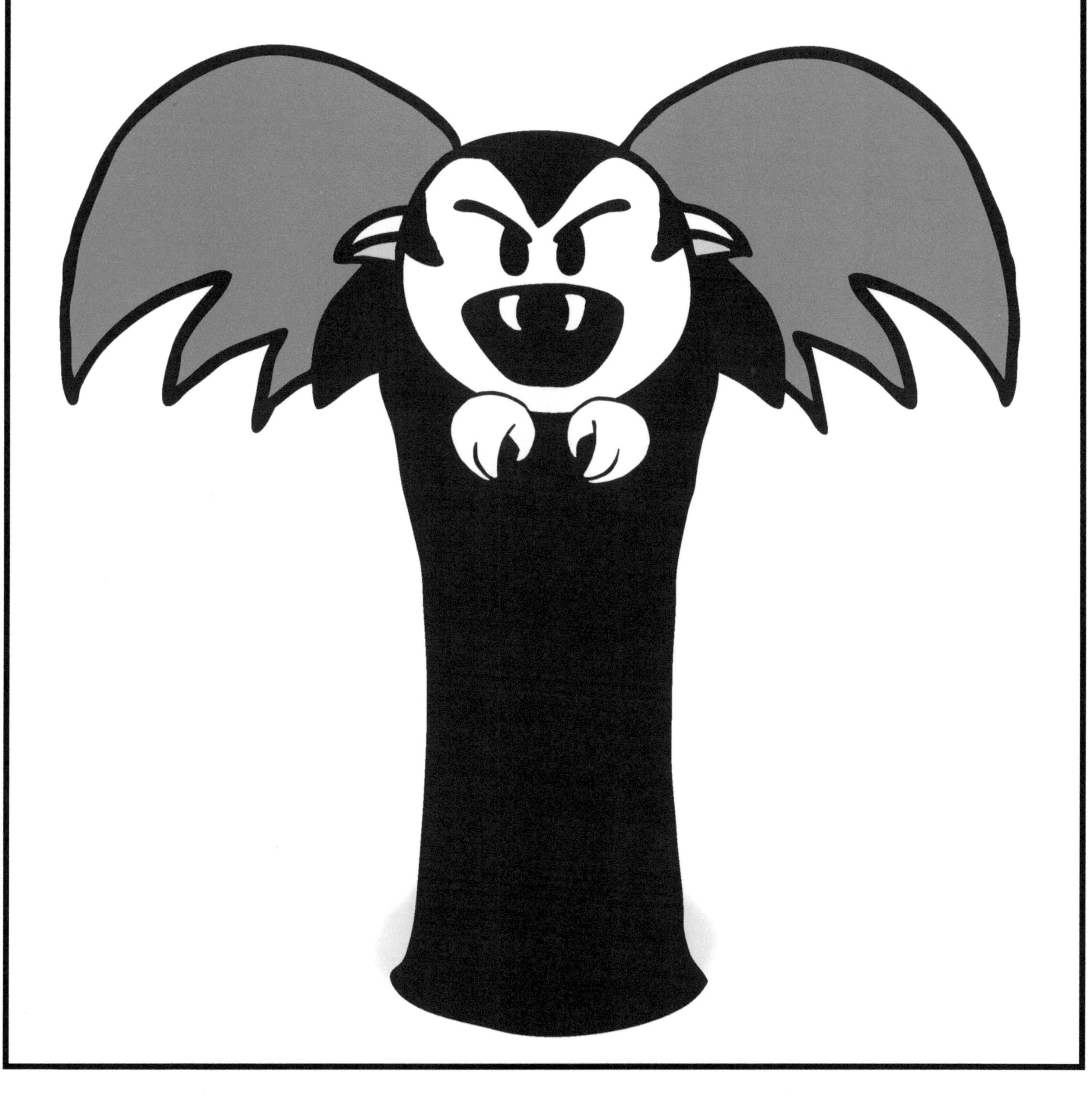

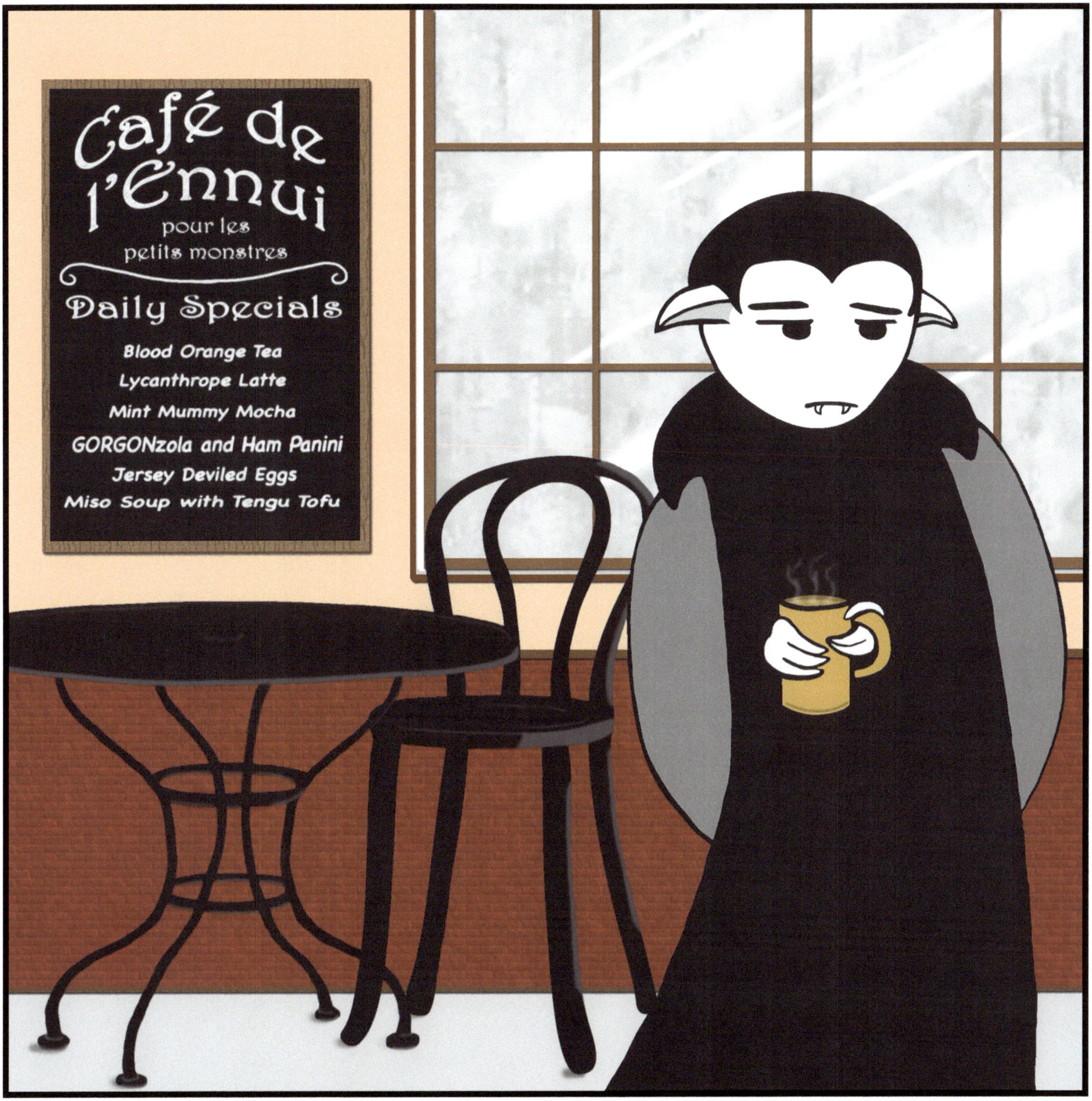
Café de l'Ennui
pour les petits monstres
Daily Specials
Blood Orange Tea
Lycanthrope Latte
Mint Mummy Mocha
GORGONzola and Ham Panini
Jersey Deviled Eggs
Miso Soup with Tengu Tofu

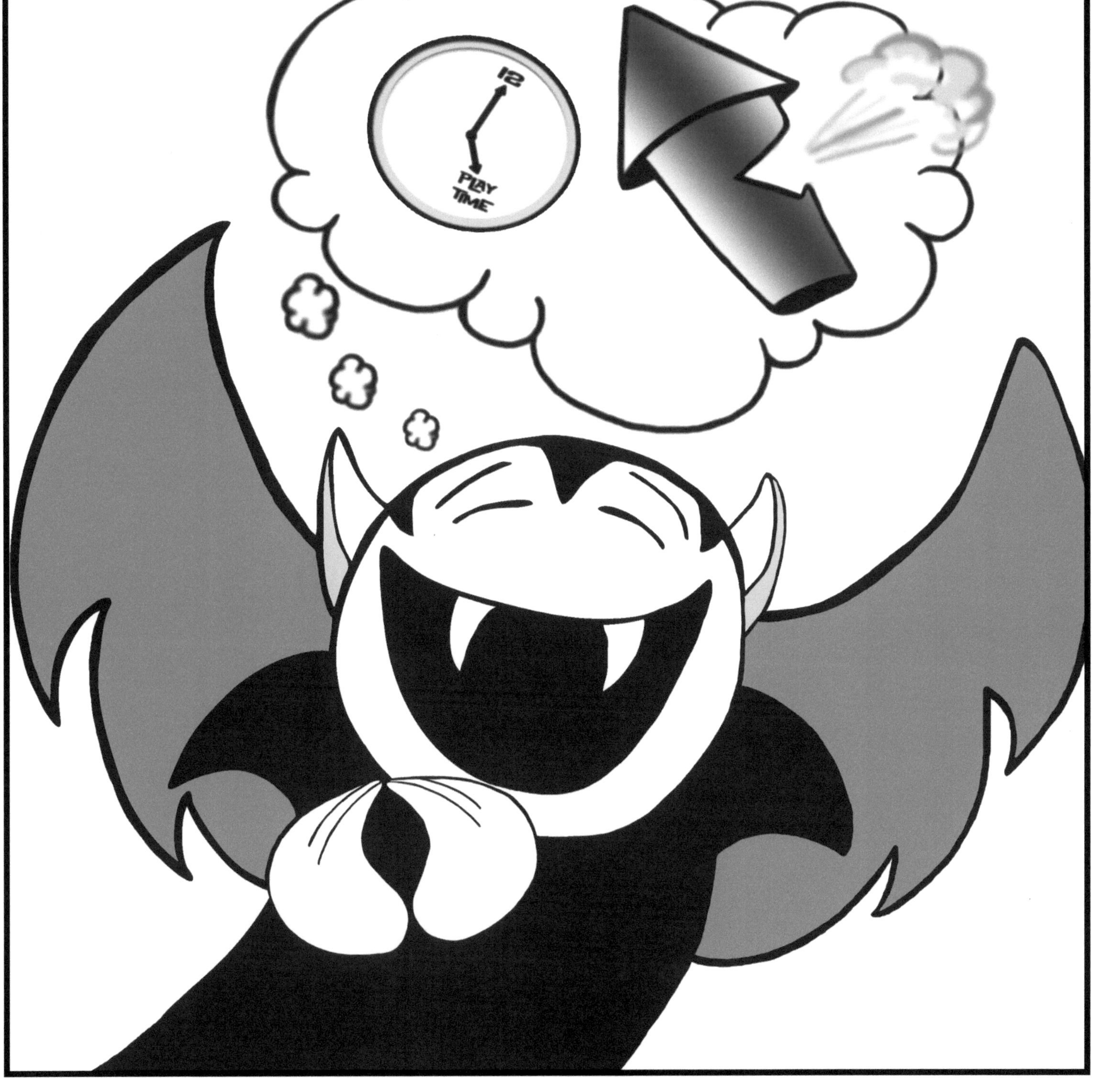
12
PLAY
TIME

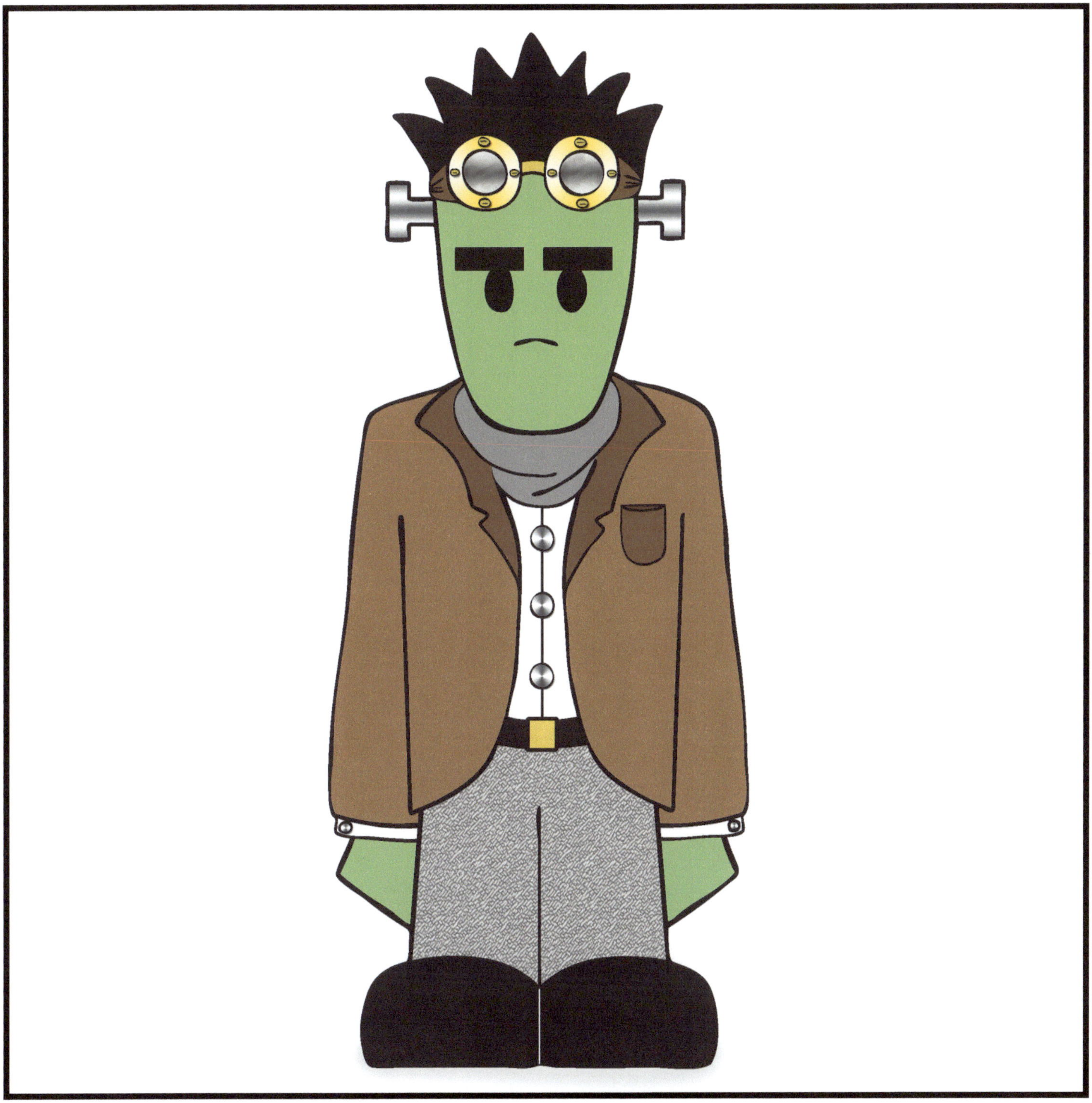

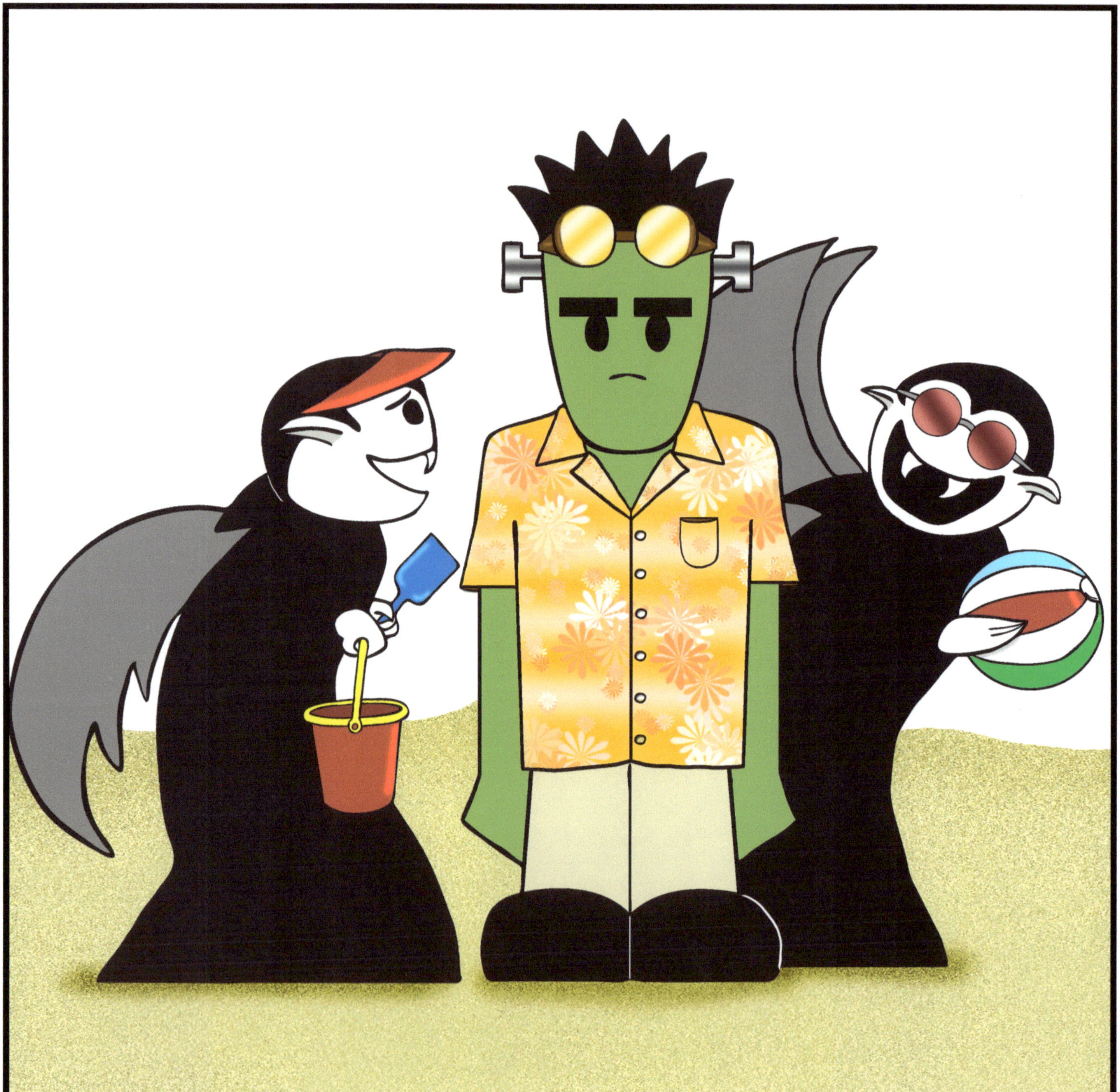

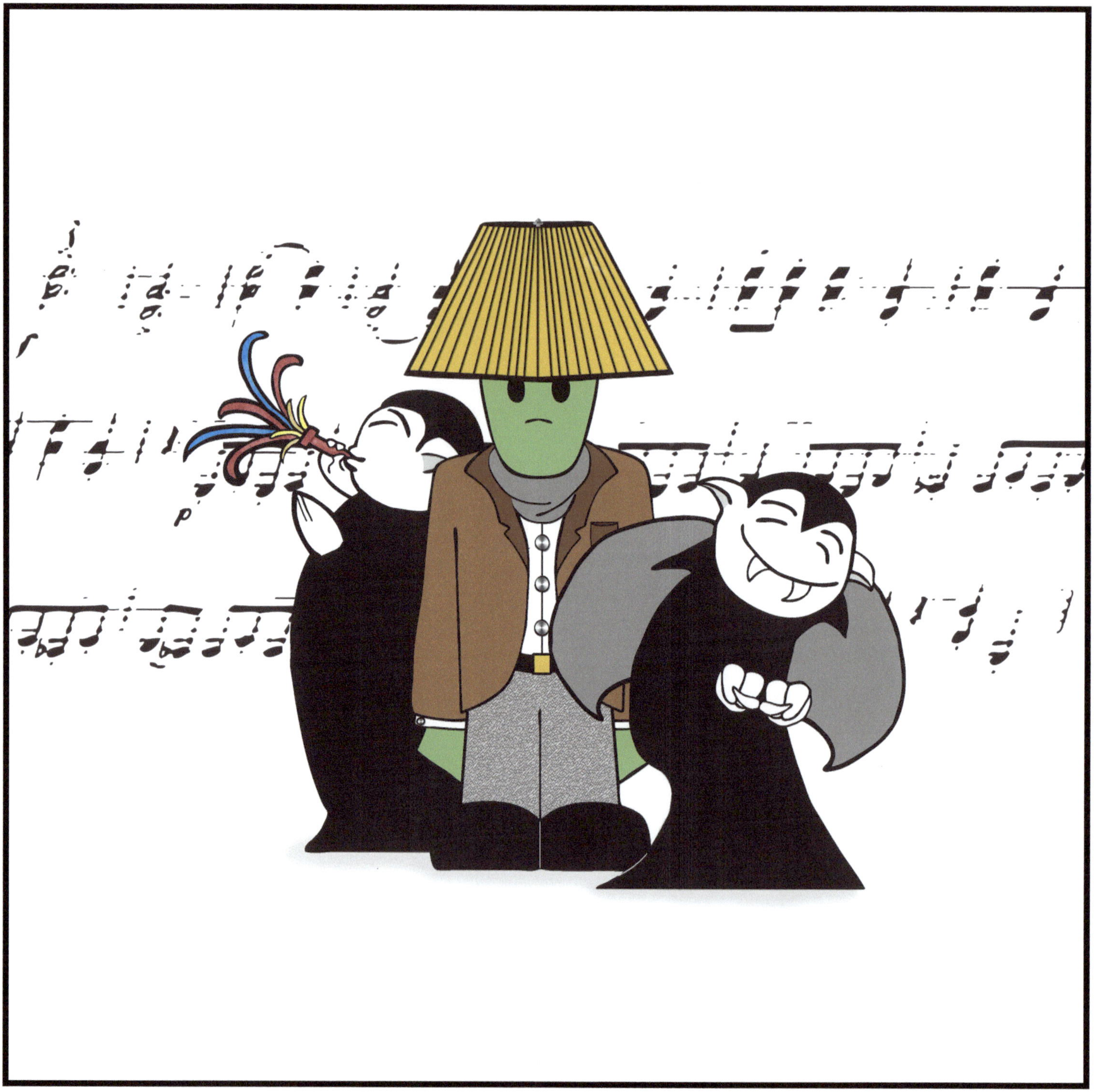

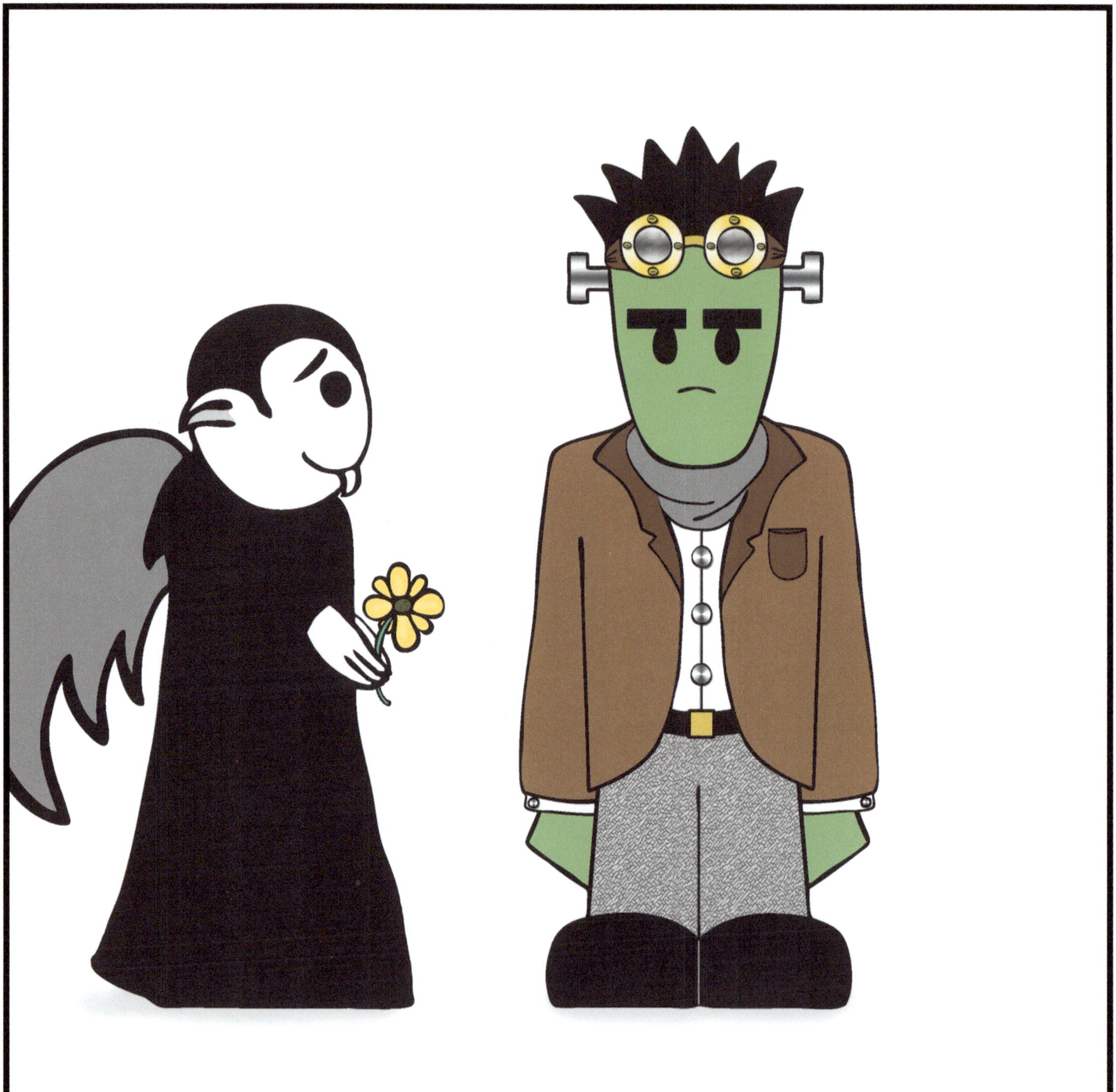

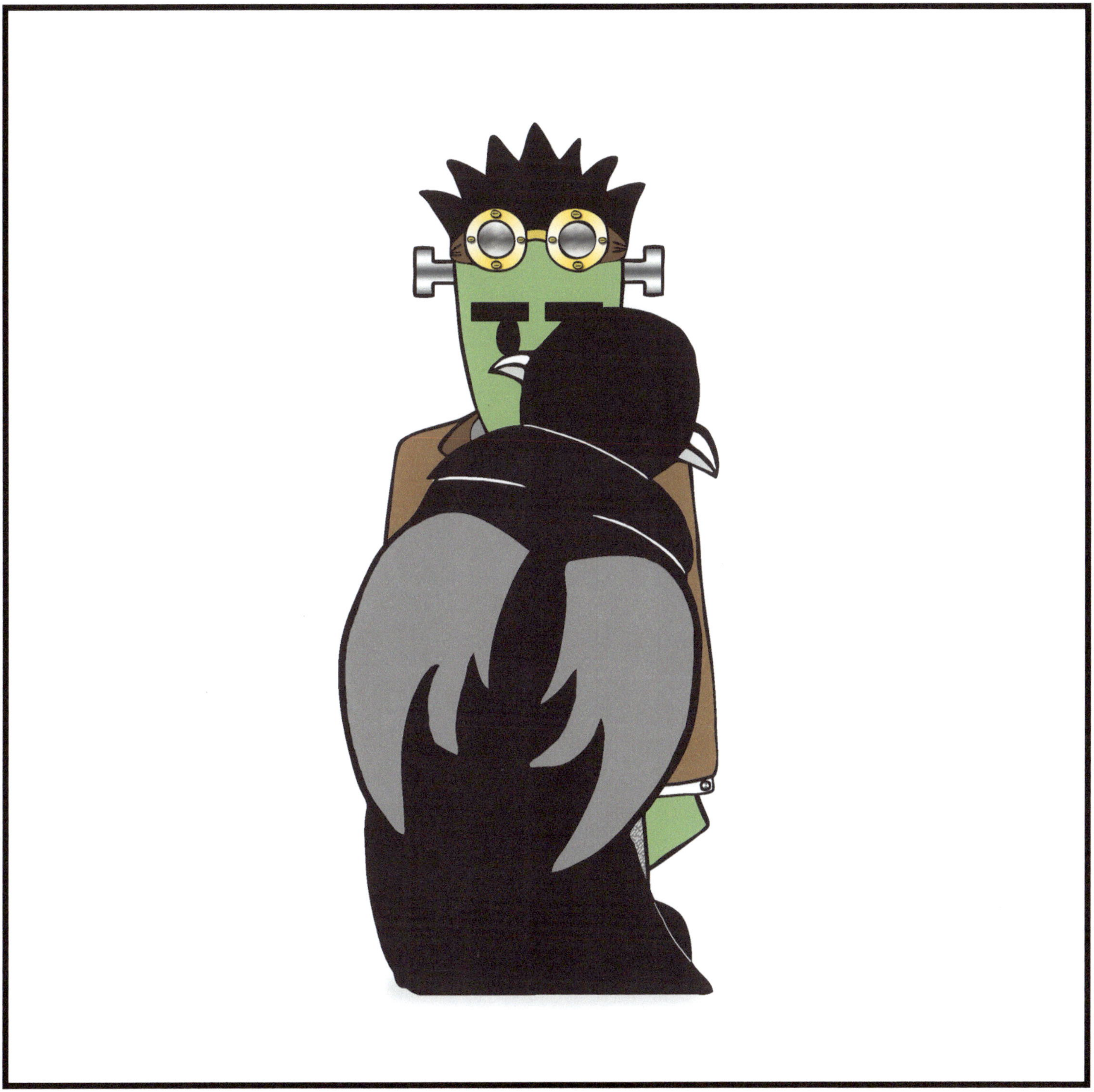

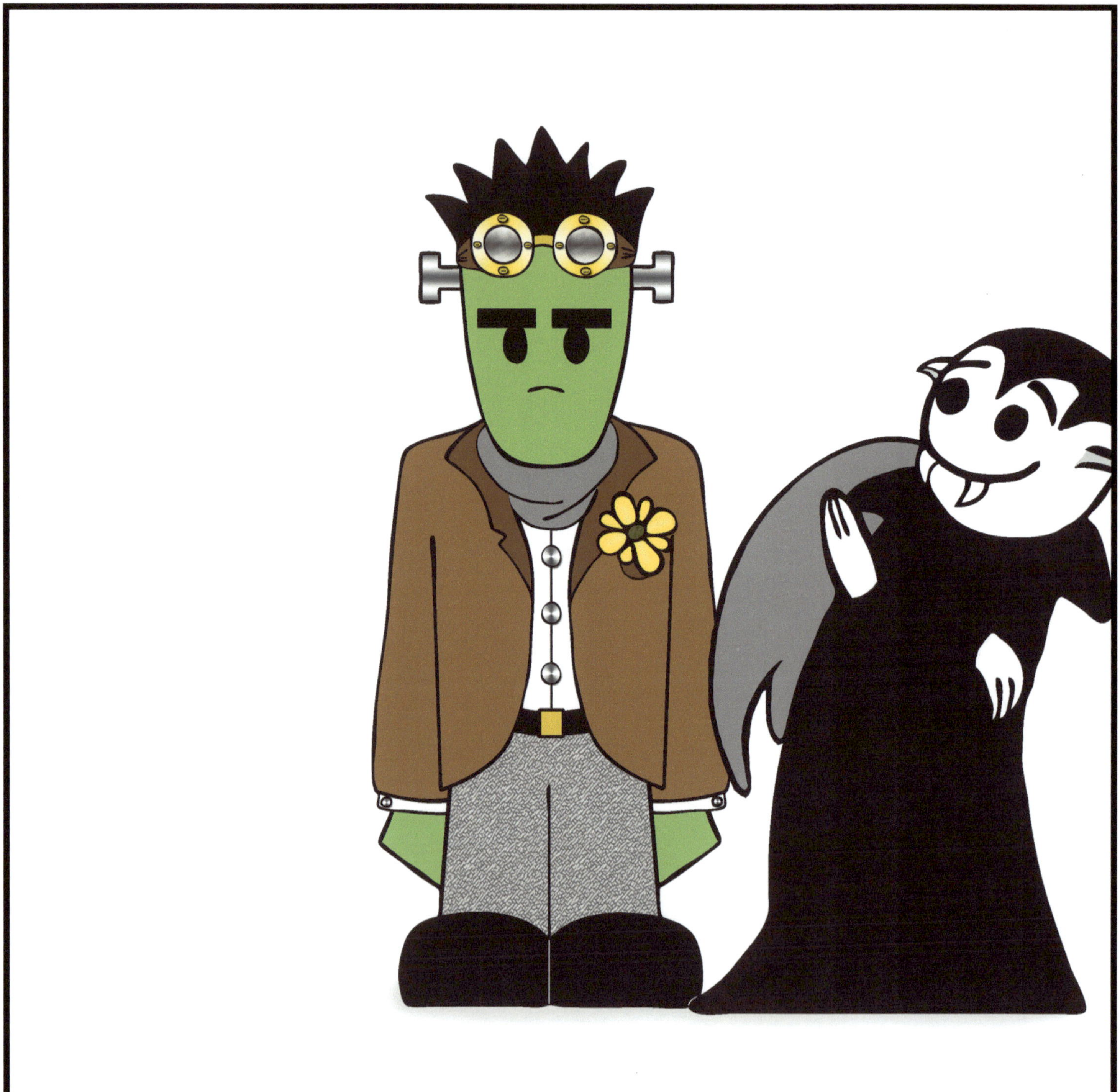

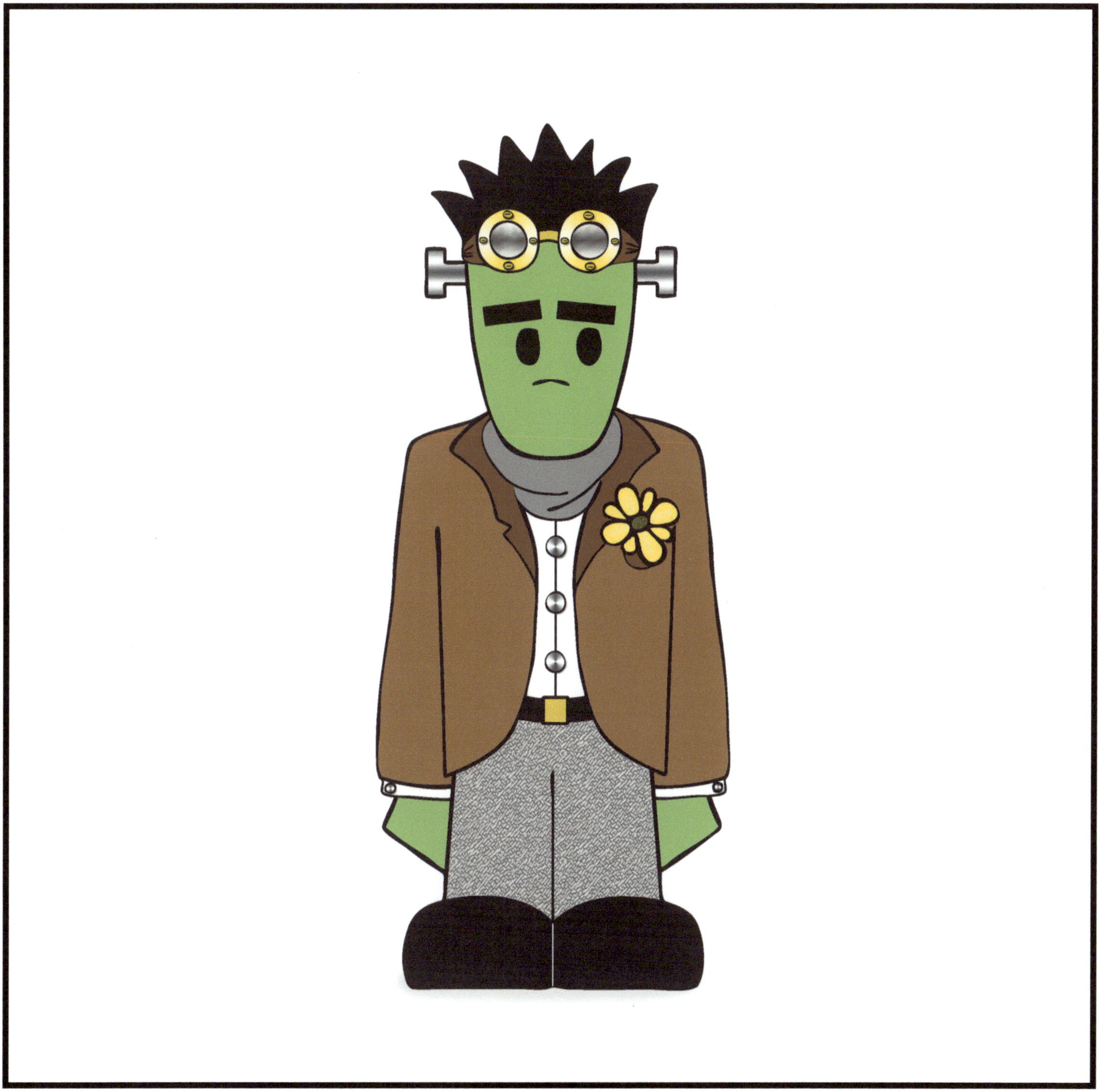

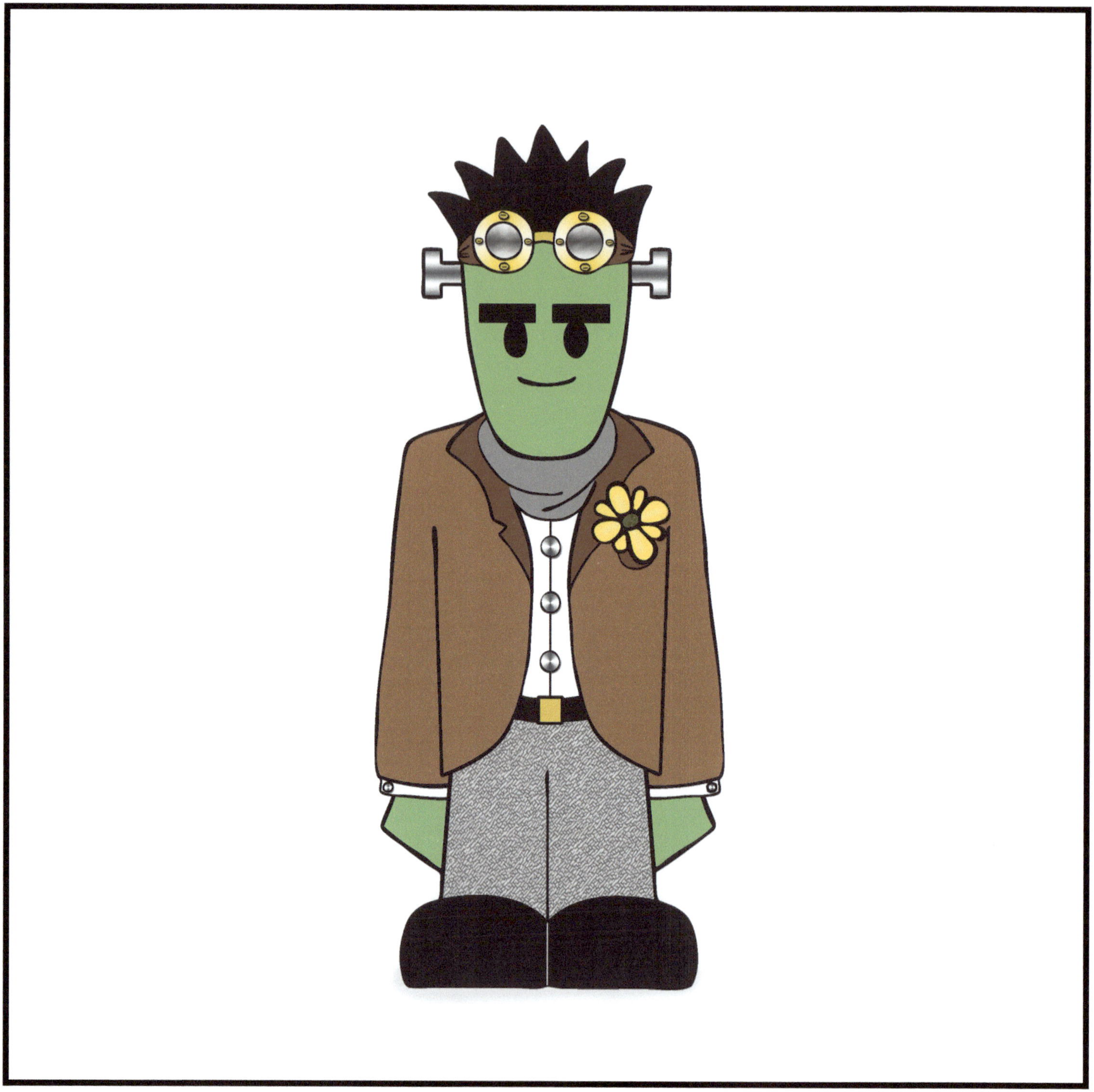

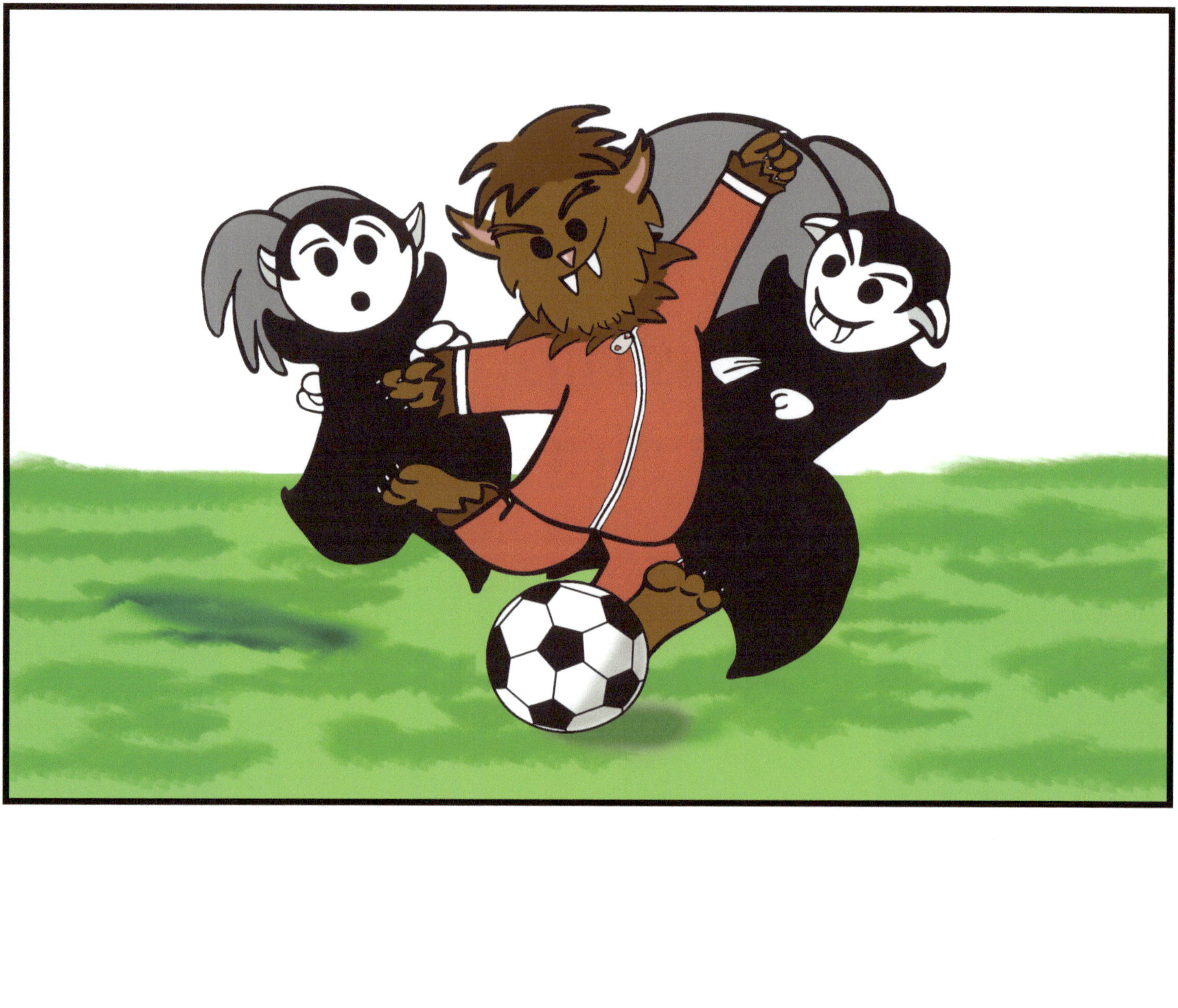

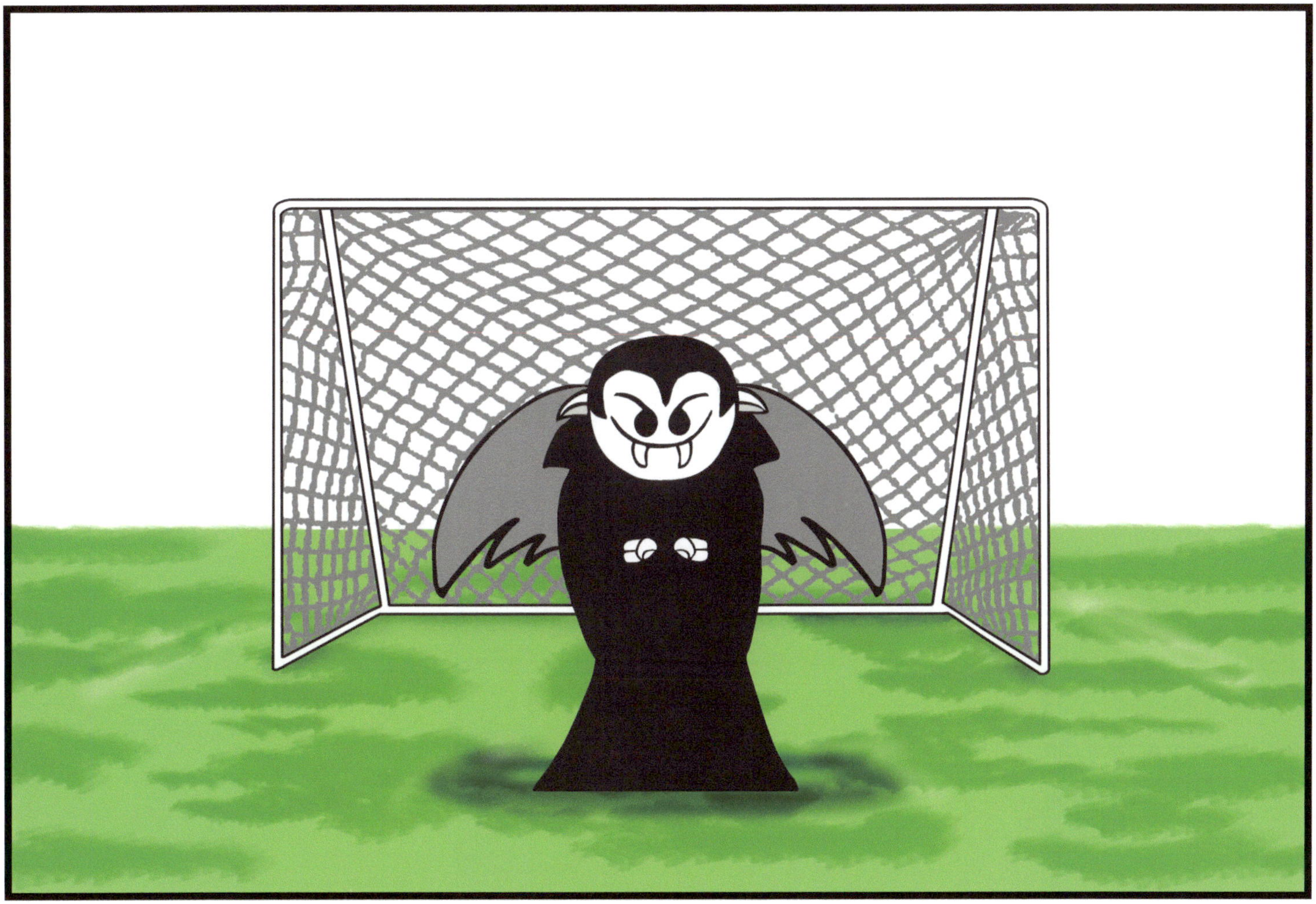